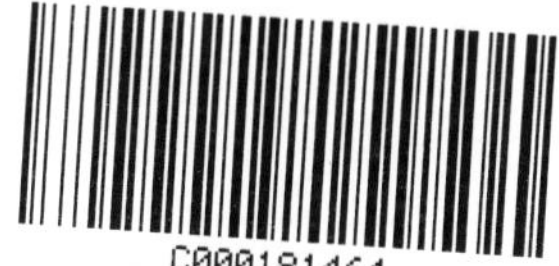

Financial Spread Betting FOR DUMMIES®

A Wiley Brand

by Vanya Dragomanovich and David Land

Financial Spread Betting For Dummies®

Published by: **John Wiley & Sons, Ltd.,** The Atrium, Southern Gate, Chichester, www.wiley.com

This edition first published 2013

For general information on our other products and services, please contact our Customer Care Department within the U.S. at 877-762-2974, outside the U.S. at 317-572-3993, or fax 317-572-4002. For technical support, please visit www.wiley.com/techsupport.

Wiley publishes in a variety of print and electronic formats and by print-on-demand. Some material included with standard print versions of this book may not be included in e-books or in print-on-demand. If this book refers to media such as a CD or DVD that is not included in the version you purchased, you may download this material at http://booksupport.wiley.com. For more information about Wiley products, visit www.wiley.com.

A catalogue record for this book is available from the British Library.

ISBN 978-1-118-63858-3 (pbk); ISBN 978-1-118-63855-2 (ebk); ISBN 978-1-118-63853-8 (ebk);
ISBN 978-1-118-63854-5 (ebk)

Printed in Great Britain by TJ International, Padstow, Cornwall.

10 9 8 7 6 5 4 3 2 1

Contents at a Glance

Table of Contents

Introduction

We've been lucky enough to have spent more than a decade working in trading or writing about the financial sector. Many people would consider that more of a punishment than a career, but it has given us exposure to a lot of people, a lot of fascinating concepts and a lot of different ways in which people manage their investments.

So, we decided to write a book sharing some of the knowledge we've gained and helping investors who are keen to take a more self-directed approach to their investments. Our aim has been to produce a guide that's as upfront as possible when dealing with the mass of different considerations that spread betting traders have to take into account when buying and selling positions. But most importantly, we hope after reading this book you'll go away thinking about how you'll include risk management as a key part of your trading process.

Financial spread betting has captivated the UK trading audience and has seen rapid growth as an investment option since the mid-1990s – and with good reason. Spread bets are simple to understand and easy to use. What requires the most effort is understanding how to manage your positions and how to fit spread bets into your wider portfolio. The many different alternatives as to what to trade can be a little overwhelming. By being patient and methodical in the way you approach any investment – and particularly spread betting – you give yourself a big advantage. There are no short cuts to successful spread betting, but you set yourself apart from the beginning by preparing yourself as well as you can for all the challenges you'll face.

A lot of people want to be short-term traders, and that's a wonderful goal to have – just make sure that you're a short-term trader who's around for the long term. No matter who you are, we recommend that you start small, remain conservative and be as methodical as you can be. Everyone wants to be wealthy and the markets can deliver that for you, but they won't provide it for free, so be prepared for a long journey that will hopefully be rewarding and satisfying.

About This Book

This book is specifically about financial spread betting – spread betting on price changes in the financial markets. It's not about sports spread betting, which is also very popular in the UK. Although you may use the same provider for sports and financial spread bets, they're quite different in their calculation and risk assumptions. So don't expect us to talk about football in this book!

Spread bets are a wonderful product for traders. They offer incredible advantages, such as built-in leverage, low entry cost, a huge range of markets to trade and the ability to profit in a rising or falling market. In addition to this, they are also free of tax and usually free of any commission costs as well. From the perspective of attracting traders, they're pretty much unrivalled in the market.

Financial Spread Betting For Dummies gives you the full picture of what this product is all about. This doesn't mean it tells you ten ways to become a millionaire – because you won't find any short cuts that way. But reading this book will help you make well-informed decisions about how spread bets fit into your overall investment portfolio.

It is also important to bear in mind that financial spread betting is only available in the UK and the Republic of Ireland. Elsewhere in the world (outside the US and Canada), you will instead be offered a CFD (Contracts For Difference) trading account.

When you're informed as a trader you can go about the task of building a strong trading methodology to follow. We applaud a 'have a go' mentality, but spread bets aren't the place for it. People may find trading satisfying, but it's not a forum in which you just make a few trades and see what happens. We've built nearly all the chapters around an awareness of the pluses and minuses of spread betting. When you properly recognise the risks you can take steps to dealing with them and try to keep them to a minimum. You can't eliminate risk, but by planning to be successful over the long term you can deal with risk effectively.

We don't want you to be afraid of making mistakes – just make sure they don't cost much money. We think the difference between the good trader and the bad trader with equal amounts of knowledge is the way each deals with losing trades. We hope you'll find all the guidance you need in this book to put yourself in the good trader camp and keep your risk and your losses conservative.

Conventions Used in This Book

To help you get the most from this book, we follow a few conventions:

- *Italic* is used for emphasis and to highlight new words or terms that we define.
- Web addresses may split over two lines – if so, ignore the hyphen that links them when you're typing the address into a search engine. If you're reading this on an enabled device, the web addresses are hyperlinked and will take you straight to the site in question.
- **Bold** shows the action part of numbered steps, and also the key introductory parts of bulleted lists.

Foolish Assumptions

Although we wish everyone would buy this book, we know it's not that simple – if you're not interested in spread betting then *Financial Spread Betting For Dummies* isn't for you. Having said that, if you're reading this, you've proved true our first assumption – that you've heard about spread betting and you want to know more.

We also assume that you have a working knowledge of markets and have as a minimum dealt in shares before. Derivatives (such as spread bets) are an extension of other markets, so you need to be aware of the underlying market first in order to make sense of the derivative.

In addition, we assume you want to take an active approach to your investing and are comfortable with the idea of applying a conservative amount of leverage to the trades that you take.

Perhaps our most important assumption involves risk management. Despite what you may have heard about traders, we assume you're not interested in the idea of getting rich quick and you understand that learning about the product is only the first step towards your trading future.

Finally, we assume that spread bets will only make up a very small portion of your overall investment portfolio, although they'll most likely make up the part of your portfolio that you more actively manage.

How This Book Is Organised

We designed *Financial Spread Betting For Dummies* so that you can jump in at any point and get the information you need: so you don't have to read entire parts or every chapter to find what you're looking for. The table of contents gives a very detailed view of what's where, so make good use of it, and then head straight to the points of most interest to you.

At the back of the book we include a handy glossary of terms. Don't let trading terminology put you off getting to know more about spread betting!

This book is split into six parts.

Part I: Getting Started

In this part, you find out what spread bets are, the key points you need to consider when deciding who you'll use as a provider and how to place enter and exit orders. We discuss the difference between trading long and trading short, and start to look at leverage and how you should manage it. There are lots of spread betting providers out there for you to choose from, and different types of spread bet and markets to trade in. Take the time to consider here what these differences mean to you before making a decision on a broker or market.

Part II: Touring the Spread Betting Marketplace

In this part, we introduce you to the main types of spread bet that are available, including shares, foreign exchange, indices, commodities and interest rate securities. All these have unique points that you need to understand before you make any trades. When you understand them, however, you're sure to find a product suitable for you in this group, whether you're a short- or longer-term trader and whether you want to trade night or day.

Part III: Keeping Risk Under Control

This section is a must-read for people who are new to the world of derivatives and spread betting. In this part, we look at keeping a lid on leverage, applying stop loss orders and the merits of sensible position sizes. Although it may be tempting to think only of the possible profits you can make from a trade, you should trade only when you have a keen awareness of the possible downsides that you may face. Any trading has risk attached to it, but you put yourself ahead of the group if you manage yours carefully at all times.

Part IV: Trading Strategies

In this part, we look at a number of different methods you can use to start your trading journey, such as swing trading and trend trading. We explore the core concepts of fundamental and technical analysis, and show how you can apply them to your use of spread bets within your portfolio. Thinking through and personalising your strategy allows you to consistently trade and pick up times when you could be doing things better. Taking a scattergun approach may be a lot easier, but it's not going to help you be profitable over the long term.

Part V: Knowing Where You're Going

Happily, this section is all about you. This is the part where we look at bringing together what you know, analysing your trading behaviour and turning this knowledge into an effective trading methodology. As part of this, we look at record-keeping and some of the perils of not making good trading plans. Some people say that you won't know whether you've reached the end of your journey unless you know where you're going. Traders don't get that luxury because the journey never ends, so you need to be sure you're moving ahead at all times and not losing money or opportunities without being well aware of what's happening and why.

Part VI: The Part of Tens

In this part, we look at a number of key considerations that can make life a lot easier when you're spread betting – ten rules or thoughts to make things go more smoothly. We examine mistakes made by beginners, strategies for better risk management and how to deal with leverage.

Icons Used in This Book

In this book we use a few icons to mark special information. Here's what they mean:

The Internet is the trader's best friend so be sure to use it. Because so much information is out there, this icon points to websites that are good reference points for the future.

This icon flags up real-world applications of the techniques and strategies we outline in the text.

This icon draws attention to a key point. Do whatever it takes to remember these points!

This icon flags descriptions of phrases or concepts that you may not be familiar with. This is usually good background or more advanced information on the market that you're dealing with – which may interest you, or may not. You can skip these bits if you choose without missing out on the main gist of the section or chapter.

Look out for these little gems – they note ways you can do things more easily or more quickly, or strategies to keep you trading more successfully for longer.

When you see these icons, pay attention! Trading is easy to do but difficult to master, so in order to keep moving forward you need to be aware of traps that ensnare the unwary.

Where to Go from Here

Where you choose to dive into the book is really up to you. If you're making a new venture into spread betting, we recommend starting with Parts I and II. If you have some experience spread betting already, you may like to just skim Parts I and II and then really sink your teeth into Parts III, IV and V.

Part I

Getting Started with Financial Spread Betting

getting started with Financial Spread Betting

For Dummies can help you get started with a huge range of subjects. Visit `www.dummies.com` to learn more and do more with *For Dummies*.

In this part . . .

- Get to grips with what Financial Spread Betting really involves, and whether it's for you.
- Weigh up what you need in choosing a provider.
- Grasp the basic strategies: trading long, trading short and getting the lowdown on leverage.
- Deal with price slippage.
- Go to `www.dummies.com/extras/fsbuk` for online bonus content.

Chapter 1

Deciding Whether Financial Spread Betting Is For You

In This Chapter

- Understanding where financial spread bets fit into the financial product spectrum
- Fulfilling your responsibilities as a trader
- Taking the preliminary steps to trading success

Financial spread bets are *financial derivatives*, instruments whose prices are based on something else – such as a share price, a barrel of oil or any of a wide range of other products. From the outset, we need to distinguish between financial spread betting and other types of spread betting in the UK. Although many people are used to spread betting on sports – football, for example – *financial* spread betting involves betting on the movement of prices in financial markets.

Financial spread bets are popular with traders because they're possibly the simplest of all derivatives and this makes them accessible to a very wide audience. This ease of understanding carries with it a tendency to create a false sense of security, however, which can lead to traders being overexposed and overlooking the fact that losses are largely unlimited in some circumstances (see Chapter 3 to find out how this occurs). When used properly, though, spread bets enable you to trade a vast array of products very easily and very cheaply, which can greatly enhance your profitability.

In this chapter, we explain how spread bets work and how you can use them as part of your overall investment portfolio. We also discuss using spread bets to benefit from short-term price movements in a number of financial markets, including shares and foreign exchange. Finally, we start you on the journey of understanding how best to manage your risk as a trader, since managing risk is critical to your success.

Grasping the Ground Rules

In this section, we look at the major characteristics of spread bets and some of the main points that you need to understand before starting on your spread betting journey.

So what are spread bets, anyway?

A *spread bet* is an agreement to pay the difference between two prices – the price at which you open the bet and the price at which you close the contract. The spread bet's price is based on that of an underlying instrument, which varies depending on the particular bet, but may be, say, a share or foreign exchange rate. A financial spread bet is typically an over-the-counter product. This means that it isn't traded on a centralised exchange or market like shares. Each contract involves only two parties: you (the trader, or buyer) and the bet's provider (the counterparty to the transaction, or seller).

When you open a spread bet you do so based on current market prices. The same applies when you close the position. What makes spread bets unique when compared with many other categories of derivatives is the way that they're priced. Other derivative products use complex formulas to determine their prices, but spread bets simply mimic the price of the underlying instrument that they track.

In essence, a spread bet puts you in a position to make a profit (or loss) from changes in the price of the underlying instrument. For example, if you enter a long trade (that is, you bet with the view that the price will rise):

- If the price rises between the time the bet is opened and closed, the seller must pay the difference in value to the buyer (you). Provided costs are covered, you make a profit and the seller makes a loss.
- If the price falls between the time the bet is opened and closed, the buyer (you) must pay the difference to the seller. In this case, the seller makes a profit and you suffer a loss.

Spread betting can be risky, especially when traders overuse leverage (see the later section 'Employing leverage') – we cover strategies for managing this risk in Chapter 8. However, spread bets also have features that make them very useful and the preferred instrument for many traders:

- **Ability to easily and practically short sell shares and other financial instruments:** This increases your opportunity to make money from good trading strategies by allowing you to profit from falling as well as rising markets (see Chapter 3 for more information).

- **Ability to trade small positions:** By staking only a small amount on the bet, you can limit your risk.
- **Access to a wide range of products from all around the world.**
- **Access to cost-effective trading platforms that provide you with a wide range of analytical capabilities:** These include real-time pricing, charting packages and financial news.
- **Leverage:** When you open a spread bet, you don't have to pay the full price of the underlying product, but simply a smaller deposit known as an initial margin (see the section 'Paying margins', later in the chapter), so you pay only a small amount to control a much larger position.
- **No physical delivery or settlement of the full value of the underlying instrument.**
- **Simplicity of use.**
- **Tax free:** Because spread betting is treated as gambling by the tax authority in the UK, you don't have to pay any tax on your profits.
- **No commission:** Unlike share trading, few spread betting brokers charge commission on your trades. The bid/offer spread contains the cost of the trade.

Spread bets have become a very popular short-term trading product in the UK. By 'short-term' we mean less than one month, but the duration can be shorter or longer than this, depending on the trader. By spread betting, you're trying to capture short-term price movements in financial markets. If you establish a solid trading methodology, you can generate profits very quickly, but – and it's a *big* but – before you rush headfirst into spread betting you must consider the potential downsides that exist. The downsides include losing more capital than you invested and seeing large swings in your capital due to the over-application of leverage. Most of these downsides relate to risk management, which we discuss at length in Chapter 8.

Spread bets are a product for sophisticated traders and you need to understand the mechanics of spread betting before placing any trades. We explain more about spread betting in general in Chapters 2 and 3.

Types of spread bets

A real highlight of financial spread betting is being able to trade in a wide range of market types and geographic locations. At one time dealing in foreign shares could be logistically quite difficult, but the Internet has changed all that by giving traders online access to markets in different locations and in different time zones. Spread betting takes this one step further by allowing you to deal in products from all around the world from a single trading platform – which means you can build trading strategies for just about anything.

To give you an idea of the different markets that these bets track, here we briefly discuss the main types of spread bets. We look at each in depth in Chapters 4 to 7.

- **Commodity bets:** They've been around for some time, but have become more popular in recent years as the commodity boom has brought the world's attention to this investment category. Commodity bets enable you to trade products like crude oil over a long trading day, which makes these spread bets very convenient. Commodity bets also offer very good portfolio diversification for traders. We discuss commodity spread betting in Chapter 7.
- **Foreign exchange (FX, Forex) bets:** This is a very popular trading tool offered by most providers. In this market you're dealing in the relative value of two currencies (the exchange rate). The market is very *liquid* (meaning it's very easy to get in and out of trades). Foreign exchange spread bets are available to trade 24 hours a day, often six days a week, so you can trade at any time that appeals to you. In Chapter 5 we examine FX spread bets.
- **Index bets:** Index spread bets have become very popular because they allow traders to take exposure to the wider market in a single trade by placing a bet over an index. This may be something like the FTSE 100 Index or the Dow Jones Industrial Average in the United States. Index spread bets are typically available to trade all day and much of the night. We look at index spread betting in Chapter 6.
- **Interest rate bets:** Interest rate (or money market) spread betss enable traders to access a market that most traders may not have dealt in before – the interest rate securities market, with a particular emphasis on short-term notes and longer-term bonds. While the underlying instruments may have a specific term (for example, ten years), this isn't an issue for spread betting, where you're only interested in capturing the price *movements*. Interest rate bets can offer real benefits to traders in the form of diversification. I discuss interest rate bets in Chapter 7.
- **Share bets:** For budding spread bettors share bets are likely to be the first step, because they're the most similar spread bet to a market you should already be familiar with – the share market. Share bets enable you to trade the price movements of domestic markets and most of the larger foreign markets. Share bets are available to trade during the same hours that the underlying market is open – so if you want to trade US markets, you're in for a late night. We look at share bets in Chapter 4.

Ownership

Ownership is a very easy to grasp part of the overall concept of spread betting, because spread betting gives you no right to do anything with the underlying instrument that you're trading. In many ways a spread bet is similar to any other bet – your broker is acting as a bookie, your trade is a bilateral agreement between you and your broker, and you can't go and sell your spread bet position to someone else. The contract states that the broker will pay you if you're correct about the movement of the underlying instrument, and that you'll pay the broker if you're incorrect. The contract mentions nothing about taking on ownership of the underlying instrument by paying the difference between your margin (the small payment you make to open the bet) and the outstanding amount (the total amount you have exposure to).

Some traders see the margin that they pay to open a spread bet as part payment for the position, and wonder why they can't just pay for the rest of it. When you understand how spread bets work, you may ask why you'd want to convert spread bets into the fully paid version of the underlying instrument. A spread bet moves directly in line with the underlying instrument – but when holding the underlying instrument you're required to pay your financing charges for as long as you hold the position open.

Even though you can't do a direct conversion from the spread bet to the underlying instrument, you can consider the price at which you open the bet as 'locked in'. This means that you can capture any price movements without the expense of having to buy the underlying instrument.

Imagine that you opened a bet on British Land at £1 per point at a share price of 500.00 pence Your total exposure to British Land would be £1 × 500.00, or £50,000. At a typical margin rate of 5 per cent, you'd need to stake £2,500. Although this bet doesn't give you the right to own British Land shares, it does allow you to profit from a gain in the price. You're betting only £2,500 initially, but your trade in the market is £50,000 - your broker is effectively lending you the other £47,500. If the price of British Land shares were to rise to 505.00, for example, your profit would be the same as if you had a £50,000 position. Your gain of 500 points would translate into £500 at £1 per point.

Spread betting providers

You can usually open a spread betting account with one of three types of providers:

- **A spread betting firm:** A specialist broker that deals in spread betting as its specialist product.
- **Your stock broker or financial adviser:** Many financial intermediaries in the UK can help you open a spread betting account. However, they go to one of the spread betting firms for placing the bet, hedging risk and so on.
- **A white label provider:** Many other firms, like banks and bookies, now offer spread betting accounts. However, behind such a service you usually find one of the specialist brokers is taking the trade.

For the lowdown on choosing a provider, head to Chapter 2.

Getting to Grips with Trading Factors

Although many of the key features of spread bets are quite simple, you need to have a very firm understanding of the factors that you, as the trader, are contractually obliged to deal with. This means not only dealing with losses but also understanding how much money you need to open a position and the conditions under which you have to provide more money to your broker. The better your understanding *before* you spread bet, the less likely you are to receive a shock down the track.

Understanding spread bet pricing

Spread bets are placed on a pound-per-point basis. *Points* or *ticks* (in foreign exchange parlance) are the smallest decimal place on the price of the market you're trading. Most prices are quoted at five digits, but not all.

When you open a spread bet, you determine how many pounds you'll risk per point that the price changes before the bet closes. This determines what your profit and loss will be, and ultimately the size of your overall position and the amount of risk you're taking on with that trade.

For example, if you bet £1 per point that the FTSE 100 index would go up today, and it rose 60 points, you would make £60 (less the spread on the trade). If you bet £2 per point, you would make £120.

Similarly, with the £1 per point trade above, if the FTSE fell by 60 points, you would be out of pocket by £60, again less the spread, usually one or two points in this competitive spread betting market.

Paying margins

Spread bets are the first product that many traders employ that requires payment of a margin. You may be familiar with margin lending, but some very stark differences exist between margin lending and paying a margin on spread bets.

- With *margin lending*, you buy a number of shares but pay for only a portion of the amount that you hold (say, 50 per cent). The remaining amount is paid by the margin lender (such as a bank or broker) and you repay the margin lender over time. The amount of money that you put up initially acts as security for the loan, as well as being a part payment over the shares that underlie the loan.

- A *margin in terms of spread betting* is a percentage of the total position that you pay to your spread betting provider to secure a holding – and the provider returns this amount to you after you close the trade.

Look very closely at your broker's terms and conditions so that you understand exactly how it takes margin from your account. In general, the broker takes margin payments from your trading account as soon as the trade takes place. Although you may prefer not to have to pay margin straight after the trade takes place, you do get the benefit of being able to use these funds as soon as the position closes.

Initial margin

The amount your broker requires upfront in order to open your position is known as the *initial margin*. The contract that you enter into with the broker requires you to pay the difference between your entry and exit price if you're incorrect in your judgement about the direction of the underlying instrument. So the initial margin acts as security for the broker for any move against you that may occur. You can certainly think of your initial margin requirement as a deposit, because the broker refunds the amount to you when the trade closes.

Brokers publish the initial margin requirements for all the markets that they offer bets on. You find that the more liquid the underlying instrument, the lower the margin requirement. So if the underlying instrument is very *illiquid* (not readily convertible into cash), the broker wants a large part of the payment upfront. This is because liquidity (or lack thereof) is one of the risks that the broker takes when entering into a bet with a client.

Liquidity refers to the ease with which a position can be bought or sold in the market and the impact that this has on price. In an extremely liquid market, like the foreign exchange market, you can buy and sell very large quantities without having any impact on the price. Conversely, trading shares in small companies in the share market readily affects price, even if the trade being made is relatively small.

The initial margin that you pay on different products varies greatly, from lows of around 1 per cent to highs of about 50 per cent. For example, you may pay an initial margin of about 1 per cent on products like index spread bets and foreign exchange spread bets. The initial margin for share bets starts at around 5 per cent and rises to a level of about 50 per cent for the smallest companies that the broker offers (for example, AIM stocks).

Financing costs

Spread bets are a *marked-to-market* product, which means that all profits and losses are settled at the end of every trading session and at the start of every session the slate is wiped clean for everyone, or the bet is rolled over to the next day. Many traders like to settle their bets on the same day, but others like to keep them open overnight, from one trading day to the next. Most brokers allow you to roll over the bet to the next day, but they apply an overnight financing charge based on the size of your bet. This is usually quite small in proportion to the overall size of your bet, but if you keep the bet open over weeks or months, the charge can start to eat into your profit margin.

Available liquidity in the banking system can affect margin and overnight finance rates. A UK broker is within its rights to change margin requirements and financing rates if it so chooses. The terms under which this occurs are in the broker's terms and conditions. Read them carefully.

Margin calls

If you open a bet and later find that you're losing money on that trade, your broker may contact you to ask you to deposit more money in your account. This happens when all your available capital held with that broker is already committed to financing trades. The call is a *margin call.*

If you fail to make the deposit your broker requires, you may find that it closes some of your trades immediately, regardless of whether they're in profit or loss. Each broker has a different policy governing how it manages client accounts in respect of margin calls. Be sure that you find out the policy in advance.

Marking to market

Traditionally, for products that are marked-to-market, all profit and loss on the positions is settled at the end of the trading session. This occurs whether the positions are open or closed. The idea is to reduce counterparty risk – that is, the risk that one party won't be able to pay the other party when the trade eventually closes. By marking to market, the risk exists for only one day, whereas for many other products settlement is at the end of the contract and so counterparty risk increases. Spread betting brokers commonly use marking to market on nearly every product that requires only a margin payment rather than full payment to open the position. Brokers can sometimes take this a step further and require this settlement in real time.

Most brokers debit and credit your account in real time as positions move in your favour and against you. Make sure that you have plenty of available funds in your account to pay for any margin calls that may be required and that you understand the conditions under which you have to supply more funds to your provider. (In Chapters 8 and 9 we look at risk management and position sizing, respectively, which can help you to avoid this type of trouble.)

Employing leverage

One of the most interesting elements of spread betting relates to using margin payments as a means of increasing the size of your position – or, looking at the issue another way, not tying up as much of your capital in holding your positions open. Brokers keenly compete to keep margins as low as possible, because doing so allows traders to open more positions with a smaller amount of their own capital.

The term *leverage* means making your capital work harder and amplifying the results of an investment by using borrowed funds to trade larger positions. Employing *leverage* is a really big component of spread betting, but you always need to be thinking about how you're managing your risk when using leverage. That is, even if margin requirements are very low, rather than thinking exclusively about the exciting part of carrying leveraged positions you should be mindful of the amount of exposure you take to the market at any given point in time and the risk that this exposure carries. (We examine some risk minimisation techniques in Chapter 8.)

Having a low level of margin doesn't always have to imply that you're taking on a massive position in the market. For example, if you look at index spread bets, these tend to trade at a minimum size of £1 per point, meaning that you make or lose £1 for each 1-point movement of the index. This type of contract usually requires only a 1 per cent margin, which means that if the index is trading at 4,500 points, you need to make a margin payment of only £45. So although this is a really highly leveraged position, because you're getting £4,500 worth of market exposure for a £45 margin, you don't get a massive exposure in the market.

The main rule that you need to set for yourself relates to the amount by which you lever your overall account. An individual position may carry a large amount of leverage, but how this relates to your overall capital base is more important. For example, if you had £4,500 in your account and paid a margin of £45 for a highly leveraged position, you wouldn't be levered at all relative to your available capital – which illustrates how margin requirements and the actual exposure that you have to the market relate to one another.

Taking the British Land trade example from the earlier section 'Ownership', with the £2,500 margin requirement for that trade, you'd eat up a large proportion of your available spread betting capital immediately, and leave yourself open to a margin call should that trade turn suddenly against you.

If you're so inclined, you can actually use spread bets as a means of gaining quick and cheap exposure to the market without using leverage at all. More commonly, though, traders want to apply leverage to their accounts. One of the principal advantages of spread betting over margin lending is the fact that with spread bets you can turn the loan on and off, depending on whether you have a position open or not.

We talk more about using leverage in Chapters 8 and 19.

Considering the effect of delta

Spread betting has become very popular as a standalone trading product and traders use spread bets to gain exposure to movements in the price of underlying instruments. Spread bets track the underlying instrument more closely than other financial derivatives, which makes spread betting much more predictable. In essence, this means that if you can correctly pick the direction of the underlying instrument, the bet moves in line with your prediction too.

One of the biggest considerations for traders is the closeness with which the derivatives they're trading track the underlying instrument. Spread bets are possibly the simplest derivative to understand in terms of how they move relative to the underlying instrument. The underlying instrument for spread bets can be just about anything, but most commonly comprises shares, indices or foreign exchange. The closeness with which a derivative tracks its underlying instrument is measured using the Greek letter delta. If the derivative has a delta of 0.5, you expect the derivative to move 0.5 for every 1 movement of the underlying instrument. Happily for spread betting, these bets tend to have a delta of 1, which means that for every point the market price moves, you see a 1 point move in your spread bet.

By controlling the amount of money you're staking per point of price action, you have a high degree of control over the risk.

Although using delta sounds like a very simple equation for successful trading, beginner traders have a long journey in front of them coming to terms with the addition of leverage and the multiplying effect this has on the volatility of their trading; that is, how quickly the price moves up and down. This is a really important issue, and we discuss it in more detail in Chapter 8.

Capital is the trader's lifeblood

For years we've been hearing people say that you should trade only with money that you can afford to lose, and yet others say that you should invest in shares only with money that you can afford to lose. Anything you invest in gives you the potential to lose, but you can control how much you risk. Our advice is this:

- Trade only with money that, if lost, isn't going to stop you paying your bills.
- Don't trade when in a position where you 'have to win'.

As you become more confident in trading, you get a better idea of what 'sensible risk' is. You shouldn't be thinking: 'I'll just take this one trade and if I lose my £1,000 then that'll be that.' Our guess is that if you think this way and make money on the trade, you'll risk it all until you lose and become yet another person who says that you can't make money from trading.

Remember: if you risk all your trading capital again and again, you need to lose only once to be finished for good.

Pulling it all together

To open any spread bet, you must have enough money in your account to cover an initial margin. While your position is open your broker constantly revalues it as the market fluctuates, and debits and credits your account with losses or profits caused by these fluctuations. If you get the trade right, your profit will be the difference between the opening price of the underlying instrument and its closing price. But how does this all play out?

Example: Say you open a trading account with a balance of £10,000. You then stake £1 per point on ABC shares at a price of 100.00 pence, with an initial margin requirement of 5 per cent. You close the position three days later at a price of 110.00, or 1,000 points, a tax-free profit of £1,000. While the position is open the balance of your account changes as your position is revalued and as your margin obligation varies. Table 1-1 shows your initial margins and account balance while you hold the position open, and your closing profit. (Note that other costs for this trade would include financing charges. For more on financing charges, see Chapter 4.)

It is important to understand that regardless of the price, if you're spread betting, it is all about the ticks – therefore whether it is £100 or 100 pence may be less relevant than the decimal point. If I'm betting £1 per point, and the share price changes by 0.97, it doesn't matter if it is pounds or pence, as there is no physical ownership – I'm just speculating on price change. No asset disposal takes place.

Table 1-1	Example Share Spread Bet Trade			
	Settlement Price	***Initial Margin***	***Total Profit (Loss)***	***Account Balance***
				£10,000
Day 1: Buy 1,000 ABC Co. £1 per point	100.0010	£500		£9,500
Day 2	100.50	£525	£500	£9,975
Day 3	101.00	£550	£1,000	£10,450
Day 4: Sell ABC Co. @ 110.00		0	£1,000	£11,000

The example shown in Table 1-1 shows a good profit from a winning trade. Remember, though, that not all trades move in your favour – or as quickly!

Managing Your Trading

As soon as you hear from your broker that your account is funded and ready to go, you'll likely want to trade right away. Try to resist doing so, however, because opening your account is the easiest part of the trading process. Most people think the first step to trading success is to work out how best to choose your trades, but before you do this you need to:

- Understand the market.
- Know how much you're going to buy and when you'll get out of a position if it moves against you (broadly referred to as risk and money management).

So, before trading a single cent, do your homework. Ask yourself:

- Do I understand the market?
- Can I control my risk in this market?

You need to be able to answer 'yes' to both questions before you begin spread betting.

As you become a more experienced trader, you'll probably want to invest in some software to help you uncover potential trades and to maintain your records. You don't need to spend a fortune, but you do need to make some very simple considerations before opening your wallet.

Understanding the market

The question 'Do I understand the market?' is easy enough to resolve: simply study the market you're interested in by reading relevant articles in the business section of the newspaper and online.

Although you need a good theoretical grounding before you start trading, understanding the practicalities of trading comes only by placing trades. You may spend a lot of time studying a market, but only after you make your first trade using real capital do you feel like you really understand the market. Many people think that paper trading has value (and it may do), but putting real money on the line teaches you lessons you won't soon forget – so start small. Chapter 9 has more information on position sizing.

Paper trading is a means of replicating actual trades without risking your money. It involves making hypothetical trades as if you were trading with real money, but without putting your actual money at risk. To get any value out of the activity, you must follow a very clear trading strategy (we discuss trading strategies in the section 'Developing your trading plan', later in the chapter, and in Chapter 16). If you think that guessing what to buy and recording the results can help you learn about trading, you're wasting your time.

Controlling your risk and managing your money

The question 'Can I control my risk in this market?' requires a more in-depth understanding of the nature of the market. The characteristic of most interest here is the amount that the price in a given instrument moves over the time that you plan to trade it. For example, if the company on which you're planning to place a spread bet moves on average 2 per cent per day, you may have more trouble trading this for a single day than a share price that moves an average of 5 per cent per day. The very short-term trader needs to be able to capture a reasonable price movement in order to make a decent profit. The longer the period over which you trade, the easier this becomes, because you have more time to capture the profits.

Finding a method in the madness

A commodities trader named Richard Dennis once created a group known as 'The Turtles' whom he trained to trade using a very specific set of rules. All the group members had to do was follow the rules that Dennis gave them. They did so, and some became very successful, accumulating huge profits. Dennis commented that he'd happily publish his methodology in the Wall Street Journal because he knew no one would follow it anyway.

Although you may scoff at this comment, following someone else's method is tougher than it sounds. Many people believe that if only they can be told what to buy, everything else will fall into place. But if you're following someone else's advice, doing the right thing is easy – until you have a losing trade, or a string of losing trades. Then life becomes a bit trickier. You need to have confidence and a firm understanding of what you're doing, otherwise you can't respond to the changing market conditions and, more importantly, to changes in your account balance.

You have two very powerful weapons at your disposal to manage your risk:

- **Position sizing strategies:** One fundamental principle of trading is that the bigger your position, the bigger your risk. So, based on your available capital and the use of stop loss orders (see the next bullet), you can work out the position sizes that mean you lose only a small percentage of your capital on any trades in which you lose money. We talk more about using position sizing strategies in Chapter 9.
- **Stop loss orders:** A *stop loss order* is an order offered by brokers that enables you to choose the price at which you admit that you were wrong about a trade that you're in and close it down to preserve your precious capital. (We explain how to use stop loss orders in Chapter 2.) Plan where to place your stop loss order *before* you open a trade, because doing so helps with your trade discipline (see Chapter 15 for more information on trade discipline).

Being consistent with your risk management is key to survival when dealing with an ever-changing market, so we strongly suggest that you familiarise yourself with Chapter 8, which deals with risk management in much more detail.

As an extension of this issue, you need to know the minimum cost to you if you get closed out of a trade. Not all spread bets are equal when it comes to how much a one-increment movement in the price impacts on the value of the position you hold. Some bets can seem very conservative, but others are anything but.

All discussions of what constitute reasonable costs for trading are quite relative. For example, traders with a high risk tolerance (who are comfortable with the potential for large percentage swings against them in the short term) can cope easily with the trading of volatile positions, whereas traders with a small capital base or a low tolerance for volatility won't cope so easily. Spend time getting used to a product to find out whether it's suitable for you.

We recommend trading in small amounts (that is, only £1 or £2 per point), when you get started, irrespective of how much capital you have to play with, because you may be surprised by how much a market can move if you don't.

Developing your trading plan

'Failing to plan is planning to fail.' If you're like us, you can't stand expressions like this – pieces of wisdom that are breathtakingly easy to dispense but infuriatingly difficult to put into practice! Obviously, if you have no planning in place then life will be much more difficult for you. However, having a plan won't work wonders for you if that plan is ineffective or you don't follow it consistently.

In very general terms, your *trading plan* represents your guide to helping you know what to do in a wide range of situations – some of which may be very unpleasant for you from a trading perspective. Your trading plan should cover the following issues:

- Why you want to trade
- What you're going to trade
- How you decide what to buy
- When you want to sell, and how much risk you take on with each trade

Pretty much everything else derives from these important aspects of trading. We give you tips on developing your trading plan in Chapter 16.

Choosing your software

Using software to help you make trading decisions is really standard these days, but the range of products available can make choosing the best software a challenge.

The following sensible considerations should help with your decision:

- Many of the features of very powerful software (which tends to be expensive and allows for extensive customisation) aren't necessary unless you're an extremely advanced analyst. Start with the cheaper software, because then you have less sunk costs working against you. As long as you can use common indicators (for example, moving averages, which we explain in Chapter 13) and draw trend lines and support/resistance lines (which we also explain in Chapter 13), you're ready to use software to start trading.
- The cost of charting software doesn't have a large correlation with your effectiveness as a trader. In other words, a good trader can be successful using cheaper software. Cheaper software limits the amount of customisation that you can do, but this isn't likely to be an issue until you're a more advanced trader.

We examine software options in more detail in Chapter 14.

Record-keeping

You need to think quite carefully about the record-keeping that you undertake. Naturally, you want to know whether you're winning or losing over time, but this isn't the only issue you need to consider. You need to think about how often you're winning compared with how often you're losing. And you also need to look at the average size of your wins compared with the average size of your losses. Such factors help you to develop the fullest appreciation of your trading success. We outline how to keep track of your progress in Chapter 17.

Chapter 2

Setting Yourself Up for Success

In This Chapter

- Getting to know the providers
- Understanding the different orders available, and how to use them

Before you can start trading, you need to select a spread betting firm or broker. The financial spread betting market is a very competitive environment for providers, so you need to consider your choice of provider carefully. There are many similarities between providers, and you may find that it's the small things that make all the difference for you and the trading you plan to do.

In this chapter, we examine some of the things you need to think about when selecting a spread betting broker. And, because after you select your provider you will be keen to start trading, we help you with the next step: examining the types of orders that you can use as part of your trading plan.

Choosing between Spread Betting Providers

In the UK, the Financial Services Authority (FSA) regulates all financial spread betting firms. This means that you have some recompense under the Investors Compensation Scheme should your broker collapse. Your first £48,000 of credit with your broker is covered under this scheme, but it may take a while before you see this. Spread betting isn't offered by firms without an FSA license, or shouldn't be. You can always check with the regulator if in doubt.

A wide range of spread betting providers compete for your money in the UK – from specialist firms, to stock brokers, financial advisers, banks and bookies. On the upside, the number of providers on offer means they need to compete harder on price and service levels to keep your business. But it also means that you need to do your homework to ensure that you're dealing with a firm that's reputable and will manage your account fairly.

Differentiating between spread betting and share betting

Although you may find spread betting firms advertising their services in very similar places to stock brokers, never forget that spread betting means trading on markets quoted to you by the spread betting firm. You're placing a bet with a broker – you're not buying shares or commodities in the market. A spread betting firm is effectively making a market itself: the market is a series of prices on different bets, just as you might see odds on a horse race quoted to you in a betting shop. The prices may be very similar to the underlying market you want to trade – the FTSE 100 index, for example – but ultimately, your broker owns that price.

A number of key factors recommend spread betting over share trading, other than the wider range of financial markets you are able to access. For starters, you don't pay commission on your trades. The cost of the trade is built into the bid/offer spread. In addition, the spread betting firms provide you with far more leverage (margin) than you would ever get from a stock broker. You are also often able to trade outside market hours. On top of all this, of course, is the fact that you pay no tax, either capital gains or stamp duty, on your trading profits.

Not all firms offering spread betting accounts are your actual counterparty – many of the big brokers now offer partnership agreements with other financial institutions and independent financial advisers, allowing them to *white label* (resell under their own brand) their spread betting platform. You can check what the spread betting provider is in the terms and conditions of your spread betting account.

The following sections help you compare providers to make the best choice for your needs.

Considering the basics

First of all, look at the basic offering of the providers you're considering:

- **Margins and spreads:** Price – the width in points in the spreads on popular markets – has become an increasingly competitive aspect for brokers, with many now offering only one point or even zero point trading on indices. In addition, margin rates vary. If you imagine your trading will be focusing on one or a small number of markets, shop around to see who's able to offer the best rates.

- **Education:** Some firms offer more education than others. If you're new to spread betting, you may want to start trading with a firm that can provide free educational material such as podcasts, guides to trading and seminars to support you early on. This can include webinars if you live too remotely to get into a major town.
- **Range of markets:** All spread betting firms aren't created equal in this respect – most offer the favourite markets, like the FTSE 100 and the GBP/USD currency pair, but if you're looking for something more esoteric, like rough rice or a mid-cap share, the larger firms are more likely to be able to help you.
- **Trading platform:** Many of the leading brokers now offer proprietary trading platforms, but some are better than others. Increasingly, the platforms are web-based, but older versions require downloading onto a computer. Other firms use third-party trading software.
- **Mobile trading:** In the last few years mobile trading has become an important factor in spread betting, with some brokers reporting over a third of their bets now coming in via mobile devices. Brokers tend to launch trading apps for the iPhone and iPad first, and then follow with Android after these have been successfully road-tested. If you think you'll want to trade on the move, check whether mobile trading facilities are available.
- **Stop losses:** See the later section on 'Placing Orders'. Some brokers are better at honouring your stops than others. Most of the time, this depends on the liquidity of the underlying market and the broker's ability to hedge risk, but generally speaking, brokers are quite efficient at this. Some now offer guaranteed stop losses. One of the best ways to check out how good a provider is at executing stops is to talk to other traders online – there are plenty of trading forums where you should be able to find current and former clients of most of the UK spread betting firms.
- **Demo accounts:** Some firms now offer demo accounts that let you trade with play money, helping you to hone your skills and learn on their trading platform. The degree of access you're granted varies – some only let you trade a small number of markets, and others expect you to fund your account after a period of time with real money.

  Depending on your provider, you may receive the software for free or pay a fee. Some brokers charge for the software, because they need to pay the company that provides them with the software. However, charges are often negotiable and depend on how much business you do with the provider during a month. The more trades you make, the lower the software charge you pay.

Keeping an eye on grey markets

A recent trend in financial spread betting is the introduction of grey markets – trading the price of a company before its initial public offering. Some of the larger brokers have been able to offer this facility, but it is not available from all spread betting firms. Recent examples include Betfair and Ocado in the UK and Facebook in the US. Traders speculate on the price of a share before it even hits the market. Because you're dealing with a market maker, and not trading the actual shares at any point, you can profit from price changes ahead of the live listing date. Look for more such grey markets going forwards.

Yet more to think about

The type of provider you choose doesn't affect your access to the market because you're still spread betting with them and not trading in the physical market.

To help you make your decision, you may also want to consider the following issues, all of which should be readily answered on the provider's website:

- **Product range:** One of the clear advantages of spread betting is the range of products that providers make available to their traders. Many providers provide access to spread bets in the following markets: foreign exchange (FX, or forex), indices, commodities, treasuries and equities (foreign and domestic). In addition, some will offer other products, like binary bets or emerging markets FX and indexes. The majority of spread betting volume (80 per cent) flows through a small number of popular products, like the FTSE 100 or GBP/USD currency pair, but some traders will be looking for more esoteric markets, like mid-sized companies or niche commodities markets. Only the bigger providers will offer these.
- **Funds on deposit:** Ask potential providers what happens to the funds that you have on deposit with them. You need to establish how safe these funds are with the provider and what happens to any interest you earn. The information will be mapped out clearly in your firm's terms and conditions. As a point of good practice, spread betting firms should be able to prove that they're clearly segregating client money – your money is accounted for separately from other customers' and the firm's own trading capital.

- **Integration of services:** Some providers enable you to deal in both spread bets and the physical share market, thus enabling you to deal using a single trading account.
- **Interest:** Check whether you earn interest on funds on deposit. Usually, you need to have more than a certain amount in your trading account before you earn interest; something like £15,000 is the likely minimum threshold.
- **Ongoing trader education and market research:** Some providers offer trader education in the form of courses or printed material, and market research such as market updates and trade strategies.
- **Other types of bets:** Some brokers offer different types of bets; for example, bets that function as options or binary bets. Many of these are unique to a given provider. Explore the online product literature for details.
- **Personal service:** Some offer a high level of client service, with your own personal sales trader on the end of a phone.

Placing Orders

After you decide which type of provider fits the bill for you, you need to examine the ways in which you can manage your account and your trades. One of the main areas of spread betting that new traders often find a bit of an eye opener is the wide range of different orders available. An *order* is an instruction from a trader to the provider to buy or sell a specified item in a market. Compared to share investments, where market orders and limit orders are the most common orders, spread betting offers a much wider range of orders as part of the standard offering. By using these spread bet orders properly you can take control of your trading and plan ahead how you'll execute your trades.

Different providers offer different types of orders, so check what your chosen provider has available and be sure that the offering meets your needs.

Spread bets are generally a *non-advisory product*, which means that you're totally responsible for making all your trade decisions and placing all your orders. We strongly suggest that you set yourself a routine for placing orders, such as always reading your order back to yourself twice or even saying the order out loud, to ensure that you aren't betting £100 a point when you want to bet £10. Such a huge error takes the fun out of your day very quickly indeed!

Market orders

A *market order* is an order to buy or sell immediately at the current market price. Market orders are probably the most commonly used orders because they allow you to get in and out of the market immediately.

Stop orders

A *stop order* is an order to buy when the price has climbed to or above a specified stop price or to sell when the price has dropped to or below a specified stop price. The stop order is one of the most important orders available to traders because you can use this order to manage your risk by selling automatically when the price reaches a level that you nominate. You can also use stop orders to automate the entry of *breakout trades*, which occur when the price moves through a support or resistance level (see Chapter 13 for more information on support and resistance levels).

A *stop loss order* does exactly what the name implies – it stops your loss. The reason a stop order isn't always a stop *loss* order is because you aren't always going to use the order to stop a loss – you may also use the order as a stop *entry* order.

Your broker places limits on how close to the current market price you can place a stop order. For example, if you're currently in a long position (meaning you expect the price to rise) and you place a stop loss order to limit your loss, the broker may execute the order as soon as the bid price matches (or is less than) the price you nominated – although some brokers wait until the market actually trades at this level before they execute the order. You may think that getting out before the market actually trades at your level sounds like a bad deal, but if you think about it, your broker doesn't know what's going to happen next, so it closes out the position as soon as possible.

Being able to use stop orders is a critical component of being a successful trader, because of the ability that stop orders give you to manage your risk. The key issue is to work out where to place your stop *before* trade opens. If you're not sure about where to place your stop orders, check out Chapter 8 on risk management strategies.

If you're dealing in the share market, stop orders are normally triggered when the price trades at the level that you nominated rather than the bid price (or the offer price if you're short) hitting that level. With foreign exchange, the bid price triggers stop orders because there's no published traded price to go by.

Stop orders versus contingent orders

In many ways stop orders and contingent orders perform the same task: allowing traders to cap the downside that they may otherwise have been exposed to. Potentially, however, stop orders may be superior to contingent orders in the event of a significant price gap occurring in the market, as follows:

- If such a gap occurs when you're using a stop order, the market maker will still close the position at the first available price and you'll be out of the position – although this may be well below your originally nominated stop loss level (an issue known as *slippage*).
- If such a gap occurs when you're using a contingent order and the market you are spread betting on doesn't trade at the contingent price that you nominate (meaning that no trades occur in the underlying market at that price), the position remains in place. As a result, unless you have access to your trading platform to close the position yourself, you'll still be in a trade that you'd rather not be in.

Contingent orders

The broker executes a *contingent order* only if it is instructed by you to execute another order first. Contingent orders are used in a similar way to stop orders. Effectively, you are asking the broker to execute one order only IF another order happens first. If this happens, you are saying, *then* do this. By using a contingent order you're saying that if the market trades at a certain price then your provider should automatically place a market order – which is how a contingent order behaves in a way similar to a stop order. If your provider offers this type of order instead of stop orders, you can use it as your primary means of managing your risk.

Limit orders

A *limit order* is an order to buy at no more than (or sell at no less than) a specified price. You use a limit order if you want to deal at a price below the current level (that is, if you want to *go long* – meaning to benefit from a rising price) or above the current price (that is, if you want to *go short* – meaning to benefit from a falling price). This means that you trade only if the price moves to the level that you nominate.

Limit orders are a popula[illegible]ns of trading for people whose strategy relies on the price coming to them, and not the other way around. Generally, there's a limit on how close to the current market price you can place a limit order: check your provider's terms and conditions so that you know how the provider handles the issue.

You may be tempted to think that using limit orders is always a good idea, and in some ways getting into a position as cheaply as possible makes good sense. Be sure that you're using the limit order for the right reason, though, because in a sense what you're saying is something like, 'I believe that this position is going to go up, but I won't buy it until it goes down.' One of the worst outcomes of trading like this is that you end up chasing the price higher but always put in the order at a lower price until you get the position – by which stage the price is already heading lower and will keep going that way.

Requotes

A *requote* occurs when the market is moving quickly, and the provider does not want to offer you the spread bet at that price. A requote isn't an order type in itself; it's something of a subset of orders. The provider will usually either offer you an alternative price, or simply say the price you wanted to open the bet at is no longer available. It is rare for this to happen these days, as many of the biggest providers now use highly automated systems for calculated trades. It can also happen if too many traders are taking the same position, and the provider is finding it difficult to hedge this in the market.

When you place an order online and insufficient volume is available to fill your order, a separate box pops up on your screen, explaining that the price at which you wanted to deal isn't available any more. Instead, you're offered a quote at a different price, although this new price won't be as good as your initial price.

You can choose whether to take the new trade or not – but you generally have only a few seconds to decide!

- If you accept the trade, your order is filled at the new price that the provider offered you.
- If you reject the trade, you can wait to see what happens to the available volume and perhaps try to place the order again at a later time.

Guaranteed stop loss orders

Using a *guaranteed stop loss order* (GSLO) from a provider helps you manage your risk even more effectively than with a regular stop order, because you pay extra to ensure that if you get stopped out, you know at exactly what price it will occur. The benefit is that even if large price gaps develop (perhaps triggered by a large fall in the US market overnight), you have the assurance of knowing where you'll get stopped out.

The downside to using a GSLO is that you have to pay a premium upfront whether the provider executes the order or not. This premium differs from provider to provider (as do policy conditions like whether you can move the order without extra charge), so check your provider's terms and conditions for clarification.

If-done orders

An *if-done order* is an advanced order type that allows you to connect two different orders together, such as a limit order and a stop order. As the name implies, if one order is done, the other order is placed. Using an if-done order enables you to plan much of the order set-up ahead of time and then execute the order automatically when certain conditions are met.

Say you start with a limit order that's below the current market price: you plan to buy if the price retracts to a level that you've chosen. When you first place this order you say that *if* a provider executes it, you want to automatically place a stop order 20p below the limit entry. This leaves you with a long position and a stop order 20 points below the price at which you entered the trade. In other words, you've got into your position and placed your stop order to manage your risk all in one step, using an if-done order.

One cancels other orders

One cancels other (OCO) orders are designed to let you have two connected orders (to get you out of the market) surrounding a position that you already have. Most commonly, this allows you to either stop your loss (if the price moves against you) or take your profit (if the price moves in your favour). OCO orders are a really important order type for many traders, but if you plan to trade a 24-hour market like FX then they're essential.

Say that you're long XYZ (you expect the price to rise) and want to take the profits if the share price rises by 30p but close out the position if the price falls by 15p. You can place both of these orders and link them together as an OCO order: if the provider executes one of the orders, the provider automatically cancels the other.

An OCO saves you from having to be glued to your trading screen to manage your orders, because the order removes the risk that the provider will execute a second order before you get a chance to cancel it. ***Note:*** Generally, the two orders need to be a minimum distance apart.

Chapter 3

Making the Most of Financial Spread Betting

In This Chapter

- Comparing long and short trading
- Getting to grips with financing charges and payments
- Choosing between different types of spread betting
- Understanding market trading conditions

When you start spread betting, the number of different products and strategies to choose between can be a bit overwhelming. The key is not to carry too many preconceived notions about how you're going to trade but instead focus on keeping your risk low and devising strategies that follow the trends in the market. In other words, look to the direction of the overall market and the individual instruments that make up the market (for example, a share index and the individual shares that make up that index) and trade in line with the way they're trending. So you want to be primarily on the long side when the market trends up, and short when the market trends down.

In this chapter, we look at dealing on the long and short side of the market – having this amount of choice to benefit from rising and falling markets will be unfamiliar to many traders who are new to spread betting. We also look at some of the key issues you need to understand about market conditions and then examine how you can adapt your trading strategy accordingly.

Examining Long Versus Short Trading

So often the things that appeal to traders about spread bets are factors like leverage and small commissions because you can take on large positions very cheaply, but an amazing (although not unique) strength of spread betting is that it allows you to trade very easily on the long and short sides of the market.

- Trading on the long side (*long trading*) means buying with the view that the price is going to rise and selling at a higher price in order to make a profit.
- Trading on the short side (*short trading*) means selling with the view that the price is going to fall and then buying back at a lower price in order to make a profit.

Many people are comfortable with the concept of long trading but have difficulties with the concept of short trading. We concentrate on short trading in this section, so that you can be completely at ease with the process.

Benefiting from a price that goes down

One of the first questions that beginner traders ask concerning short trading is: 'How can I sell something that I don't own?' The answer is really simple, because with spread betting you don't own anything anyway – even if you're buying to go long. Remember that a spread bet is simply a contract between you and the provider, so instead of thinking about ownership, just remember that buying and selling determine only whether your contract value rises or falls as the price rises or falls.

Many people continue to look past short trading even after they understand the concept because they feel that it's a step too far for them. Others are happy dealing on the long side, because it's more akin to dealing in the share market. Of course you need to be comfortable with your trading strategy, but make sure that you consider some of the potential advantages of short trading before closing the door on short trades for good.

A closer look at short trading

One of David's colleagues used to tell a brilliant story illustrating how short trading works, which he's been dining out on for years – so another rendition can't hurt. Imagine that you're at work and you need to go up the road to buy your lunch, but it's raining outside. You borrow an umbrella from a colleague and head off. In the doorway to the building, you're approached by someone with a mass of paperwork who offers to buy the umbrella for £30. You agree and take the money. Then you head across the road to the umbrella store and buy an identical umbrella to the one you just sold for £20, grab your lunch and head back to the office. When you get back to the office you return the umbrella to your colleague.

This scenario is very similar to a short trade because you sold as your opening trade and then bought back to close the trade. You pocketed the difference, which in this case was £10 and is your profit to keep, because all parties were returned to their original state.

Yes, we realise that you need to get rained on for this example to work, but hopefully you can look past that!

- Markets spend a lot of time heading lower, and trading on the short side of the market is the best way to take advantage of this. Over the long term, even though historically the share market has risen quite consistently, it has spent not much less than half the time going down and the average magnitude of the down days is only a little smaller than the average up day. This means that in *bull* (generally rising) markets and *bear* (generally falling) markets you have plenty of opportunity to find positions that are falling in value, which give you opportunities beyond those that would be available if you were only dealing on the long side of the market.
- Most markets tend to fall more quickly than they rise, so if you're keen to find some very short-term trading opportunities, the short side of the market may be just the place for you. The good thing is that you can use most of the same analysis as you would for trading on the long side – you just have to reverse your thinking. (Check out some of the methods we mention in Chapter 13 on technical analysis.) Basically, methods such as a support/resistance breakout or a moving average crossover are the same whether in a rising or falling market – you just approach the analysis from the opposite direction.
- You may be able to reduce the *volatility* of your overall portfolio (that is, sharp movements in the value of the positions) by maintaining a combination of long and short exposure. A big part of this reduction comes from not relying so heavily on market direction as a driver of your profitability, which is a significant benefit for traders who prefer to see fewer up and down swings in the value of their portfolio.

You may have read that 80 per cent of share movements follow movements in the index. This concept doesn't really make sense, because the index value is calculated using the movement of the shares and not the other way round. Nonetheless, the overall market is a major driver of the broader market moves that are seen on a day-to-day basis, and being caught up in the wider up or down movements of the market can be difficult to escape. However, if you're not quite unidirectional in the make-up of your portfolio and you carry a portion of long *and* short positions, these movements may improve your portfolio – or at least make it less volatile, which a lot of traders really like.

Understanding that FX trading has built-in short trades

If you choose to trade foreign exchange (FX), you need to be comfortable with trading on the short side. This is because FX doesn't have any inherent directional bias and has as much opportunity on the long side as it does on the short side. More importantly, though, you can't trade on just one side of the market in FX, because to buy one currency you must sell an equal-sized amount of another currency. This means that you go long in one currency and short in the other. For more on FX trades, see Chapter 5.

Keep in mind that the maximum downside to trading short is actually worse than the downside to trading long. The reason is that there's no limit to how high something can go in value but it can't go any lower than zero. This is worth remembering, but within reason. An author whose name eludes us once wrote that he'd seen many stocks go to zero but he hadn't seen any go to infinity, so you can make your own judgement on this concept.

Your most likely concern is a takeover bid being made for a company while you're short, making a large gap upward in the price of the shares – with very little you can do about it.

Recognising the Costs and Benefits of Doing Business

Financing charges are the costs that your spread betting broker charges to you if you have long side exposure (long trading) to the market. You can think of this cost as interest on a loan that's been made to you by your spread betting broker to allow you to take on this exposure to the market. Most providers charge financing based on your total exposure to the market (that is, the number of share spread bets you have multiplied by the price of the spread bets), rather than your exposure minus the margin that you put up.

Margin isn't part payment for a position: it acts as security for the spread betting broker.

Conversely, your spread betting broker pays you financing payments on short positions. We examine how this works for different types of spread bets in Chapters 4 to 7, but the main thing to note here is how the provider calculates payments and pays you. The standard method of calculation in the UK is to add or subtract from the official cash rate. For example, for short positions you may receive the LIBOR (London Interbank Offered Rate) rate minus 2 per cent (and for long positions you may pay the LIBOR rate plus 2 per cent). (If the cash rate is less than 2 per cent, you'll be charged for the short mode.)

Although you're unlikely to earn a huge amount of money from your short position financing, the payments provide an interesting offset for you if you carry long and short exposure. In fact, if you were equally long and short in the market then, using the example of the LIBOR rate plus/minus 2 per cent, your overall financing charge would be 4 per cent, regardless of what happens to the LIBOR rate. This may not necessarily be the most realistic outcome for you, but it shows how short positions can benefit you beyond capturing falling prices.

Making Sense of Spread Betting

One of the simultaneously most exciting and most daunting aspects of spread betting is the large variety of different spread bets that are available to trade. In fact, some several thousand different instruments are available, so you could be forgiven for being a little unsure about where to start trading! However, in actual fact most beginner traders are fairly sure where they want to begin – for most people the choice is spread betting on shares, but for others it may be FX or commodities. No right or wrong choices exist, and you certainly don't need to feel like you have to trade everything that's on your broker's product list. How many traders do you think spread bet on lumber? Very few, we suspect.

The goal of spread betting is to make money for you, not for your provider. Your broker makes money off the spread and from financing charges, so the more you trade, the more money the provider makes. There's no such thing as a free lunch, so trade the most appropriate product for you, not the one that seems cheapest to trade.

One of the things about spread betting that has always captivated us is the idea that you can run something that closely resembles a hedge fund from your personal computer. This is because with spread betting you can trade both long and short, as well as across a massive range of different products – enabling you to take a view on a range of different markets. Although you may think that this is too much for a beginner trader to take on, this isn't the case for someone who's willing to dedicate a reasonable amount of time to trading.

Coping with Market Trading Conditions

You don't need to view your spread betting portfolio in isolation from the rest of your investment portfolio – and, indeed, you can create quite a bit of interactivity between the portfolios. For example, you can use your dealing on the short side with spread bets to hedge the market exposure you have with physical shares, and even to potentially reduce the overall volatility of your portfolio. Similarly, you may find that because of the wide range of asset categories you can gain exposure to with spread betting, you may get diversification benefits that otherwise would be difficult to achieve.

Getting fancy: Hedging your bets

One of the huge upsides that comes from spread betting is the fact that trading on the short side can offer strategic opportunities. One such opportunity is *portfolio hedging*. Typically, in the past the main form of defence that traders have undertaken for their portfolios has been diversification. This tactic relies on spreading money widely enough so that a fall in the value of a small number of positions should be offset by rises in other positions. The main problem with diversification occurs when the wider market falls heavily – the benefits of diversification are then seriously limited.

In such a falling market a more direct defensive approach – hedging – can yield greater benefits. When you hedge your position you take on exposure to another instrument that moves in a different direction to the investment you already hold.

Imagine that you're long 1,000 XYZ shares. You've held these shares for a long time and although you believe the company to be very sound, you expect a short-term downturn in the share price, which you want to defend against. With hedging, you simply go short on XYZ shares as a spread bet, so that for every penny the share price moves down, you lose £10 of your floating profit on your XYZ shares but make the same amount of money on your XYZ share spread bets. You can see that spread bets offer a great deal of precision in the way they deliver the hedging benefit.

If you were feeling a little more adventurous, you could increase your short exposure to XYZ share spread bets, so that you go from being net long XYZ shares to being net short XYZ shares as spread bets. Note that you still hold your original shares, but you switch your exposure to being short in order to benefit from the falling share price. Because you control the amount of money you stake on a per point basis, you also have a high level of control over the degree to which you enhance your short position.

Many products are available to help you with hedging, among which options are the most notable, but with spread bets you can be a lot more direct with this type of method because the underlying share price and the price of the spread bet precisely offset one another, which is an ideal situation when hedging. In Chapter 1, we briefly look at the concept of delta and how it helps you to determine how one instrument is likely to move in relation to another instrument. A spread bet will closely mirror the underlying asset it is based on, but because you can also trade on the short side of the asset – that is, in the opposite direction – this means a spread bet can be used to offset losses in the original asset. In effect, it can be used as a form of insurance for an investment portfolio.

Although a hedging strategy seems like a relatively harmless way of dealing in the market and it does protect you from losses that you'd otherwise be exposed to when the market turns against you, hedging has its disadvantages:

- You receive no benefit if the underlying share price rises.
- Even though you earn financing payments on the short spread bets, this strategy doesn't pay for itself because the money you have tied up in the physical shares isn't earning anything for you other than any dividends paid out.

Such considerations must remain in your mind at all times when spread betting. Remember, there's no such thing as a risk-free trade, and for every reward a risk is attached.

Coping with FX volatility

You need to have a keen understanding of the nature of the markets that you're dealing in. For example, if markets are inherently volatile, you need to ensure that your strategy evolves to cope with this volatility. In this section, we explain how to deal with volatility and how allowing for volatility is a necessary skill that you need to adopt in order to avoid the frustration of being stopped out frequently on trades that would eventually have gone in your favour.

The FX market is one of the most volatile markets, but it's also the market where your risk management can be the most effective. This is because the huge volumes that people trade mean that you're very likely to be able to close out your losing positions at precisely (or very close to) the level that you nominate, even in times of high volatility – which is something you won't see in any other market.

Importantly, though, just like in any other market, you need to take account of the prevailing level of volatility and adjust your expectations accordingly. So if the market is volatile, you need to set wider stop loss orders to avoid getting stopped out too quickly and unnecessarily. You can judge volatility in several ways. The average true range indicator is a good option and we explain this in Chapter 13.

In addition, you find that although the FX market frequently offers good trending opportunities over periods of weeks and months, in the short term (which often seems attractive to new traders) periods of high volatility and largely directionless trade occur. In order to illustrate this concept, consider Figures 3-1 and 3-2.

Figure 3-1 is a five-minute chart showing the value of sterling against the US dollar. The chart provides a new price candle every five minutes (a *candle* shows the open, high, low and close for that period; see Chapter 13 for more details). In the space of about eight hours the value of the dollar ranges from 1.555 to 1.54600 and then back again. Most spread betting brokers offer a minimum position size of between 25p and £1. Although you may not think that this cost sounds too bad, you have to consider its impact on your overall risk and reward:

- If you're happy to take a 40-pip profit (a *pip* being the smallest price movement of an FX rate) – which equates to £10 if you deal on the smallest position size – you can't reasonably risk more than about one-third of this profit amount on each of your trades.
- You need to consider the spread your provider charges on the risk side of the proposition because it costs you money. This is a cost that you can't avoid and it impacts you as soon as you open the trade.

In other words, if you're always looking for small profits, you need to be even more aware of the risks and costs of doing business because you have fewer gains to offset them against.

Figure 3-1: Short-term directionless trade.

Figure 3-2: More time can equal more profit potential.

Now look at Figure 3-2, an hourly chart of the sterling–dollar relationship. This chart covers a different time scale to that used in Figure 3-1. The hourly chart shows a greater range or volatility being achieved, but it also illustrates that your profit potential is significantly higher, which means that on a winning trade you expect much bigger profits. Of course, the opposite also applies, because in general terms you need to be able to take larger losses in order to generate larger profits.

In adapting to a given set of market circumstances you must look to the expected volatility of a position and set your stop losses accordingly. If you were to look at any FX chart and aim to take a profit of 100 pips, but place your stop loss 5 pips away (which is about as close as any provider will allow), very likely you'd be stopped out of your position before the position had any reasonable chance to be successful. Although you may think that stopping your loss if the price moves against you even a little bit sounds perfectly reasonable, it actually isn't very sensible, because you're very unlikely to be able to pick the precise moment to get into an FX trade such that the price only moves higher from that moment on.

Wiggle room: Allowing the market to move

We've often heard traders say: 'I always put my stop *x* points away on my trades.' Although being disciplined enough to use stops is certainly a plus for such traders, the resulting plan of attack may not be as effective. As an example, if you're dealing in a £50 stock and a £1 stock and you always put your stop 10p away, your stop is almost certainly too close in the case of the £50 stock (it absorbs too little volatility) and too far away for the £1 stock (it absorbs too much volatility).

Some people refer to allowing the market enough room to move against you in order to absorb normal market volatility as *wiggle room*. This means setting your stops far enough away that you can benefit from broader market moves without your trade being closed out. Although you want to keep your downsides small, you don't want to get taken out of positions only to have them move in your favour afterwards. The idea that you need to let the market move against you a sensible amount takes a little while to digest, but you can see that different trading methods are available to help you find the right mix of return and volatility absorption. The average true range indicator is great at measuring this (see Chapter 13).

Dealing with slippage and gaps

Depending on the markets that you trade, you may see a great degree of slippage and gaps in prices. *Slippage* means your provider executes an order at a worse price than the order you placed, and *gaps* are movements in price where no trade occurs – for example, if one trade occurs at a price of $1 and the next trade occurs at a price of $1.10, the market has 'gapped' 10p.

This high degree of slippage and gapping in prices occurs for two main reasons:

- Conditions changing when the market is closed, such as economic news being released
- Low volumes, which see prices move more erratically than in high-volume markets

Because the FX market has a high turnover and trades 24 hours a day, it has the lowest likelihood of slippage and gapping. To reduce your risk in this market, you can use stop losses. The reasons that stop losses work so well in managing your risk are twofold.

Big volume for low slippage

The FX market is the most liquid of all markets. This is particularly notable when you're looking at the more liquid currency pairs, such as the EUR/USD. As a result of this liquidity, slippage on your trading is much less likely.

Slippage usually occurs when your order is too big for the buyers/sellers to absorb, but it can also occur in times of high volatility. Happily, because the FX market has so much turnover, slippage is less likely to be an issue in this market than in any other market.

Index bets trade in both day and night sessions, but the night sessions see significantly lower volumes and as a result have a much greater likelihood of slippage occurring (some brokers don't offer index bets outside the trading hours of a particular market – check before opening a live bet). So if you trade large volumes on indexes in a night session and a ruction occurs in the market, you may get slipped quite aggressively. This doesn't mean that you shouldn't trade at night, but if you do, exercise greater caution. However, if you trade large amounts, you may be best avoiding night-time trading altogether.

If you get slipped on a position that you're trading, the natural temptation may be to blame your spread betting broker. Sometimes spread betting brokers are to blame, but make sure that you know the characteristics of the product you're dealing in before racing to the conclusion that your broker is at fault. Spread betting brokers generally give you no more volume to trade than is available in the underlying market, so if you're quickly trying to unwind a large position in an illiquid market, you'll certainly experience some slippage.

Frequent gaps in prices

Gaps in prices occur as the market absorbs new information. In the UK (and indeed in most countries) traders focus on events in the United States overnight and these events have a major impact on the local market when trade begins. A big move higher or lower in the US market may see companies locally 'gapping' higher or lower. The frequency with which gaps occur depends on the market. For example, the share market closes every night, so each day when it opens gaps may occur, whereas the FX market closes only once a week and so has fewer opportunities for gaps.

No trading takes place in these gaps, and if you place your stop loss within the gap, you won't get out at the price you hoped to. This is one of the most common examples of slippage that occurs.

Gapping occurs regularly during trading sessions in low liquidity instruments, so we suggest you stick to the more liquid products. We're not trying to dissuade you from any type of trading that you want to get involved in, however. If you prefer illiquid instruments, just make sure that you thoroughly plan ahead how to handle the gaps in prices that occur. You need to recognise that when trading in less liquid markets, more frequent slippage is essentially an additional cost of doing business. When you trade in the longer term, slippage is less of an issue because you're trading less frequently. In other words, the more frequently you trade, the more of an issue slippage becomes.

Part II

Touring the Spread Betting Marketplace

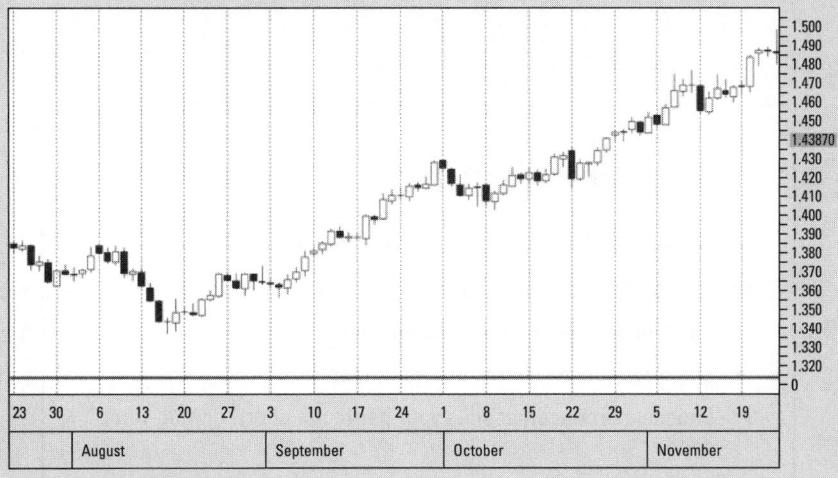

For Dummies can help you get started with a huge range of subjects. Visit `www.dummies.com` to learn more and do more with *For Dummies*.

In this part . . .

- Find your way through the maze of markets.
- Dip your toe into foreign exchange trading.
- Come to grips with trading commodities.
- Secure profits on shares and securities.
- Choose a product that suits your particular short- or long-term needs.
- Go to www.dummies.com/extras/fsbuk for online bonus content.

Chapter 4

Spread Betting on Share Markets

In This Chapter

- Comparing physical shares and share-based spread bets
- Understanding dividends, share bonuses and splits
- Looking at spread bet financing charges
- Trading in foreign share markets
- Comparing short- and medium-term trading
- Trading in other time zones

Spread bets based on share prices have a number of similarities with their underlying market, and these similarities can ease your transition from trading in the share market to spread betting on single company prices.

In this chapter, we describe how shares and spread bets relate to one another and how you can incorporate share-based spread bets into your trading portfolio. We also examine how spread betting shares on both the long and the short side can help balance your trading portfolio while dealing in the inherently volatile share market.

Spread bets are a derivative product and should make up only a small portion of your overall investment portfolio because of the high degree of leverage they carry. If you need a refresher on derivatives, refer to Chapter 1.

Understanding How Shares and Spread Bets Differ

A big part of the overall difference between shares and spread bets comes down to ownership. Perhaps you've noticed that shares in UK companies are referred to as 'fully paid shares'. Fully paid in this context means that you have nothing left to pay on the shares and that ownership of the shares gives you certain rights, such as a right over company dividends and the right to vote on matters concerning the company.

Spread bets never allow you to take ownership of the underlying instrument. So, unlike holding shares, share spread bets don't entitle you to vote at the company's annual general meeting. Some spread bets do pay dividends; see the section 'Dividend payments', later in this chapter.

Other derivatives such as options, warrants and futures allow you to take ownership of the underlying instrument, but that's because different maturity features are built into these products. Maturity features can also exist in a spread bet, but there is no delivery of a physical asset when the bet expires – it is either closed or rolled over to the next period for a small fee.

When you open a spread bet, you make a margin payment, but this payment doesn't give you ownership of the underlying shares – it isn't like a margin loan, which provides a part payment of the shares. Rather, this margin payment acts as security for your spread bet provider, ensuring that you can pay for any losses that occur due to normal market activity.

The easiest way to think of a spread bet is as a derivative that mirrors the price of the underlying shares. This means that if ABC Ltd shares increase in value by 50p, so too does the ABC Ltd spread bet.

Traders spread betting on share prices are interested in only one thing: capturing movements in price. Spread bets aren't designed to be a long-term investment.

Accounting for Dividends and Other Corporate Action

Several common occurrences in the share market move the price of shares and in turn the price of spread bets. It's very important that share-based bets reflect these share price changes because otherwise the ability of spread bets to mirror the price of the underlying shares breaks down – and this mirroring is the reason that spread bets are so popular in the first place.

Dividend payments

The most important time for those betting on or holding shares in a particular company is the ex-dividend date. On this date the value of the dividend is removed from the value of the shares. So, if on the day prior to the ex-dividend date the share price is £5 and the company pays a 20p dividend then, all other things being equal, when trading begins on the ex-dividend date the share price starts at £4.80.

No problem, you may say: why not go short on the company as a spread bet the day before the dividend is paid and collect a very likely profit? When the price falls – and it will – you could pocket an automatic profit. Unfortunately, spread betting companies didn't blow into town yesterday and dividend payments work a little differently with spread betting:

- If you're trading a long share spread bet into the ex-dividend date, you *receive* the dividend.
- If you're trading a short share spread bet into the ex-dividend date, you *pay* the dividend.

If you think that it sounds great to be long on share spread bets on the ex-dividend date and lousy to be short, the story isn't quite that simple: the payment of dividends offsets the movement of the share price whether you're long or short. Think of it as a compensation payment from the spread betting firm to those traders who are long on the share, and would otherwise be out of pocket after the ex-dividend date. It also stops traders from lining up on the short side of share prices going into the ex-dividend date.

The best way to understand what's actually going on is to look at Table 4-1, which shows two spread bets on XYZ shares: Trader A, who's long, and Trader B, who's short. In this example, XYZ Ltd is trading at £3 and is about to pay a 10p dividend. On the ex-dividend date the share price falls from £3 to £2.90. Yet, as you can see from the table, both traders end up in the same overall position. How come? Trader A, who's long, sees a benefit from the receipt of the dividend but loses on the falling share price; and Trader B, who's short, loses on the dividend payment but benefits from the falling share price.

If dividend payments weren't handled in this way, traders would just go short before the ex-dividend date, which wouldn't be fair to either the traders on the long side of the market or spread betting companies.

Table 4-1 The Impact of Dividend Payments

	Trader A: Long 1,000 XYZ Spread Bet	Trader B: Short 1,000 XYZ Spread Bet
Value before dividend payment	£3,000	£3,000
Dividend payment	£100	–£100
Profit and loss due to share price movements	–£100	£100
Net position	£3,000	£3,000

Share bonuses and splits

In general terms, whatever happens to shares happens to share spread bets. For example:

- **Share bonus issue:** If one new share is issued for every five shares held, as a spread bettor on a share, your old bet is closed and a new one opens to account for the change – that is, your position is added to.
- **Share split:** If two shares are issued for every one share held, and you have an open bet on that share, it closes automatically and a new one opens to reflect the change in the size of your position. For example, a bet of £10 on 1,000 shares would become £20 on 500 shares.

As with dividend payments (see the preceding section 'Dividend payments'), share spread bets adjust to share bonuses and splits so that traders on the long or short side of the market don't get an unfair advantage.

Familiarise yourself with your spread betting broker's terms and conditions document and use it as a point of reference. Terms and conditions can vary from company to company. Although the terms and conditions document is a long one, it provides full details about the way in which your provider does business with its clients, including:

- How prices are struck
- The conditions under which positions can be opened and closed
- The rights and obligations that you have as a client

Financing Charges

The difference between trading shares and spread betting on share prices is that when you buy shares you have to pay the full amount in order to take out the position, whereas when you spread bet you pay financing charges in order to replicate the cost that share buyers incur on purchasing the position. In other words, *financing charges* are what you pay in order to take out spread bet positions with only a small amount of cash upfront (*your margin payments*). Because a margin payment is only a small percentage of the overall market exposure that you're receiving, you can apply a great deal of leverage to your spread bet.

Your broker almost certainly charges you financing on the total exposure that you have in the market and doesn't take your margin payment into account. You may think this doesn't sound right, but you mustn't see the margin you pay as part-payment for your position. Your margin acts as security for your broker to allow for any losses that you may have. We look at the margin payment mechanism in more depth in Chapter 1.

Spread betting companies calculate financing charges differently, but usually they take the local cash rate (the LIBOR or London Interbank Offered Rate) and add what's known in the trade as a *haircut* – an addition to the cash rate that's generally in the region of 2 to 3 per cent. This premium is the way providers make additional profit above the cash rate. So if the cash rate is 4 per cent and your provider charges a 2 per cent haircut, you pay 6 per cent per annum in financing charges.

Note that financing charges apply *each night* that you hold the position open. This is one reason many traders like trading intra-day with spread bets, because then they don't pay any financing – but you wouldn't want to turn to intra-day trading based on this one factor alone.

On short positions, you *earn* financing payments on the positions that you hold. In this case, though, the haircut works the other way round: you earn the cash rate minus 2 to 3 per cent. Although this is unlikely to be a big earner for you, it can make all the difference when you use hedging strategies (which we look at in Chapter 3). Keep in mind that if interest rates are really low, you may not receive any financing payments for short positions. Check your provider's terms and conditions for the exact details.

When you deal in foreign share markets, the financing charge that applies is generally based on the cash rate of the country from which the shares originate. This means that if you're dealing in a French company, you're liable for the Euro zone interest rate plus the broker's extra clip, and if you're dealing in a US company, the finance charge is based on the US Federal Reserve cash rate. The rates in different countries can vary significantly. For more information on financing charges when dealing in foreign exchange, see Chapter 5.

Dealing in Foreign Share Markets

With the advent of online trading, investors could more easily gain access to different share markets around the world by opening an account with a foreign stockbroker. Unfortunately, doing so involved sending cash overseas to settle your trades. However, using the right spread betting firm you can now gain exposure to international share markets from a single trading platform, so you can monitor prices and positions very easily. In addition, your spread betting company allows you to trade using sterling (or Euros in Ireland), so you don't need to worry about exchanging currency upfront.

Normally, when people talk about the benefits of dealing in foreign share markets, they consider points such as the diversification of industries and the potential for growth beyond what's available domestically – and these are valid points. When it comes to short-term trading, though, a potentially bigger consideration is *opportunity*.

Proficient traders look for the same characteristics in each and every trade that they make. Say you have a really good trading strategy but this strategy offers you only one trade a week in your home market, which is too infrequent for you. By looking outside the limited opportunities that you have in your home market you may be able to use your trading strategy in foreign markets and so take advantage of greater opportunities.

On the edge

Many trading books refer to a trader's 'edge', which is the way in which a trader's methodology allows her to consistently make money. If you have an edge, obviously you try to apply it as widely as you possibly can.

The best example of using an edge is a casino, because all the games that you can play have the odds stacked in the casino's favour. As a result of this stacking, the casino doesn't have just one table open for people to play on, it has as many as it can possibly fill – because even though players often win, the casino always wins more. The casino's actual edge may be only a couple of percentage points over the players, but over thousands of rolls of the dice this small percentage really pays off for the casino.

We're not suggesting that you open a casino so that you have the best trader's edge! But we recommend developing your edge and then exploiting your advantage in the market – or across many markets. For more information check out Chapter 16, in which we outline ways to develop your trading plan.

Foreign market trades are generally denominated in the currency of the country in which the company trades. One of the core advantages of spread betting is that you're betting in pounds per point. This means you win or lose depending on how many points that share price moves. Whether the share in question is originally denominated in US dollars, Euros or Hong Kong dollars doesn't affect you. Spread betting lets you trade foreign shares without the worry of foreign currency risks.

So although foreign shares may be denominated in another currency in the physical market, when you're spread betting, you're effectively just trading their prices in your home currency. Your spread betting broker hedges out the foreign currency risk. Meanwhile, as a trader, you focus purely on the number of points a share price moves, which in turn translates to pounds earned or lost for you. At no time do you have to take on foreign currency exposure.

Daily changes in foreign exchange (FX) prices are incremental, so unless you're taking out an extremely large bet, they're unlikely to have much impact on the sort of short-term trade that a spread bet typically represents. But what if you're long on a US share and the pound falls against the dollar – won't this affect your profit? Well, currency markets are moving nearly all the time, and this would be a consideration if you were trading actual shares, but with spread bets the change in FX price doesn't impact your bet significantly. Your bet is held with your broker – you aren't buying or selling actual foreign shares. Be aware, however, that some other forms of trading, like Contracts for Difference (CFDs), are priced differently and, consequently, can generate an element of foreign exchange risk.

When you start dealing in foreign share markets, you most likely want to look at markets in a similar time zone, because this makes monitoring easier. Be aware that some share markets still take a lunch break and may close for an hour or more in the middle of their session. Make sure that you know whether the market you're interested in takes a lunch break before you make any trades, otherwise you may not be able to buy or sell at the time you planned to do so.

In addition, some spread betting firms are now able to quote bets on shares outside market hours, often because they're using the price of futures based on that share price (which trade outside normal market hours) to inform the price of the spread bet. Remember that the price you're trading on isn't the price generated by the stock exchange – it's being quoted to you by your spread betting company. Whether the company chooses to base the price on the futures market or the stock market is its call.

Trading Over Different Time Frames

With share spread bets you can trade from the very short to moderate time frames. By very short, we mean less than one day and by moderate we mean several months. You can hold share spread bets for longer than several months, but if you're thinking about doing this you may want to look into whether using margin lending on physical share trading rather than spread betting is a more effective trading strategy. The choice boils down to the cost of financing: don't forget that most brokers charge you an overnight rollover fee for open bets, and the charges can start to accumulate if you're long on the share (that is, you're positioned to make money if the price goes up). Although the charges seem negligible for a few days, the same bet held open for more than a month starts to look expensive unless you see some decent profit accumulate.

Whatever time frame you prefer for your share spread betting, be sure to stick with your strategy. Each type of trading requires a very different skill set and you certainly won't reach the required skill level for proficient trading if you're constantly chopping and changing your market strategy.

Trading over the longer term

The almost universal rule of trading is that the longer your time frame, the bigger your profit potential, but this statement needs to be qualified. If you're looking at a stock with a share price that's consistently rising and decide to buy that stock, there's a good chance that the price uptrend will continue. But remember that the price won't only move upwards: over a period of a month the price may go up for 13 sessions and down for 7. In all probability, however, making as much money from several short trades on the down days compared with holding your long position all through the trend (particularly when you incorporate paying multiple commissions) is almost impossible.

Trading over a longer time frame also helps you benefit from the fact that spread bets are commission free. Most spread betting companies don't charge commission on share-based trades, although a few still do. The market for spread betting companies has become so competitive that most have waived all commission charges, making spread betting a more cost-effective way to trade shares on a frequent basis. Be aware, however, that a hidden cost remains in the size of the spread – with smaller companies (like those listed on the Alternative Investment Market, for example) you can still find a substantial spread between the buy and sell price, making them more expensive to trade.

Trading over the short term

There are, of course, pluses to short-term trading. One of the most distinct advantages is that you tend to be exposed to less market risk – that is, the risk that the market as a whole will fall in value. One experience you may be familiar with is waking up in the morning and looking to see what the US market has done overnight (the rationale being that this movement is one of the key leads for other world markets on any given day). If the US market has fallen 4 per cent overnight then in all probability you're in for a very 'ordinary' session on local markets. Generally speaking, very short-term traders can avoid this overnight exposure and simply deal with the subsequent trading session (at least until the US markets open at lunchtime). Of course, day trading does require you to time your trades very precisely and to make profits from potentially very small market movements.

If you're willing to monitor your positions carefully, another advantage to day trading is that you may be able to carry more highly leveraged positions, because they're not exposed to as much chance of slippage. This doesn't mean that you can be any more relaxed with your risk in this case, though, because your chances of picking the correct market direction are lower over such a short period of time.

You can also reduce your overnight financing bill by trading in and out on the same day. However, keep in mind that this is generally a pretty weak reason to trade frequently, because any reductions in financing charges are always outweighed by share prices making a decent move in your favour.

Prospective traders often have romantic ideals about day trading: the idea of making potentially large amounts of money very quickly is very attractive. However, you need to always remember that to generate greater returns, you have to take bigger risks. This rule applies across the world of finance, so never assume that because an investment is short term in nature that somehow the risk reduces itself. The roadside of trading is littered with folk who were looking for a quick turn of profit but instead discovered how the potential for a quick profit can turn into an even quicker loss.

Capturing trend moves

If you're new to financial spread betting, we suggest that, instead of opting for either short- or longer-term trading, you focus on capturing trend moves in the market. The downside of trend following is that you have to be willing to absorb more volatility – a trade-off that you'll have to make repeatedly throughout your trading journey. However, you certainly won't have to spend all day looking at the market, and trend trading done well is arguably the most profitable method of trading, so you won't be losing out on the profit front either.

Perhaps you're thinking that trend following may cost you a lot in financing charges? Imagine that you hold a £5,000 position. If interest rates are 4 per cent and your spread betting provider adds a 2 per cent haircut, your financing charge is 82p a day. This cost would prove inexpensive if, by holding the position, you were able to secure a much larger percentage gain over the next few months.

To understand trend following in action, take a look at Figure 4-1, which shows a consistent upturn in AOE's share price over several months. From mid-January 2009, the company's share price rose from around £2 to a high of around £4 over a period of 130 days – a gain of about 100 per cent. (We're certainly not suggesting that all your spread bets are going to generate absolute returns of 100 per cent! But in the right trade you can easily exceed the cost of carrying the position resulting from financing charges.)

Figure 4-1: Trend following with spread bets.

Here's how the profit and loss break down over the 130 days (note that in order to make these calculations we averaged the gains over the time frame):

Opening exposure to AOE (£2.50 per point spread bet at £2.00 per share)	£5,000
Initial margin payment (5 per cent)	£250
Days in position (130)	Interest rate 4 per cent + hair-cut 2 per cent = 6 per cent
Approx. average daily financing charge	82p
Approx. total financing charge	£107
Commission payments	None payable in most cases
Closing exposure to AOE (£2.50 per point spread bet at £4.00 per share)	£10,000
Gain after costs	£4,893

As your position grows, of course, so too does the cost of financing the position.

The most important thing to take away from this example is that you can definitely carry a position for several months and remain profitable, so long as you're capturing a decent trending move. Although this example delivers a very large gain in share price, you can see that even a relatively modest gain can easily outweigh the cost of financing the position each day.

Now consider Figure 4-2, which shows AOE's share price movements on an hourly basis. The share price has traded over quite a modest range during the course of the session (5p). On its own this trade doesn't sound like a lot and represents less than a 2 per cent movement on the share price, but that gain may be enough for the short-term trader. However, to capture this price movement you would have to be either extraordinarily precise in your timing or very lucky!

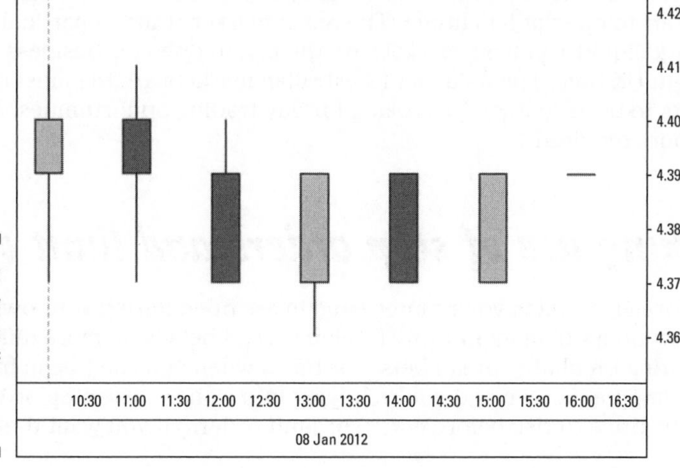

Figure 4-2: The day trader's view of spread betting shares.

Dealing with Different Time Zones

You can look to markets all around the world in an effort to gain exposure or diversification, or to exploit your trading edge. However, if you become serious about following share trading in US or Asia Pacific markets, managing your life and getting a decent night's sleep can be tricky. Although trading 24/7 sounds great, working all hours doesn't make for a contented home life or a socially well-adjusted human being. You need to find a happy medium.

Some tricks you can use to ensure your life is well balanced include dealing in sympathetic foreign markets and employing some tactics so that your orders are executed automatically when your specific price targets are met. Using such tactics requires you to plan your trades carefully in advance and to place orders to be executed if your expectations are met.

Checking out sympathetic markets

As the sun moves around the world, share markets open and close. *Sympathetic markets* are those that are relatively easy to fit into your trading schedule. For UK traders the main European markets are a natural starting point. The best examples in Europe are the French and German markets, which open slightly earlier than the UK but include some major blue chip shares (which also make up a significant slice of the Euro Stoxx 50 index). While not as liquid as the London market, the European share markets, when viewed as a whole, offer plenty of trading opportunities and price action that you can readily access using a spread betting account.

The North American markets are quite sympathetic for UK traders because they start to open at lunchtime. The Asian markets (and in particular the large and liquid Japanese market) are the last to open for business at around midnight UK time. The Asian and Australian markets are the most difficult markets to trade in if you're looking for day trading opportunities, due to the late hours required.

Making use of stop orders and limit orders

If the foreign markets you're interested in are open during your own normal business hours then monitoring foreign spread bets is no more difficult than monitoring UK share spread bets. For times when you can't be in front of your computer screen and you're buying into a share, use stop orders (if you want the price to rise before entry) or limit orders (if you want the price to fall before entry) to enter your positions. (Refer to Chapter 2 for more information on these different types of orders.)

However, if you want to enter a position during the night and open the trade with a buy order, we recommend that you use a stop order to enter, rather than a limit order. The reason is as follows:

- If you use a stop order, the trigger price will be above the market price (from the previous session's close). This means that for the order to trigger, the share price (initially at least) has to rise, which is what you want to happen.
- If you use a limit order and the market falls very heavily on opening, your spread betting company will still open the position for you, even though you may not be so keen to hold the position anymore.

Conversely, if you want to go short (that is, open the trade with a sell order), you need to place the 'stop to sell' order *below* the market price.

Always tie your entry order to an if-done order (see Chapter 2 for more information on if-done orders). The if-done order automatically adds a stop order in when the entry order has been triggered (for more information on placing stop orders, see Chapter 2).

REMEMBER

Manage your risk first and worry about taking profits second.

Foreign companies are everywhere

We find it interesting that many traders aren't comfortable with the idea of dealing in foreign shares or spread betting on foreign shares, citing that they feel they know UK-listed companies better than foreign companies. Take a detailed look at the FTSE index, or indeed the FTSE 250 index: the London market is one of the favoured stock exchanges in the world for secondary listing by foreign companies, and much of the FTSE's performance is driven by companies from outside the UK.

If you're not sure which offshore companies may be good investments, your broker may be able to offer you some starting points for researching different foreign companies. You can also dig up plenty of free information about foreign companies online using your preferred search engine.

Chapter 5

Taking on the World of Foreign Exchange

In This Chapter

- Understanding foreign exchange trading
- Handling a 24-hour market
- Managing short- and medium-term trades
- Following data releases

The foreign exchange (FX) market is the world's largest financial market – although, interestingly, it isn't really a market in the conventional sense because it has no central meeting place for buyers and sellers beyond the computers into which they place their orders. Banks and huge corporations dealing with one another around the world strike the prices paid for currencies, and because these groups have the most money in the world, the FX market is the most liquid trading environment on the planet, with plenty of volatility too. Not surprisingly, the market attracts huge numbers of traders trying to take advantage of this remarkable trading environment.

In this chapter, we outline how you can apply trading techniques you may already be familiar with to the popular FX market. One of the great features of the FX market is that it's open for trade day and night, which means you can trade foreign currency to suit your schedule no matter where you are. Although the FX market is renowned for short-term trading, we also describe how you can capture and profit from larger trending moves in the market. In addition, we explain how information that central banks and other agencies release into the market can impact the market and your trades.

Understanding Foreign Exchange Spread Betting

Spread betting on the FX market differs from trading any other financial products. Essentially, the main difference is that, in the FX market, you never trade just one product (in this case currency) – you always trade one product (currency) *against* another product (currency). To understand this concept, consider the way in which your trading screen displays prices on currencies: you always see the price of one currency quoted against the price of another currency. If you're interested in buying the euro (EUR), for example, you need to sell another currency in order to pay for the euro. You may see the price of the euro expressed as EUR/USD 1.3467, which means that 1 euro buys 1.3467 USD (dollars). So, if you want to buy 1 euro, you need to sell 1.3467 US dollars.

Grasping FX terminology

You need to fully understand several key items of terminology before you can begin FX spread betting:

- **Currency quotes:** You may have noted that your spread betting broker quotes the price of a currency to four decimal places. The fourth decimal place is important in FX trading because almost all currencies show prices to the fourth decimal place (with the notable exception of the Japanese yen). A movement of one increment in the fourth decimal place is known as a *pip*. A currency quote is the price at which your broker is prepared to let you trade that currency pair.
- **Currency pairs:** The two currencies combined in any currency quotation. The first currency in the pair is the *terms* currency and the second currency is the *commodity* currency. So, in the example EUR/USD, the euro is the terms currency and the dollar is the commodity currency.

  The quotation depicts how many units of the commodity currency you can buy with one unit of the terms currency. Thus, in the quote EUR/USD 1.3467, 1 euro buys 1.3467 dollars.

  However, we find it easier to think of the first currency in the pair as *fixed* and the second currency as *floating*, because you can think of the first currency as always representing 1 and the second currency as representing however many that 1 unit buys you.
- **Spot price:** The price quoted in a currency quotation – that is, the price that you can buy and sell that currency for at that particular moment.

In addition, to complete your understanding of FX terminology, you need to become familiar with the terms 'spot rates' and 'cross rates'. We remember hearing British comedian Ben Elton doing a skit on TV in which he said the words 'cross rates' on the evening news were a signal to go and make a cup of tea. For many people, spot and cross rates are unexciting, but as a trader you need to understand them:

- A *spot rate* is the price of an FX contract at any particular moment in time.
- A *cross rate* is any currency quotation that doesn't include the US dollar.

That wasn't too difficult, was it?

Every currency has a three letter acronym. FX traders will use these rather than currency symbols. Examples include:

- USD: US Dollar
- JPY: Japanese Yen
- EUR: Euro
- GBP: British Pound
- CHF: Swiss Franc
- AUD: Australian Dollar
- NZD: New Zealand Dollar

If you compare the charts of currency pairs such as the EUR/USD, GBP/USD and USD/CHF, you see they often look quite similar because they all trade against the US dollar. In contrast, cross rates such as the EUR/GBP look quite different. Traders using cross rates can get a real diversification benefit because they allow you to trade currencies without being impacted by movements of the US dollar.

One final word on cross rates: they're so-called because you need to *cross* two different US exchange rate quotations in order to work out a separate rate – because you can only trade the spot rates directly. So, to work out the value of the AUD/NZD rate you need to compare the value of the AUD/USD rate and the NZD/USD rate.

If you buy AUD/USD (which means buying AUD and selling USD) and sell NZD/USD (which means selling NZD and buying USD) then your overall position is long AUD/NZD (which means buying AUD and selling NZD). The USD is out of the equation because you buy it in one transaction and then sell it in the other.

Don't worry – you won't have to put a cross rate together; your spread betting broker does this for you automatically. Still, at the very least you can impress your friends by showing that you know what a cross rate is.

Starting small

Most spread betting brokers set their smallest trade at £10,000 exposure. This may sound like quite a lot of money, but it's not quite what you think. For a start, the margin requirement on FX spread bets is generally no more than 1 per cent, so for a trade of £10,000 you pay a margin requirement of £100. Second, for $10,000 exposure your profit and loss are £1 per pip movement in price.

Although the minimum exposure of £10,000 means only £1 profit or loss for you for each pip movement, don't think of this profit or loss as a trivial figure. Foreign exchange prices can move several hundred pips in some sessions, which even on the smallest exposure can mean a loss of £300 or more. We don't say this to put you off FX spread bets but to make you realise why you don't want to start out with position sizes generating profits and losses of £20 per pip.

We generally suggest that even experienced traders start out at the minimum position size of £10,000 exposure on FX spread bets until they become more familiar with FX spread betting.

Settling your trades

Different spread betting brokers have different ways of accounting for your outstanding profits and losses from your FX spread bets. In most cases, when you're spread betting your entire trade is denominated in sterling. Even if you're trading USD/EUR, your profits and losses are still in pounds per point. By spread betting on FX markets, you're not taking on any direct foreign currency exposure – you're simply betting on the change in the price of the currency pair in pounds. Check with your provider's terms and conditions to see how it manages your accounts.

Dealing With a 24-Hour Market (and Getting Some Sleep)

One of the most interesting features of the FX market is the fact that it trades from late Sunday night all the way through to late Friday night in Greenwich

Mean Time. Throughout this period the market has peaks and troughs in terms of the volume traded and its volatility, but it's always on the move and open for action. Even keen and inspired traders have to sleep sometime, so you need to have a plan in place for managing your trade while you sleep.

Building in stop orders

Much can change in the FX market in a very short space of time, so you always need to look at ways to protect yourself in order to minimise your risks and losses. One of the best ways to manage your risk is to set up stop loss orders, which you place with your spread betting broker. A *stop loss order* is an order to sell when the price drops below a specified price: the order kicks in automatically, even if you're asleep, so you don't always have to have one eye on the market. (You can also use stop orders to buy new positions as well. We talk more about using and placing stop orders in Chapter 2.)

One of the things that beginner traders frequently note about the FX market is its huge volume of turnover. This volume is an advantage not only for entering and exiting positions (because you're much less likely to experience any price slippage) but also when using stop loss orders. Even in times of high volatility, you should be able to get stopped out of your position at – or very near to – the price that you request on your order, because the real FX market has so much volume.

If your chosen trading strategy requires you to be in front of the trading screen all the time, you may think that stop loss orders aren't necessary. But when it comes to spread betting on FX markets, it's better to be safe than sorry. Like all trading strategies, you need to know where you're going to get out *before* you get in. If you know where to get out, it shouldn't make any difference whether you close out the position manually or your spread betting broker closes the position for you automatically via a stop loss order.

Even if you plan to always keep an eye on the market, remember that using a stop loss order has two advantages to closing manually, because your spread betting broker's trading system:

- Won't be tempted to give the position the benefit of the doubt, as you may do, leaving the position open
- Has a lot faster reflexes than your own

If you plan your trades well, you'll get the best outcome when you let the technology manage the execution for you.

Make room for volatility

When you're deciding where to place your stop loss order, you may be very tempted to place your order extremely close to the point where you enter a position. The downside to this strategy is that you're much more likely to get stopped out of the position before the trade has an opportunity to move in the right direction. So, whether you're trading on the five-minute chart or on the daily chart, you need to allow for a reasonable amount of volatility. Several indicators can help you determine volatility, but one of the best is the average true range (ATR) indicator, which is specifically designed to help you factor the recent volatility of an instrument into your determination of where to place your stop loss order. We explain the ATR indicator in Chapter 13.

By using your spread betting broker's trading platform in the form of various orders you can execute many (if not all) of your transactions without being in front of the trading screen day and night. This means that you can sit down with your charts well in advance and determine where to enter trades, where to place your stop loss orders and where to take profits. You can accomplish all this planning by linking orders that execute the trades when the market you are trading reaches the appropriate price level. We talk more about the various types of orders that you can execute in Chapter 2.

Placing profit target orders

If you're not trading based on trending movements, you're probably looking to earn specific profit targets. To avoid having to trade 24/7 to keep an eye on the market and maximise your profits, you can ask your spread betting broker for a *one cancels other (OCO) order* to link two orders on your position. As the name suggests, the OCO order automatically cancels one of the two orders if the trading platform executes the other order.

For example, you may want to link a stop loss order and a take profit order (a type of order that closes a profitable trade when it reaches a specific point) on a position. If the trade drops, you want your broker to execute your stop loss order; and if the trade rallies, you want your broker to execute your take profit order – but you don't want your broker to execute both orders or you could lose money. An OCO order is a good option because it cancels orders that you no longer need in the market and so reduces your potential losses and risks. By using an OCO order to link the two orders, if the market triggers the stop loss order your broker automatically cancels the take profit order.

Consider what could happen if you place two orders – one to stop loss and the other to take profit – that *aren't linked* in a volatile market: you may easily end up in a position where the market you are trading triggers the stop loss order, followed by the take profit order. The stop loss order sees you out of the trade and the take profit order puts you back in – but in the opposite direction and losing money!

Charting Methods for Short- and Medium-Term Trading

Don't make too many assumptions about the time frame over which to trade your FX spread bets, because the FX market has opportunities for all sorts of traders. You can choose to trade for less than an hour or for several weeks with the right FX position, so don't fall into the trap of thinking you have to trade in and out every few minutes.

Short-term trading

The FX market is one of the best markets for short-term trading. Here are some points to consider if short-term trades are your goal:

- **Charting methods:** Look at charting methods that incorporate charts with a time value of less than one hour per bar/candlestick (we explain charting methods in Chapter 13). Using this time period you can isolate short-term trends as well as support and resistance lines to trade with (see Chapter 13 for more about support and resistance strategies). However, you need to be careful of getting *too* short term with your charts (such as time values of five minutes or less), because managing the inherent short-term volatility in FX trades is very difficult.

  Alternatively, you may choose to incorporate oscillating indicators (such as the Relative Strength Indicator (RSI), the Stochastic Oscillator or MACD Histogram) as a means of looking for changes in market direction, but we suggest that you start with support and resistance lines because they're easy to identify but still allow you powerful trading opportunities.

- **If-done orders:** You can incorporate if-done orders to enter the market when the market reaches the optimum price point (that is, the price where you determine it's best to enter your trade), because no matter how keen you are, you can't stay in front of the trading screen all the time. We examine if-done orders in Chapter 2.

In Figure 5-1 we've marked a resistance line that the market has shied away from a number of times – meaning that the price has touched the line and then reversed itself. Short-term traders can either wait for the resistance to break or assume that the resistance will hold and trade accordingly. In either case, you can place your stop order close to the resistance line. By so doing you can potentially set yourself up for a solid risk/reward trade because your risk is very small.

Numerous authors suggest that support and resistance lines may not be very effective in spread betting foreign exchange, because every trader can identify where support and resistance occur and can use this knowledge as an opportunity to unload the position if the support or resistance line breaks. (A line *breaks* when the price suddenly moves through a previous support or resistance level – this is referred to as a *breakout.*) Certainly plenty of evidence supports this theory, but not always. Your best option is to form your own opinion of support and resistance lines by studying a wide selection of charts, using either those available on your spread betting broker's platform or your own standalone charts. We explain support and resistance lines in more detail in Chapter 13. A firm understanding of support and resistance strategies is a key skill for any trader to have, so don't ignore their benefits.

Figure 5-1: Support and resistance strategies can make excellent trade set-ups.

Medium-term trading

Although very-short-term trading may carry certain appeal for traders looking to make quick profits, taking a slightly longer-term approach to FX trading has its advantages:

- You don't need to watch your trading screen the whole time.
- You can capture some of the bigger moves that occur in the market over time (that is, by trend following).

One of the great characteristics of FX trading is that consistent trends often appear in prices over weeks and even months, which means that, like share spread betting, FX spread betting offers you the possibility of significant gains over the duration of a trade.

Figure 5-2 is a daily trending chart that shows a consistent increase in the value of the Australian dollar against the US dollar, driven largely by the expectation of strengthening commodity demand. As the trend progresses the traffic certainly isn't all one-way, but plenty of gains exist to be captured.

Of course, you have to consider the amount of volatility that your open trade needs to absorb over the course of a medium-term trade. Even if you trade the smallest amount, you can easily see swings in the value of your position of +/- 300 pips (or £300 at the minimum trade size for many spread betting firms), which means it won't be all one-way traffic for you. For some traders this amount of money isn't significant, but for others such a loss may stretch the risk tolerance of their account beyond the reasonable limit.

For the most part, you don't want to risk more than 2 per cent of your capital on any given trade. This is referred to as a *fixed percentage risk model.*

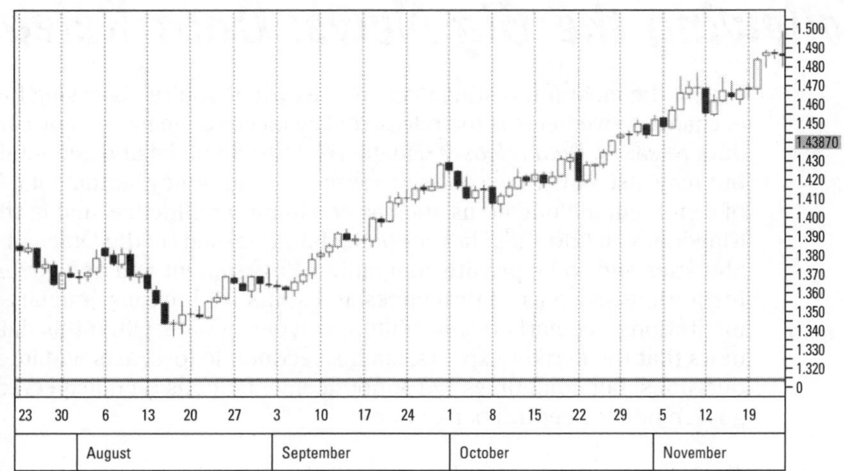

Figure 5-2: Bigger trends can mean bigger profits.

As an alternative to a fixed percentage risk model you can place a stop loss order within the appropriate range allowed by your maximum percentage loss. This strategy involves working out how many pips against you your account can stand, and then placing your stop accordingly. We're against this type of strategy because you're taking a fairly random approach to the placement of your stops, and common wisdom suggests this isn't the most sensible approach because you give no consideration to the behaviour of the individual instrument that you're trading.

We discuss different position sizing strategies in Chapter 9.

In medium-term FX spread betting, you need to find a balance between trying to capture trending effects and absorbing volatility.

- Absorb too much volatility and you may get stopped out of a position too late, causing you a very large loss.
- Absorb too little volatility and you won't give a position enough room to move, which makes a small loss very likely and a large profit very unlikely.

Be mindful of the risks that you take on all your trades and try to ensure that any risk isn't too big for your available trading capital. We talk more about managing your risk in Chapter 8.

Following the Big News: Data Releases

One of the most interesting occurrences when you're observing foreign exchange movements is the release of key pieces of financial information, called data releases. *Data releases* usually relate to financial and economic news, but may also cover measures of sentiment and policy statements. Measures of sentiment include items such as consumer confidence, and in the United Kingdom you find them in economic data released by the Office of National Statistics and some private companies. Government and non-government institutions, such as central banks and statistics bureaus, and large financial institutions, regularly release different types of data. Often this data presents news that the market expects, such as economic forecasts and interest rate decisions, but sometimes the announcements focus on unexpected shifts in government or central bank policy.

Traders pay attention to data releases because the announcement of new information can have an impact on prices in a market. Of the data released, economic news is the most watched category in the market and, given the country's place at the top of the economic ladder, news that comes out of the United States is easily the most important. Traders usually pay less attention to measures of sentiment, policy statements and more minor economic data.

Before data is released, the market often predicts what the announcement may be, based on a consensual forecast from various sources. When the data is released, if the difference between the forecast figure and the actual figure is huge, the market tends to move very quickly to buy or sell currency to accommodate this news. This is because the market prices in expectations about what the future holds into current FX values. *Pricing in* means working out what a financial instrument should be worth based on expectations. When expectations prove incorrect, the market very quickly changes its expectations and buys or sells currency, depending on whether the information makes the currency worth more or less than people previously thought.

The FX market can get very volatile very quickly as news is announced, so some people use data releases as a trading opportunity. Traders often place limit and stop orders just before data is released (for more on these orders, refer to Chapter 2) in order to capture sharp swings in the market. Although news trading can be profitable, it's a highly speculative way to trade because during data releases a currency pair can swing sharply one way and then the other before you have enough time to react.

Some experts warn that you should never trade in the FX market during data releases, because the way in which the market responds to the new information can be very violent and unpredictable. However, we need to qualify such advice:

- If you're a short-term trader then we couldn't agree more with holding off trading until the dust has settled after an announcement, because during the data release your risk can become very difficult to manage. The potential exists for you to make a great gain – but also to make a significant loss.
- If you're trading for weeks or months with the goal of capturing a trending movement, you have little choice but to trade during data releases such as interest rate decisions – such releases are hard to avoid, because organisations make financial announcements every day somewhere in the world.

Keeping advised of the latest data releases is important. Your spread betting broker should give you details of upcoming economic releases and may also send you electronic alerts when the data is released. We suggest that you also search the Internet using key words such as 'Economic data releases'. Your search should reveal a number of good news sources such as Bloomberg (www.bloomberg.com) and MarketWatch.com (www.marketwatch.com).

Figure 5-3 shows the type of data that's released in the United States over a period of one week. People don't watch all these releases closely, but some are very important. Probably the most-watched news items from the United States are Federal Reserve interest rate decisions and the Nonfarm Payroll (NFP; this gives the major US employment data). As we note in the section 'Grasping FX terminology', earlier in the chapter, all currency quotes either directly follow the US dollar or are derived from it (cross rates), which explains why US economic data has such a widespread impact on all the currencies around the world. When newly released economic data impacts the value of the US dollar, the US currency in turn affects all currencies that are priced relative to the US dollar.

US data releases aren't the only announcements to have a big effect on FX values. UK data releases, such as the unemployment data released by the Office of National Statistics, also affect FX trading locally, although often such news doesn't have as widespread an impact on currency values globally. You can check websites such as Bloomberg (www.bloomberg.com) to find out what consensus expectations are for a particular data release. If the actual results are different to expectations, currency markets will react quickly.

The chart in Figure 5-4 shows just how swift market reaction can be when a data release contains a surprise. In this case, unexpected news about unemployment data caused an immediate change in the AUD/USD exchange rate, which moved from 0.8050 to 0.8200 in less than a day.

Of course, such a data release doesn't only impact the AUD/USD rate: it can also affect other currencies such as the NZD and GBP. You see this same sort of impact when other countries release data as well.

By watching how a short-term chart responds when organisations release data, you can learn an awful lot about how FX markets behave. The best example in the UK time zone is the release of interest rate decisions by either the Bank of England (affecting the GBP/USD pair) or the European Central Bank (affecting the EUR/USD pair). After banks announce most interest rate decisions, you see some very swift price changes in the market, which gives you a good idea of how volatile the FX market can be. And simply watching the market reaction is good fun, because you have no money at risk.

Region: North America					Country: United States	Type: Economic releases				
Date 07/12/09					11:43:23		United States: Economic releases			
	Date	Time	A	M	Event	Period	Survey	Actual	Prior	Revised
106	08/06	22:30		×	Continuing Claims	JUL 26	—	—	—	—
107	08/07	01:00		×	ICSC Chain Store Sales YoY	JUL	—	—	–5.1%	—
108	08/07	22:30	×	×	Change in Nonfarm Payrolls	JUL	—	—	–467 K	—
109	08/07	22:30		×	Unemployment Rate	JUL	—	—	9.5%	—
110	08/07	22:30		×	Change in Manufact. Payrolls	JUL	—	—	–136 K	—
111	08/07	22:30		×	Average Hourly Earnings MoM	JUL	—	—	0.0%	—
112	08/07	22:30		×	Average Hourly Earnings YoY	JUL	—	—	2.7%	—
113	08/07	22:30		×	Average Weekly Hours	JUL	—	—	33.0	—
114	08/08	05:00		×	Consumer Credit	JUN	—	—	–$3.2 B	—
115	08/11	22:30		×	Nonfarm Productivity	2Q P	—	—	1.6%	—
116	08/11	22:30		×	Unit Labor Costs	2Q P	—	—	3.0%	—
117	08/12	00:00	×	×	Wholesale Inventories	JUN	—	—	–0.8%	—
118	08/12	00:00		×	IBD/TIPP Economic Optimism	AUG	—	—	—	—
119	08/12	07:00		×	ABC Consumer Confidence	AUG 10	—	—	—	—
120	08/12	21:00		×	Bloomberg Global Confidence	AUG	—	—	—	—
121	08/12	21:00	×	×	MBA Mortgage Applications	AUG 8	—	—	—	—
122	08/12	22:30	×	×	Trade Balance	JUN	—	—	–$26.0 B	—
123	08/13	04:00	×	×	Monthly Budget Statement	JUL	—	—	—	—
124	08/13	04:15	×	×	FOMC Rate Decision	AUG 13	—	—	0.25%	—

Figure 5-3: A week of US economic data releases.

Figure 5-4: Economic data can rock the market.

Chapter 6

Following the Big Guns: Spread Betting on Indexes

In This Chapter

- Introducing index trading
- Understanding how spread betting on indexes works
- Dealing with changing local market conditions
- Branching into foreign index spread betting
- Coping with catastrophes
- Trading over the short and long term

One of the first instruments that many beginner traders find out about in financial markets is an index. In market terms, an *index* is a way of tracking and measuring broad movements that occur in a particular market. There are major indexes, called indices, for currencies, commodities, bonds, property and shares; but in this chapter, we talk only about share indices. Traders follow numerous share indices in the United Kingdom and around the world: each index is made up of a 'basket' of shares and given a value. When the average value of the basket moves higher, so too does the index value, and vice versa. The real value of indices for traders is that they can use them to track broad movements in a related set of shares.

By spread betting on indices you can track the value of a whole index, rather than one or several individual shares. Such a strategy can be very valuable as a means of hedging to reduce risk or speculating to make profit. Many traders spread bet on indices exclusively, which underlines what a powerful and flexible product they can be.

In this chapter, we describe the key features of index spread betting and detail how you can use index bets in your trading portfolio. We also explain how you can apply many of the technical analysis techniques that you would use with other tradeable products in spread betting indices. In addition, we outline some of the key considerations you need to be aware of if you want to spread bet on foreign indices.

Understanding the Basics of Index Trading

Index trading is all about taking a broad view of future movements in a particular market. Even though all traders and investors track market movements, they mostly trade shares and spread bets on shares to try to profit from their view of a market. By spread betting on indices instead you're taking a much simpler approach, because you're speculating simply that a particular market *as a whole* will either rise or fall in value over the period in which you trade – you don't have to specify which individual shares you think may rise or fall. Like share spread bets, you have the opportunity to spread bet on indices from all around the world, which means that you have additional opportunities to speculate for profits or spread your risk.

All countries that have shares listed on an exchange offer an index (or several indices) over a basket of shares of the biggest companies so that investors can track changes in value that occur over time. Many countries have only one index that an investor can trade on.

For example, in the United Kingdom the main index of interest to traders on the share market is the FTSE 100 Index, which was first calculated in 1984. The basket of shares for this index is the top 100 companies listed on the London Stock Exchange (LSE). Traders track movements in the basket of shares by monitoring changes in the index value. Of the companies in the index, 73 contribute less than 1 per cent, 20 companies contribute between 1 and 3 per cent and the remaining 7 companies each make up between 3 and 8.25 per cent. In addition, the largest company in the United Kingdom, HSBC Holdings, makes up 8.25 per cent of the index.

In the United States, the world's biggest market, the focus is mainly on three indices: the S&P 500, the Dow Jones Industrial Average and the NASDAQ.

When you spread bet on indices you get immediate exposure to the market in a single trade. If you couldn't do this, potentially you'd have to buy hundreds of individual shares to get the same market exposure. So trying to replicate this exposure with individual shares or spread bets on shares is hugely unfeasible.

Looking at your share portfolio, you may notice how similar its movements are on any given day to the movements in the FTSE 100 Index as a whole. This is hardly surprising considering the index value derives from the value of individual shares.

How Index Spread Bets Are Priced

Spread bets on indices, like other spread bets, derive their price from an underlying instrument. However, in the case of spread bets on indices the underlying instrument isn't an index itself, but rather a futures contract on the index (for the lowdown on futures, head to the later sidebar 'The importance of futures'). Why a futures contract? Spread bets track only tradeable underlying instruments (that is, instruments that can be sold). An index itself isn't tradeable, because the index value derives from the value of a *basket* of shares, not one individual share – so it's just a number. However, a futures contract is a tradeable instrument, which is why the underlying instrument for index spread betting is a futures contract on the index. The futures contract tracks the value of the index, and the index spread bet tracks the value of the futures contract.

Different spread betting brokers price their bets on indices slightly differently. Some providers offer spread bets that directly follow the futures contract, whereas others offer spread bets that track a recalculation of the contract. This recalculation is often the index value minus the *fair value* – the value of upcoming dividends on shares within the index. Both pricing methods follow the index, but the method that directly tracks the futures contract is a little more transparent because you can more easily see the underlying price.

Not all brokers offer spread betting on indices, but for those that do, spread bets on indexes have become one of their most popular products.

Understanding price spreads

A *price spread* is the distance between the price the highest buyer is willing to pay and the price the lowest seller is willing to sell for. The buyer's price is referred to as the *bid* and the seller's price is referred to as the *ask*, or offer. How does the price spread affect you as a trader? Simply put, the closer the price spread in a market, the smaller the price move required in your favour before you start making money on a position.

The importance of futures

Futures contracts are one of the most important (and often misunderstood) types of derivatives (financial instruments). A *futures contract* gives the holder the right to buy (or sell) a set quantity of a commodity at a set price in the future. Futures contracts usually cover physical commodities like oil, gold and wheat, but they can also cover financial commodities such as government bonds and indices. Just as a spread bet on shares tracks the price of a share, an index spread bet tracks the value of a futures contract.

Depending on the type of futures contract that you're trading, settlement may be in cash or physically. You settle commodities like gold or oil physically: at the expiry of the futures contract, the final holder purchases the commodity at a set price. You settle index futures in cash: the holder pays in cash the difference in value between the price at which the trader opened the contract and the price at which he closed it.

Imagine that you want to spread bet over the FTSE 100 Index and the current price of the spread bet on the index is quoted as 6,310/12. The first figure in the quote is the bid price and the second figure is the ask price, which means that you can buy the spread bet at 6312 points, or £6312 if you are betting at £1 per point.

The bid price is the price you use to *buy* the index – that is, you expect it to go up, and to make money if it goes up. The offer price is used to sell the index, that is, if you expect the market to go down, and you want to short it.

If you have an open long trade, and you want to close it, you will be using the offer price to close the trade, not the bid price.

When you first enter a spread bet position you will probably see a loss, which in this example is £2. Why a loss? Because the price you can sell at is £6,310, which is 2 points *below* the price at which you entered the trade. In order for you to break even, the price needs to rise by 2 points.

Sometimes the market determines the price spread, such as you may see with shares where the difference between the buyer and seller isn't artificially inflated – it's simply the price at which people are willing to buy and sell. The varying price spread often reflects the liquidity of the underlying investment – how much people are trading it in the real market.

Most spread betting brokers charge a certain price spread during market hours (essentially daytime business hours) and a higher price spread after market hours. In general terms, expect to pay a 2-point spread during market hours and a 4-point spread after market hours. This difference arises because, after market hours, the underlying market has less liquidity and price spreads will likely increase – so spread betting brokers increase their spread to account for this increase. But as the UK spread betting market becomes increasingly competitive, many brokers are cutting their spreads on flagship products like indices in order to attract business – many major index bets are now priced at a point or less in terms of the spread, and some are even now available with no spread at all.

Following market movements

The current trading price multiplied by the number of pounds per point you're staking determines the value of a spread bet on an index. The amount of exposure is easy to calculate because each index is already measured in points, so the value of the spread bet is the current index value multiplied by your stake. Thus, if the FTSE 100 Index is trading at 6,300 points, one spread bet at £1 per point gives you £6,300 worth of exposure.

Spread bets on indices are a popular choice for traders because you can trade broad market movements in a single trade, which is easier and cheaper than trying to replicate the index by purchasing all the shares individually. This means that if you believe the market as a whole will rise or fall over a given time frame, you can go either long or short on the index, respectively. You can carry an index position for as long as you like, but short-term movements are likely to prove most attractive for traders. In the section 'Looking at Short- and Long-Term Trading', later in this chapter, we explain how you can use spread betting on indices to *reduce* your exposure to the market by trading on the short side of the market.

Examining sector trades

Sector bets are a specific type of index spread bet. They allow you to take exposure to a broad (but nonetheless similar) category of shares in an index, rather than all the shares in the index, in a single trade (saving you commission charges and fees). Several large companies dominate most of the larger market sectors, and companies within the same sector are likely to be heavily correlated, so in many cases taking exposure to them all make sense, rather than trying to pick several of the best companies.

For example, you may want to concentrate on only finance sector shares covering banks and insurance companies. So instead of trading all 200 shares in a bet covering the FTSE 100 Index, you can use a sector bet to trade only the 10 or so largest shares in the finance sector of that index.

You can also use sector bets along with spread betting indexes to undertake the hedging strategy of index stripping. *Index stripping* generally involves being long on the index (taking the view that the value will rise) and then going short on the sector that you believe will underperform (taking the view that the value will fall). Because the index is an average of share price performances, if you can remove the underperformer(s) then naturally your returns should improve.

Spread Betting On Local Indexes

In general, the index market doesn't quite trade for 24 hours a day. For example, the FTSE 100 Index trades between 8.00 a.m. and 4.30 p.m.

Importantly, unlike the share market, the index market isn't asleep when you are. The Dow Jones Industrial Average in the United States trades between 9 a.m. and 4 p.m. Eastern time, and the Australian S&P/ASX 200 Index trades in two blocks between 9.50 a.m. and 4.30 p.m. and between 5.10 p.m. and 7.00 a.m. local time. Also, Dow Jones Industrial Average futures trade all day.

This means that when you wake up, any new information that's been released overnight may have impacted on the value of your spread bet, so how your profit and loss statement looks before you go to bed may be quite different to what you see in the morning. In this section, we describe some of the factors you need to be aware of at these times to help you deal with changing market conditions.

Taking care when volumes are low

One aspect you need to consider if you let your positions run overnight is that at night the volume of trade goes down and the volatility goes up, which increases your risk at a time when you don't have your eye on the market. If you're trading only one or two spread bets at a time, this risk may not be a particularly significant issue for you, but if you're trading multiples of ten spread bets, this becomes much more important.

Say you're trading 20 spread bets overnight and a major move in the market sees the price move over your stop loss such that you experience a 10-point slippage – *slippage* happens when no trade occurs at the price you nominate as your stop loss, and can result from volatility or low liquidity, or both. Your spread betting broker will execute your trade at the next available price, which means you make an additional loss beyond what you anticipated based on where you placed your stop loss. Although this may not sound like an overly large amount of money, many people trade in volumes far outweighing 20 spread bets and so would experience greater losses in such a situation.

Trading overnight can be beneficial, because you can respond immediately when news is released in other parts of the world, whereas daytime traders can't respond until trade begins the next day. This isn't always an advantage, though, because short-term movements may reverse themselves by the opening of trade the following day!

We know several traders who don't allow their positions to run overnight because they find it too difficult to manage their risk in the event of an increase in volatility. You don't necessarily have to follow the same rule, but you do need to be aware of the potential outcomes of leaving your positions open overnight. To improve your understanding of coping with risks, see Chapter 8.

You can see that no single, easy answer exists for traders, so you need to be very thoughtful about the strategy that you employ and be sure that it's suitable.

Putting in stops

A lot can change in the index market in a very short space of time, so as with other types of spread betting you always need to protect yourself, and this means using stop orders with your spread bets on indices. However, just as you need to be mindful about not throwing caution to the wind when you aren't paying commission, you also need to avoid being careless with where you place your stop orders.

Putting your stop orders as close as you can to your entry price in the hope of reducing your risk isn't a good idea because:

- You'll very likely get closed out simply due to normal market volatility and so miss out on the opportunity to make bigger profits. This is a very real risk beyond more obvious things like major market announcements, which can cause the market to move suddenly and sometimes unpredictably.

- Although your loss may be relatively minor, you've a much better chance of locking in more losing positions overall because you'll likely have a smaller number of winning trades.

We talk more about how to place stop orders to reduce your risk in Chapter 8.

Spread Betting on Foreign Indices

Spread betting on foreign indices gives you the same advantages as spread betting on the FTSE, but over different baskets of shares: you can take on immediate exposure to baskets of shares in the United States, France, Germany, Australia, Hong Kong and Japan, among others. Trading different baskets of shares has two specific advantages:

- You gain new trading opportunities, which increase your chances of making a profit.
- You may increase the diversity of your portfolio, which can reduce your risk in the marketplace. Keep in mind that often a very strong correlation exists between different share markets on a day-to-day basis, so these diversification benefits may not be as great in the short term as you may hope.

Before you rush to your trading screen to make a foray into the foreign index market, you need to be aware of a couple of distinct issues relating to the times at which these markets are open and the currency in which you trade.

Timing your trades

Most indices trade an extended session (by which we mean almost 24 hours) broken down into a day session and a night session. Invariably, the day session offers higher volumes, which tends to make trade less choppy; and the night session trades lower volumes, which tends to increase volatility.

- **Day trading:** To trade during the day in the United Kingdom you may want to focus your energies on the German and French index markets, because these two countries are in a similar time zone to the United Kingdom. In addition, some United States indices offer good short-term opportunities and are suitable for UK traders because these indices start their sessions in the early afternoon local time. You also have the pan-European Euro Stoxx 50 index, which tracks 50 of the biggest shares in Europe.

- **Night trading:** If you're a bit of a night owl and want to trade at night in the United Kingdom during a foreign market's day trading session, the S&P 500 Index and the Dow Jones Industrial Average in the United States are probably the most popular indices in the world to trade and should offer you plenty of opportunity. Other large markets of note are the Australian S&P/ASX 200 in Australia and the Nikkei 225 in Japan.

Always check with your spread betting broker to see what indices it offers and what times it trades.

Knowing which currency to use

Spread betting on foreign indices doesn't require complex foreign currency calculations. The underlying shares that compose the index may be denominated in a foreign currency, as are the futures contracts, but your spread betting account is in sterling and you make all your bets in sterling. Your bet is with the broker you deal with, and it's left to the broker to worry about hedging any currency risk your trading might incur. You make your stake in pounds and receive your profits in pounds. You're saved the cost and the bother of hedging your foreign currency risk, and can simply get on with trading.

Guarding Against Bad News and Market Catastrophes

The announcement of major business, economic or disaster-related news can turn a trading position on its head – whether this is your index spread bet position or your trading position in general. Some news announcements you can plan for, but others you can't foresee. In the last 30 years two market events stand out due to the speed and severity of their impact:

- The share market crash of 1987.
- The shock to the markets that occurred after the terrorist attacks in the United States on 11 September 2001.

In retrospect, we think there was some early warning about the 1987 share market crash (due to the extraordinary increase in share values in the lead-up to the crash), but of course there was no economic precursor to the September 11 attacks.

A survivor's tale

Renowned US hedge fund manager Paul Tudor Jones became a market icon following the 1987 share market crash. While most traders around him were taking a hammering, Tudor Jones was carrying a large short index position (which means he'd sold short a number of index futures contracts) and a large long bonds position (which means he'd bought a lot of treasury futures). Both of these strategies benefitted from the collapsing share market and allowed him to make an extraordinary profit in what proved to be a dire time for the vast majority of investors.

What made Tudor Jones even more remarkable was that in order to make these trades he had to be in a position contrary to the majority of other traders, who were riding a very exuberant bull (rising) market at the time. His success serves to illustrate that while following the prevailing direction of the market can be beneficial to traders much of the time, you're likely to encounter episodes where you need to go your own way.

So how can you manage your positions with these potential drops in market value in mind?

To answer this question you need to balance how much potential damage a catastrophe can do with the potential gains you'd miss out on if you didn't invest when the market wasn't in full-blown catastrophe mode. Although over a number of years the overall trend of the stock market is to rise, in any given year the market goes regularly up and down. With that in mind, you can't expect the market to go your way every session.

The only way to defend yourself completely against drops in market value is to invest entirely in risk-free assets (that is, cash), but such a strategy won't get you returns that are particularly exciting. At a more extreme level, you can see that defending against very large scale events is impossible without damaging your returns when a catastrophic event isn't occurring.

To manage your risk against such market shocks, we suggest you carry no more leverage than you can manage to cover immediately with the cash that's in your trading account. Say that you have £10,000 in your trading account and are fully levered using index spread bets. Spread betting brokers typically charge a 1 per cent margin for index bets, so this means you're carrying £1,000,000 worth of exposure to the market (£1,000,000 × 0.01 = $10,000). A 1 per cent movement in price against you will cost you £10,000 and you'll have no money left in your account . . . a 2 per cent movement in price against you and your account won't cover your debt and you'll be left owing your spread betting broker £10,000 on top of the £10,000 you lose from your account.

A conservative measure is not to lever your account by more than three times – that is, if you have £10,000 in your account, you shouldn't have more than £30,000 exposure to the market.

See Chapter 8 for more information on risk management.

Mentally stress-test your positions on index spread bets (in fact, your whole trading portfolio) by looking at the current value of your positions, wiping off 20 per cent and then determining what you'd do next. After drying your eyes you'd need to take action, but would you sell out, wait it out or buy more? This is the type of decision that you'd face in a severe market shock.

Looking at Short- and Long-Term Trading

Many traders think that index spread bets are aimed at a very short-term time frame. They've good reason to think this, because index spread bets are a liquid trading instrument that you can access over long trading hours. However, you don't have to approach index spread bets as short-term trades only, because you can incorporate them into your overall portfolio to perform such functions as reducing your total market exposure.

Short-term strategies

The charts that your spread betting broker gives you update in real time and enable you to make trading decisions in the short term. Many of the trades you're likely to deal with in the short term arise as a result of what you see on your charts. We suggest that you look towards support and resistance lines as a starting strategy in index trading. This strategy involves looking for prices that are hitting the same price level repeatedly and then reversing. Support and resistance points are useful because you can easily identify them and they allow you to clearly set profit targets. For more information about support and resistance lines refer to Chapter 13.

When you're looking at your charts you often see prices trading between two distinct areas of support (the lower horizontal line) and resistance (the upper horizontal line). Commonly, traders take long positions if the price moves above the resistance line or short positions if the price moves below the support line – this is referred to as a *breakout* and is an opportunity for traders because it shows the price moving in a new direction. These trades often see sharp price movements. We explain more about these support and resistance strategies in Chapter 13.

Long-term strategies

You have a choice of several different approaches to long-term trading strategies for index spread betting. Some approaches are quite conventional, but others are more unusual and involve modifying your exposure to the market by adding or removing exposure. By 'removing exposure' we mean offsetting other exposure that you have to the share market. For example, if you have a diversified share portfolio that's all 'long' side (that is, you benefit if the price rises) then going short on an index spread bet reduces your market exposure in line with its value (the number of index points – such as 4,800 × your stake in pounds per point).

Here are two long-term trading strategies:

- **Capture trending movements in the overall market.** This is one of the more conventional ways in which you can approach trading the index. If you have a view of a specific market (such as the UK share market), you can try to time your entry into the trending movement. For example, if you think the market is going to rise (that is, it's bullish), you may buy index spread bets to reflect this view and then hold them for as long as you believe the market will remain positive. The benefit of this type of approach is that you maintain your exposure to the market continuously: one of the things that can be quite frustrating about trading is missing moves in the market due to lack of exposure or having the wrong exposure.
- **Hedge against falls in share value.** Such a strategy would have been difficult for many retail traders to implement before the advent of spread betting. Given the fact that index spread bets give you a relatively small amount of exposure, you can use them to hedge against falls in the value of even a small share portfolio or share spread bet portfolio. If you have a well-diversified portfolio, chances are it's quite highly correlated to movements of the index. For this reason, if you believe that a downturn will occur in the market in the short term, you may choose to hold your physical share/share spread bet positions and simply short the index as a means of defending value within the rest of your portfolio, which is eroded without your short index spread bet exposure. Index spread bets won't provide a perfect hedge for your portfolio, but they can go a long way toward defending against falls in the market.

Although we discuss hedging strategies quite lightly, they're very serious and you need to plan your strategies carefully before you execute them. Even though the downside to your hedging strategies is limited, the risk lies in the potential opportunity cost that you may lose: if you hedge your long share portfolio and the market surges, you receive little to no benefit from that movement. For this reason, you should implement hedging strategies sparingly.

We explain more about hedging strategies in Chapter 3.

Chapter 7

Venturing into Commodities and Interest Rate Products

In This Chapter

- Discovering the different commodities products available
- Understanding the workings of the commodities market
- Dealing in interest rate products
- Handling important economic news

Commodities are physical products that investors buy or sell, usually via futures contracts. The main commodities that people trade are oil, gold and agricultural products such as grains and livestock. In addition, people also trade financial products such as interest rate products. Because traders don't want to transport the actual products that they trade, they instead trade *futures contracts* on the commodities or financial products, which are agreements to buy or sell the products at an agreed price on a nominated date.

Traditional commodities, such as gold, oil, wheat and oats, are some of the more interesting products around because they have a tangible quality – that is, you can picture what they look like.

In this chapter, we look at the major types of commodity-based spread bets that are available for trading and some of the main factors that may impact on the price of these bets at any given point in time. We also look at some of the main characteristics of interest rate products and the factors that impact on the value of these tradeable instruments. You will see that the factors that affect both commodity bets and interest rate bets differ to those you'd normally be exposed to in other financial markets.

Check out where commodities are traded

A number of different exchanges around the world quote different types of commodities, so make their websites a stop on your journey to maximising your knowledge of commodities and commodity spread bets. Try starting with the websites of the following commodity markets:

- Chicago Mercantile Exchange (CME): www.cmegroup.com
- Intercontinental Exchange (ICE): www.theice.com
- London Metal Exchange (LME): www.lme.co.uk

Understanding the Terminology: What Are Commodities, Anyway?

In general terms, you can think of commodities as valuable natural products that are the same no matter who produces them. For example, oil is oil no matter who produces the oil, and gold is gold no matter who produces the gold. Virtually anything that you can grow or take from the ground is thus a commodity. Commodities cover a broad range of products but basically fall into three groups:

- Agricultural commodities:
  - Grains and legumes
  - Meat and livestock
  - Softs
- Energy commodities:
  - Gas
  - Oil
- Metal commodities:
  - Base metals
  - Precious metals

Sometimes, financial products such as interest rate products like bonds and treasuries are traded on the same exchanges as these types of commodities, and for this reason you may occasionally see such financial products referred to as commodities. However, we think it's clearer simply to define commodities as natural products such as metals – otherwise, the term starts to lose its meaning. We deal with financial products in the section 'Interest Rate Products', later in the chapter.

Although the commodities market has witnessed something of a decline lately due to the slowdown in the global economy, overall traders are very interested in commodities, and in recent years a number of commodities, such as gold, have shown a great deal of strength.

Agricultural commodities

Agricultural commodities are basically anything that's grown – or anything that a farmer makes and sells. Agricultural commodities include grains and legumes (such as wheat and soy beans), and livestock (such as cattle and pigs). So, unlike money, some agricultural commodities *do* grow on trees! However, investors don't trade all commodities on an exchange, and of those commodities that are traded only some have spread bets available to trade over them. You need to check with your broker which commodities it makes available for trade.

Agricultural commodities form a very important part of the financial world, from enabling farmers to lock in the prices at which they can sell their goods in the future to providing trading opportunities for speculators. You can assume that suppliers have bought some part of many of the food products that you eat through commodity markets. Major processors are also big users of agricultural commodities: processors include groups such as flour millers and textile mills. These companies use commodities to hedge the future costs of products that their businesses require. Traders and speculators (who don't want the end products) add liquidity to the market, which makes the buying and selling of commodities easier for everyone.

If you spend time researching more about commodities, you'll see that a number of interesting factors go into their production, such as methods of sowing and harvesting. Sometimes such information can be useful and give you a good idea of how weather can impact on harvests, which in turn can impact on price. The standard rules of supply and demand apply in the commodities market, but you'll see them expressed in different ways. For example, if a cold snap in the weather destroys large amounts of wheat then supplies will likely be lower, which will drive prices higher. This explains why traders of agricultural commodities often take a huge interest in the weather. Some traders even deal in weather futures to defend against negative impacts caused by the weather!

One of the fascinating things about the commodities market is the fact that its products impact on the daily lives of virtually everyone, because people rely on them in order to survive. In the following sections we outline the main agricultural commodities and some of their key characteristics so that you know exactly what you're trading.

Grains and legumes

Some of the most widely traded grains and legumes, such as corn, oats, soy beans and wheat, are used in foods for both human and animal consumption:

- **Corn:** Used widely for human consumption, as the carbohydrate part of a balanced diet. Corn also makes up a large component of animal feed. In the United States, corn is used to make ethanol fuel, and although you'd expect this extra demand on the product to reduce supply (and therefore drive up prices), instead farmers plant more corn crops, taking advantage of the new source of demand.
- **Oats:** Most people are familiar with oats as porridge, but farmers also use this valuable cereal widely in livestock feed.
- **Soy beans and their derivatives:** Appear in products such as tofu, soy milk, soy bean meal (a high-protein animal feed) and soy bean oil, which can be used as a vegetable oil.
- **Wheat:** Grown in a large number of regions around the world and used widely for human consumption; flour is the most notable product.

Livestock

The main animal products that people trade on the commodity market are cattle and pigs (listed as hogs on the market).

The cattle market falls into two categories: live cattle and feeder cattle. The key difference between the categories lies in where the cattle are in their life cycle when they're sold: *live* cattle, somewhat paradoxically, are slaughter-ready, whereas *feeder* cattle are still being fed and are sold to different farms to be grown out ready for slaughter. This feeding takes place at feedlots, which fatten cattle for sale.

The best place to find out more about cattle and hogs is the Chicago Mercantile Exchange website (`www.cmegroup.com`).

The pig (or hog) market is divided into lean hogs and pork bellies. *Lean hogs* are whole carcasses of a specific grade. *Pork bellies* are the parts of the carcass that butchers use to make bacon.

The softs: Coffee, cocoa, cotton and more

The softs category includes sugar, coffee, cotton, lumber (timber), orange juice and cocoa. Some people think of the softs as breakfast commodities, because the category includes orange juice, sugar and coffee. This categorisation falls down a bit, though, because it omits key products – unless perhaps you think of cotton for your PJs and timber for the breakfast table!

Energy commodities

Energy commodities cover a relatively narrow band of product categories, the major ones being crude oil, natural gas, heating oil and gasoline. Of these products, crude oil is the most actively traded and is possibly the most politically sensitive instrument traded anywhere in the world – you've no doubt already noticed that when any major political upheavals happen in the world (particularly in any country that produces oil), the oil price responds. In addition, a relatively small number of countries control vast amounts of the world's oil supply. Some of these countries make up the Organization of the Petroleum Exporting Countries (OPEC). The OPEC cartel aims to influence oil prices around the world by controlling the level of supply that goes to market.

Crude oil is one of the most important commodities in the world because it's universally used by consumers: few consumers can escape its grasp. Even if you cycle everywhere and never use a car or bus, you'll use products like plastics that are made from oil derivatives.

Oil prices have an inflationary effect, because for consumers everywhere, higher oil prices mean having less money to spend on other things. Furthermore, higher oil prices may lead consumers to defer spending in other areas of the economy in order to fuel their cars – people who drive to work may have no other choice. Thus other areas of the economy, such as retail and tourism, may suffer as a result of increases in the oil price.

Oil markets can be very active and very liquid (no pun intended) – key characteristics that traders should be looking for. You can spread bet on oil from all over the world, such as Brent Crude from the United Kingdom and West Texas Intermediate from the United States. The various contracts available worldwide have their differences in terms of standard viscosity and sulphur levels, which you can investigate simply by looking online. However, spread bets that use the prices of futures that trade on exchanges in the United States and the United Kingdom are likely to be of most interest to you, given their great *liquidity* (meaning fewer gaps in the price) and long trading hours.

Oil: Sweet crude stuff

Understanding a little more of the terminology that traders use when describing oil is worthwhile because you sometimes see these terms in the name of the contract when you spread bet. Often you see the words *light* and *sweet* used to define oil, as in light sweet crude.

Light simply refers to the viscosity of the oil – the lighter being better.

Sweet (or sour) refers to the sulphur content of the oil – the less sulphur, the better.

The lighter and sweeter the oil, the less refining it needs, which means the less it costs to turn the oil into other products like diesel and gasoline.

The contract that traders most trade is the US West Texas Intermediate. You can check out this contract at `www.cmegroup.com` as a great example.

Although you can't spread bet in the US, you can spread bet on crude oil contracts traded on US exchanges. These are among the most popular energy contracts and are available in the following contract sizes:

- Heating oil: 42,000 gallons
- Natural gas: 10,000 million British thermal units (MMBtu)
- Unleaded gasoline: 42,000 gallons

As with any spread bet, you don't pay for the full amount – expect your margin requirement to be in the region of 3 to 5 per cent. In addition, the size of the spread bet may be a lot smaller than if you were trading the actual futures contract. For example, the WTI Crude Oil contract trades in Chicago at 1,000 barrels of oil per contract, whereas spread bets generally trade over 100 or even single barrels of oil. The price moves in the same fashion, but spread betting brokers have less exposure per contract than futures traders. In addition, as with other financial markets, the spread varies widely in commodities markets depending largely on the liquidity of the underlying futures market.

Metals: All that glitters

The prices of metals commodities clearly reflect the overall state of the global economy, and dictate the cost of expenditure in areas such as housing and infrastructure.

Two important subsets of metals commodities are industrial (base) metals and precious metals. You'd be largely correct if you said that the difference between the two is the price, but that isn't entirely accurate. The actual difference is that *industrial metals* react with oxygen whereas *precious metals* don't react with oxygen.

Precious metals

The main precious metals that traders are interested in are gold, silver and platinum.

Gold is the most important precious metal, and not just because it looks nice. It actually has a wide range of industrial uses, particularly because it conducts electricity very well – significantly better than copper, in fact. More important still, though, is gold's use as:

- **A store of value.** Given that gold never corrodes, you know that any value you hold in this metal will stand the test of time.
- **A hedge against inflation.** Because you have to trade US dollars to buy gold, the gold acts very well as a hedge against inflation. This is because as the dollar falls in value, the price of gold conversely rises in value – which is extremely useful for investors keen to defend the value of their money. This isn't a guarantee, though, because if you buy gold when it's highly priced, it won't prove to be a good hedge against inflation at all.

Gold's characteristic as a hedge against inflation is the reason many people refer to gold as a currency unto itself – in fact, spread betting brokers often list gold in with the currencies.

Platinum and silver also have important applications in the industrial world. In addition, a big part of demand for these metals comes from jewellery manufacture, so low prices and a strong global economy can see a very sharp upswing in prices due to increased buyer demand.

Industrial metals

The industrial metals include copper, zinc, lead and aluminium. Many industrial metals are heavily traded in both the United Kingdom and the United States.

Demand for industrial metals is fairly representative of the overall state of the general economy. Copper is often one of the most interesting from this perspective, because of the large amount of copper used in the construction of new buildings (in wiring and plumbing). For example, in the late 2000s the copper market saw a big swing downwards as the US housing market started to fall away and demand for one of the key uses of this metal started drying up.

Getting Ready to Trade in the Commodities Market

Once upon a time traders took exposure to the commodities market either by investing in managed funds or, more indirectly, by buying the shares of listed companies that dealt in commodities – for example, buying a copper mining company to gain exposure to the changing value of copper. Although these types of investment can be a very effective way of investing in specific commodities, they're not nearly as direct as many people would otherwise like. For example, movements in the price of gold, as well as factors such as the wider movements of the share market, impact on a gold company's earnings. This means that even if you can predict the price of gold correctly, the gold company's share price may not reflect the gold price itself, because other factors influence the share price.

Spread bets take the best parts of the futures market (that is, direct exposure to the price movements of commodities) and convert them into products that are much easier for traders to deal with because they can trade them at a much smaller size, which makes risk easier to control – gold, silver and oil are examples of the most popular commodities to spread bet on.

We believe that a big part of successful trading involves having good mental aspirations of what you want your trading to achieve. This doesn't mean simply daydreaming in the hope that big profits will come your way – you need to think about something inspirational that can give you actual goals. Try watching the 1983 John Landis film *Trading Places*, primarily for a chuckle but also for the brilliant backdrop of the commodities market, which should get your mind racing with the possibilities of spread betting on commodities.

Although a big part of trading relates to trying to predict price movements and managing your risk, don't underestimate the importance of understanding the fundamental characteristics of the market you're dealing in.

Asking questions of your spread betting broker

One thing we must stress is that if you don't understand how a product operates, a condition under which a product trades or anything else to do with spread betting, call your broker and ask for a clear explanation. Your broker should be more than happy to help you with any questions you have. Don't assume that you're asking something silly – you'll simply be the latest in a long line of people who have trouble understanding the same issue. In fact, the more people who ask about a particular issue, the more likely your broker is to make changes to the way he explains the issue in the future.

Sadly, watching a movie doesn't count as a rounded education on the commodities market! So the following sections tell you some other things you need to know to help with your understanding of the workings of the commodities market.

Of course, you also need to look into the characteristics of the product you're trading before actually dealing in the product. The section 'Understanding the Terminology: What Are Commodities, Anyway?', earlier in the chapter, outlines the basic commodities that spread bettors are interested in trading.

Cost structure

When spread betting on commodities, as with other markets, you need to know how much each tick of the price (that is, each movement of the smallest price increment) will cost you if you bet the minimum amount per point your broker will allow. This is sensible regardless of what you're trading, because otherwise determining your risk is impossible.

For example, if the cost is £1 per £0.001 movement, you may have difficulty managing your risk if you want to put your stop £1 away, because this equates to 1,000 ticks, which may be more risk than you want to take on a single position.

Expiry of the underlying futures contract

Spread bets track the price of an underlying instrument, and in the case of commodities that instrument is a futures contract. A mismatch exists here, though, because futures contracts expire and spread bets don't: commodities have underlying futures contracts that expire at certain times during the year. Some expire five times a year – for example, in March, May, July, September and December – but others may expire quarterly or monthly.

So how can you ensure that your spread bets keep trading? The answer is simple: your spread betting broker automatically rolls over each spread bet near the expiry of the underlying futures contract. However, in real terms this means that your spread bet stops tracking the price of one futures contract and starts tracking the price of the next futures contract in line.

When your spread bet rolls over, the value of your exposure changes – for better or for worse. You need to be firmly aware of when the rollover will occur to assess the impact it will have on the value of your holding. You may even prefer to close out your position rather than rolling it over.

Your spread betting broker's terms and conditions should outline how your provider handles the rollover of futures contracts from one expiry period to the next. In general terms you always deal in *front-month* contracts, which are the next contracts to expire and are also the most liquid of the contracts available for you to trade. Some brokers will also quote you the price of the next contract as well, particularly if the front-month is close to expiry.

Limit-move rules

Several specific trading rules impact on each session in which the commodities market is operating, but the *limit-move rules* are key. They stop the underlying market (such as the Chicago Mercantile Exchange) changing by more than a specific value (up or down) from the close of the previous session – the particular market dictates the exact value.

The idea is that in times of very high volatility, the market will simply stop trading, limiting price swings that may otherwise occur. This means that if the underlying market locks limit up or limit down (meaning that trade halts during the normal hours of a trading session), you won't be able to exit your position.

There's great academic debate as to the benefit of the limit-move rules (many argue that imposing the rules just saves up volatility for another day), but nevertheless expect your spread betting broker to follow the rules.

Before you make a single spread bet in commodities, check the underlying market for the specific value that the limit-move rules place on the different commodities.

Liquidity

One of the key criteria that you need to consider about spread betting on commodities is liquidity. *Liquidity* refers to the ease with which you can enter or exit a position without impacting adversely on the price of that position. If you trade very illiquid positions, getting in and out of trades can become difficult, which in turn makes your risk management more difficult because you may not be able to get out at your stop loss price (we discuss risk management in more detail in Chapter 8).

Lack of liquidity in the underlying commodities futures market translates into erratic price moves and, occasionally, into re-quotes from your broker. It may also limit the size of the trade your broker is prepared to take on in that market.

Trading on the floor

Like a lot of futures contracts, commodity futures trade on the floor as well as electronically. *Trading on the floor* refers to the time when contracts trade in their home country during business hours using what's known as an *open outcry system*, where traders deal face-to-face with one another – this is the time when contracts are most actively traded. In the United Kingdom and United States, exchanges combine open outcry and electronic trading during the day (for four to eight hours) and use electronic trading at night, although many exchanges worldwide operate electronically for all trading sessions.

Generally, your spread betting broker offers trading during the same hours as the underlying market. Unfortunately, this timing is very inconvenient for many traders around the world because it corresponds with when they need to sleep. Luckily, with electronic trading contracts you can trade almost around the clock.

Interest Rate Products

Interest rate products represent one of the most important products within financial markets because they're a major way in which entire economies borrow funds – generally speaking, in order to fund a deficit. *Treasuries* are debt obligations undertaken by national governments, usually in the form of government bonds. In exchange for this revenue, governments promise to repay the money lent plus interest. Because governments guarantee treasury bonds, they're extremely low risk – as long as they're issued by a government with a strong economy (there have been some occasional – though big – government defaults in history). Some traders hold the bonds until they mature, and others sell them on to other investors on the open market.

Because of the huge amounts of money involved, the treasury market is one of the biggest markets in the world. Happily for spread bettors, interest rate products give you another string to your trading bow, because often you find that interest rate products move in an entirely different way to other asset classes, such as shares, because they're impacted by other factors, such as interest rates and the expectation of interest rate movements in the future.

Many interest rate products are available throughout the world, but not all are available for spread betting. In fact, the main offerings for spread bettors come from the United States, the United Kingdom, Europe and Japan. This restriction on offerings isn't likely to represent too much of an issue for you, though, because the greatest liquidity lies in these four markets (traders like liquidity because it makes for less erratic price movements and tighter spreads).

You can spread bet on interest rate products issued for the short term all the way out to long-term bonds. A good starting point for spread betting on interest rate products is the Eurodollar contract, and US Treasury bonds and notes:

- **The Eurodollar contract:** This is a highly liquid contract that's based on a 90-day debt issue, with the term actually referring to any US dollar-denominated fixed-interest investment made outside of the United States – not just Europe.

  European contracts also offer very high levels of volume, which makes them popular with short-term traders. The Euro-Schatz, Euro-Bobl and Euro-Bund are some of the best known products. The term structure of each of these is progressively longer, meaning that the underlying interest rate product has a longer and longer life span. In the United Kingdom, the Short Sterling and the Gilts are the main short- and long-term offerings, respectively.
- **US Treasury bonds and notes:** In simple terms, a *note* is generally an issue that's short term in nature, whereas a *bond* is much longer term – some bonds run as long as 30 years. You don't have to worry about a treasury maturing, because you aren't planning on holding on to it that long. However, you do need to consider the impact that rollover at maturity of the spread bet will have on the value of your trade. The prices of these instruments move up and down as economic expectations change and as market emotions drive prices higher and lower, so when your current contract rolls over automatically, you may pay a higher price for the new one. This rollover isn't the same as the maturity of the bond, though, which occurs at the end of the 30-year life span.

The key thing about spread bets on interest rates isn't the products themselves but what they represent for the market. When investors buy shares, they don't expect a set level of payment when they sell those shares, but with interest rate products traders know upfront the amount that they'll be paid in the future if they hold the product until maturity. So although returns on interest rate products aren't usually as high as returns on shares, interest rate products are more certain. As a result, in times of economic uncertainty you may see a rush of investors moving into interest rate products. Conversely, if the wider market has a growing risk appetite, you may see money flowing out of interest rate products and into higher-paying but riskier instruments.

Prices and yields

The price and yield of interest rate products have an inverse relationship, meaning that as the price falls, the yield rises, and vice versa. Here's why:

- If a bond starts life priced at £100 and pays a *coupon* (the term used to describe how interest is paid) of £10 then the interest rate is 10 per cent per annum (10/100 × 100).
- If prevailing interest rates are expected to fall, investors will lock in existing high interest rates, which may drive the bond price higher to, say, £110. The bond still pays a coupon of £10, but the yield has fallen to a little over 9 per cent per annum (10/110 × 100).

Yield is a way of expressing what investors will earn in interest if they buy the bond at the current price. If the price moves higher or lower, the yield changes too. You calculate yield as coupon/price multiplied by 100 (to make it a percentage).

Following Important Economic News from Around the Globe

No matter what products you're trading, you always know that the balance of supply and demand determines their price:

- **Demand:** For many commodities, like wheat, demand remains consistent, because people need it all the time. For other commodities, like copper and aluminium, the level of demand reflects the strength of the global economy (or the outlook for it). This means that your view on the outlook for the economy can have a large impact on your view of commodities that are impacted by economic growth levels.
- **Supply:** You can often find information online to help you determine supply levels of various commodities. For example, the exchanges themselves may give 'warehouse reports' and organisations such as OPEC give their own expectations for oil supplies. If demand increases and supplies remain constant, prices will rise. As an illustration, if companies stop mining copper but demand for copper grows (for example, due to huge numbers of houses being built) then the price for copper will rise. Similarly, even if demand for some types of crops remains quite consistent, expectations of falls in supply due to drought or unseasonable weather destroying crops may cause prices to rise. Alternatively, if crop harvests are very good, supplies will be high and – all other things being equal – prices will fall.

Seasonal conditions heavily influence agricultural commodities. That's why spread quotes can be very different at different times of the year. For instance, cattle prices may be relatively low in December if there's a drought, but much higher the following June if people expect the drought to break and farmers are holding on to stock to rebuild their depleted herds. Conversely, grain prices will be high if there's a drought due to lack of supply, but prices will be lower in the future if people expect the drought to break and the next harvest to be large. It's always more interesting to perform analysis if you can visualise a story around what's happening in the market you're interested in.

When you start spread betting on commodities, you need to develop an understanding of how money flows through national and global economies. The wonder of commodities is that you get a great feel for cause and effect. For example, when a long drought strikes in a certain area of the world (such as Australia) you may see wheat prices in Chicago going higher because global supplies are lower.

Here's another example of cause and effect in commodities: if inflation and inflationary expectations are on the rise, people may want to defend the value of their assets by buying gold and pushing its price higher. People may have the same expectation of movements in oil. A series of ructions in the Middle East may cause concerns about a drop in supplies of oil, which in turn pushes gasoline prices higher and drives up inflation. Traders may again turn to gold to defend the value of their funds.

For more information on broader economic factors and how cause and effect can move prices, see Chapter 10.

The following roundup highlights some of the key market and economic factors that traders look at when considering whether to buy or sell commodities and interest rate products:

- **Energy stocks:** Nothing moves energy prices more quickly than geopolitical tensions. The market immediately assumes that supplies are going to be limited, so prices rise.

  Several regular reports impact the market when they're released, particularly the US Department of Energy inventory report. This report outlines the status of US supplies: if supplies are lower than expected, this tends to have an upward impact on prices.

  Seasonality broadly impacts on prices too, particularly the northern hemisphere winter. If the weather is colder than expected, demand for heating oil rises, pushing prices higher. OPEC decisions also impact oil prices. The general rule is that when OPEC reduces supplies, prices go higher; and when OPEC increases supplies, prices go lower.

- **Grains:** Much of the wider price impacts on grain prices come from the stocks that are available at the end of the growing season. The lower the stocks, the higher the price. The US Department of Agriculture releases crop reports regularly to help with estimates. Not surprisingly, the weather impacts on prices too, with less-conducive growing conditions increasing prices due to short supplies.
- **Industrial metals:** In general terms, the higher the overall level (and expected future levels) of global economic activity, the more industrial metals will be in demand. When you consider that industrial metals have such a wide range of applications, you may wonder how countries can achieve economic growth without them.

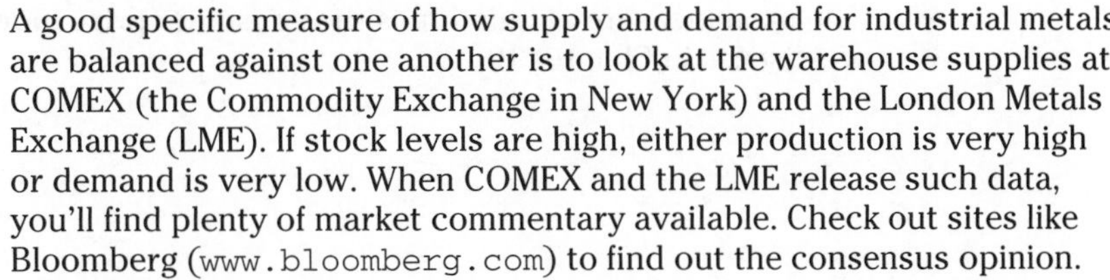

A good specific measure of how supply and demand for industrial metals are balanced against one another is to look at the warehouse supplies at COMEX (the Commodity Exchange in New York) and the London Metals Exchange (LME). If stock levels are high, either production is very high or demand is very low. When COMEX and the LME release such data, you'll find plenty of market commentary available. Check out sites like Bloomberg (`www.bloomberg.com`) to find out the consensus opinion.

- **Livestock:** Some of the same factors that affect the grain market impact on the livestock market. A colder season can see cattle gaining less weight, which makes them less valuable to farmers. In addition, a bad growing season for corn and soy beans may see prices for feed climb, and if cattle prices aren't high, farmers may prefer to sell their cattle cheaply rather than pay for expensive food – which can negatively impact cattle prices.
- **Precious metals:** Demand for precious metals can come from the industrial side of the market, the retail side of the market and from investors looking to store value. Some of the key holders of gold looking to store value are the central banks around the world. Central banks choosing to buy or sell gold can have a large impact on supply and demand. The state of inflation globally can also have significant impacts on gold prices as other participants in the market try to hedge against weakening currencies.
- **Treasuries:** Inflation is one of the major factors that impacts on the yields (return; see the sidebar 'Prices and yields') paid by treasuries. In most treasuries the interest payment is a fixed amount, say £4 per £100 bond: the yield is simply the return expressed as a percentage (in this case, $4/100 \times 100 = 4$ per cent). This relationship means that as the price increases, the yield decreases, and vice versa. This is referred to as an *inverse correlation*. If you hold a treasury that pays 4 per cent per annum and inflation is running at 3 per cent per annum, you're making a *real return* (the return you receive minus the rate of inflation) of 1 per cent. If inflation rises to 4 per cent, your real return is 0 per cent. As inflation

and, equally importantly, inflationary expectations increase, so too do treasury yields to compensate for the negative impact of inflation.

Inflation can also impact on future interest rate expectations. If inflation is high, the market may consider that interest rates are more likely to rise. You see interest rates on existing interest rate products move higher in anticipation of this type of change in expectations, because as people sell the existing bonds (which are now less attractive) the yields rise. This movement in the value of bonds is why the market watches the central banks for guidance on future interest rate movements, as well as combining guidance with the broader economic picture (determined by analysts and economists) for a better lead on overall expectations.

The main measure of inflation is the consumer price index (CPI), which we discuss in Chapter 10.

Part III

Keeping Risk Under Control

% Risk Models

Capital £

10,000
9,000
8,000
7,000
6,000
5,000
4,000
3,000
2,000
1,000
0

10% 5% 3% 2% 1%

1 16 31 46 61 76 91 106 121 136 151 166

For Dummies can help you get started with a huge range of subjects. Visit www.dummies.com to learn more and do more with *For Dummies*.

In this part . . .

- Keep a lid on leverage.
- Apply stop loss orders with confidence.
- Get a sense for a good position size.
- Understand all the risks and downsides involved.
- Learn to manage potential exposure to loss.
- Go to `www.dummies.com/extras/fsbuk` for online bonus content.

Chapter 8

Managing Risk: Your Key to Trading Survival

In This Chapter

- Deciding how much leverage to use
- Controlling losses with stop loss orders
- Taking care with foreign exchange betting
- Diversifying to reduce risk
- Balancing the long and short exposure in your spread betting portfolio
- Playing it safe and planning your trades

Using leveraged trading products is easy and fun, up until the point when you begin losing money and realise financial security is even farther away than you'd hoped. One of our favourite Homer Simpson quotes illustrates this: 'After years of disappointment with get-rich-quick schemes, I know I'm going to get rich with this scheme . . . and quick!' This is funny, but don't ever let anyone tell you that trading is a sure-fire way to get rich quick.

A good friend of ours rides a motorbike, and when he was learning to ride, his instructor told him that he always needed to be wary of reaching the point where he felt comfortable on his bike – he'd relax, then go faster, and then have an accident. Think of your trading in the same way. Just when you think you've mastered it, you're usually about to get a lesson in humility. The one thing that makes for successful trading – more than any other factor, such as picking the right position – is your ability to manage risk.

In this chapter, we explore some of the major issues surrounding risk management and look at how you can start managing your own trading portfolio based on a carefully thought out plan that involves the use of stop loss orders and other risk-reduction strategies. We talk about the special care you need to take when spread betting on foreign exchange markets and how to use diversification and exposure to minimise risk. And we also discuss how you can get too cocky and start playing with spread betting rather than being conservative and planning. Dreaming about winning trades is fun, but you're better off spending time thinking about how you manage the losing trades in order to survive.

Keeping a Lid on Leverage

How you manage risk varies depending on the type of product you're trading, because some trades are inherently more volatile than others, and some trades are more liquid than others. You need to take these factors into account when considering the overall *leverage* (the deposit which allows you to handle a much larger trading position: More details in Chapter 1) that you're willing to apply to your spread betting portfolio.

When you're spread betting, one of the things to remember is that you can employ a lot of leverage. When we say a lot of leverage, we really do mean *a lot!* However, a line we've been using for years in reference to trading parallels life: 'Just because you can do something, doesn't mean that you should.' This line rings true for leverage too. No hard and fast rules dictate how much leverage is too much, but you should exercise caution and minimise your risk.

Before you start spread betting you need to decide the maximum amount of leverage that you're willing to apply to your capital. This is one of the best ways that you can manage your risk. We suggest that you incorporate no more than 3× leverage for the majority of your spread bets. At this level you're still attaining significant leverage on your capital without being overly aggressive.

These days a lot of spread betting on shares only requires a 3 per cent margin payment, so if you put all your capital into spread bets with that requirement then you'd have 33× leverage. To calculate how much leverage you're currently employing, take the total exposure you have to all markets in your spread betting account and divide it by the amount of cash you have in your account. Simple, right? *Exposure* is simply another way of referring to the total value of all the positions that you hold with your spread betting broker and it can act as a fantastic guide to tell you whether you're carrying too many positions or positions that are too large.

If your account has £60,000 worth of positions (trades) and you have £20,000 cash in your account then you've applied 3× leverage (60,000/20,000) to your money.

Avoid falling into the trap of thinking that if you apply a huge amount of leverage to your account, you only need a small move in your favour to make a lot of money. Instead, consider that, at 33× leverage, you only need a 3 per cent move against you and all your money is gone!

Using more moderate amounts of leverage also provides returns, but allows you to absorb a lot more movement in the share price against you.

Table 8-1 outlines the way in which the application of leverage can have a negative impact when prices move against you. The table shows leverage applied to an account of £1,000. The figures in italics illustrate where the total loss of your trading account has occurred and you actually owe money to the broker. If you fully lever on a spread bet that requires a 3 per cent margin and then the share price moves against you by 3 per cent, your money is all gone. Each column shows the application of leverage growing the returns in both directions – you can see that when you apply a lot of leverage, it doesn't take a lot for you to lose all your money, no matter how much you have.

Table 8-1 Applying Leverage to Trades

Share Price	*1×*	*3×*	*6×*	*10×*	*20×*	*33×*
0.95	–50	–150	–300	–500	–1,000	–1,650
0.96	–40	–120	–240	–400	–800	–1,320
0.97	–30	–90	–180	–300	–600	–990
0.98	–20	–60	–120	–200	–400	–660
0.99	–10	–30	–60	–100	–200	–330
1.00	1,000	3,000	6,000	10,000	20,000	33,000
1.01	10	30	60	100	200	330
1.02	20	60	120	200	400	660
1.03	30	90	180	300	600	990
1.04	40	120	240	400	800	1,320
1.05	50	150	300	500	1,000	1,650

Why luck doesn't figure

Some people adopt a 'have a go' approach to spread betting. Simply having a positive attitude isn't enough – a lack of planning inevitably leads to losses. The most likely outcome is that you'll lose money and stop trading after becoming very frustrated. You may decide to have another go down the track, but you'll simply make the same mistakes.

Don't let yourself be lulled into thinking that trading involves some magic strategy or the need for a lot of luck. If you think that you only need a few wins in a row to get ahead, you're in for a shock if you've been sharply increasing your position sizes with each winning trade. When you make the inevitable losing trade you'll end up right back where you started, because the big loss at the end wipes out the smaller profits you accumulated along the way. See the sidebar 'Messing up with martingale', later in the chapter, for information on betting strategies and the weaknesses inherent in doubling up your losing positions.

Don't give losing trades legroom

Some people are inclined to want to close out winning positions quickly and give losing positions the benefit of the doubt. Why do traders do this? We suspect that these decisions reflect the way that people mentally account for things. If you close out a winning position then you can add another tick to the wins column, regardless of how big the win might be, right? If you let a losing position continue to run then as long as it remains open it could come good. Yes? If you leave losing trades open then they 'might' come good again.

Get into the habit of closing losing trades quickly; losing trades might bounce back but the ones that don't can significantly weigh on your capital.

If we ask you 'Will the next move of the share price be up or down?' what would your answer be? You might respond that you don't have enough information and so you can't answer. What if we let you look at a chart? Or last year's earnings report? Or a broker recommendation? All these things may help with your predictions of future movements, but they won't help you work out the problem in front of you. No matter how talented the trader, picking the next movement of price is no more accurate than flipping a coin.

Spread bets are generally a non-advisory product, so no one is going to stop you making a trade that is very large, like some of those we list in Table 8-1, especially the 10×, 20× and 33× columns.

Whatever percentage margin you pay (for example, 2 per cent or 5 per cent), if the share price moves against you (falls), you'll lose your margin payment. How much margin you pay is up to you, and you decide your margin by determining your position size (see Chapter 9).

Using Stop Loss Orders

A *stop loss order* allows you to close out a losing position to minimise the loss of capital. It allows you to plan ahead with your trading so that you know when your trade has failed and the position has moved too far against you (refer to the definition of a stop loss order in Chapter 1).

Although you don't need to place a stop with your provider when entering into trades, we recommend that you do. Experienced traders sometimes prefer to close out the position themselves when the market reaches their perceived stop loss point. However, we don't suggest that new spread bettors do this, even when constantly monitoring the trade. Stopping a trade this way requires a high degree of discipline. In a situation where a position reaches the point where the trader needs to close it, often the trader does nothing and waits to see what happens next. If the position continues to slide then the trader may find it even more difficult to close it out.

Depending on what you're trading, you need to allow a decent amount of wiggle room when placing a stop loss. The industry expression *wiggle room* refers to the room that you give a position in order for it to survive minor downward movements. Although you should use stop loss orders every time you trade, don't place them too close to your entry point.

Putting your stop loss order only a few pence away from your entry point may seem like a good idea, but the problem with doing this is that you greatly increase your chance of getting stopped out if the price drops slightly. Sure, all traders aim to enter a position and see it move immediately in their favour (rather than downwards towards the stop order), but this won't happen all the time.

Messing up with martingale

Remember that, in all things finance, if you think you've found an invincible risk strategy then you should safely assume that you're wrong – there's no such thing as a sure thing!

The way that smaller and larger positions relate to one another in gambling or betting strategies is referred to as *martingale*. Martingale requires you to increase your position size each time you lose in the hope that an eventual win will recover all previous losses. The anti-martingale approach increases bets after wins, while reducing them after a loss.

The best example of martingale in action is at the casino when you're betting on red or black on the roulette wheel. Each time you lose you bet on the same colour next turn but double your bet. This way you benefit from a big win when you actually win.

Sound foolproof? It's not – the casino has table limits (the maximum amount that you can bet) in place for this very reason, because even from the minimum bet you'll hit the table limit very quickly. This is also why you have to bet a little bit more to play colours so that you hit the limit even more quickly.

Translating principles of martingale ideal into trading leads to very high risk and very poor risk/reward trades and you should avoid these types of strategies at all costs.

The opposite strategy, anti-martingale, is more sensible because it allows you to add to your position size as you're winning.

We look in more detail at a number of rationales that traders can apply to the thought process of trading in Chapter 15.

The best rule to follow is to place your stop loss order at the point where you know you were wrong about the trade – the point where your *original* reason for being in the trade no longer exists.

The reason we stress 'original' in the preceding paragraph is because, through a combination of technical and fundamental analysis (or gut feeling), you can always come up with a reason for being in a trade. Just take a look at the hundreds of different indicators that exist in charting software. If you want a chart to tell you that you should stick with the trade, you'll be able to find one. However, talking yourself into staying in a losing trade makes for very poor risk management.

In the chart shown in Figure 8-1 the position has broken through a resistance level (which, to many traders, indicates a buy). It fails to continue to move higher and eventually falls below the old support level. This means that your reason for being in the position no longer exists.

Stop loss order hybrids

Keep in mind that spread betting firms are, by definition, market makers: you're not placing a trade in the real market, nor is anyone really buying what you're selling. The relationship between you and your broker is more akin to that between a punter and a bookie. On the upside, because spread betting is treated as gambling, you're also benefiting from the tax-free status of your profits.

Figure 8-1: A breakout chart showing it's time to close out.

In terms of managing your risk, spread betting providers offer you the purest form of stop loss, as ultimately they are controlling the price: when the market reaches the price in question, your broker closes your position. In physical share trading, if you are using a stop loss order, brokers can execute your order at what they refer to as 'the first available price'. This means that if the market doesn't trade at the level you wanted, they execute your stop at a level somewhere below that. Even though you may not get your exact price, at least the position will be closed.

Spread betting brokers (like traders) don't know what the market will do next, so they execute your orders as soon as they have to so that they have the best chance to execute the stop at the price the trader wants. This may mean that as soon as the bid price matches the stop loss price the client has nominated, the broker executes the order. (Although some wait until the instrument actually trades at the nominated level before executing the stop order.) If you wait then the bid might become lower and the price you receive becomes worse. Sometimes this turn of events is frustrating if the price starts to move higher, but this is nothing to do with the spread betting broker – it's just bad luck.

With a spread betting firm you sometimes receive a 'requote' for a single price. Talk to your broker to find out exactly how it deals with this type of issue. Requoting is becoming rarer in the spread betting industry, but if you are used to placing large trades, you may need to allow your broker time to ensure she can hedge your trade in the market (that is, protect herself by taking the same position in the physical market). This is particularly true of bets on illiquid shares like AIM-listed stocks, where the broker has no liquid futures market to turn to.

As a general rule, the larger your broker, the more likely it is to be able to manage big bets, sometimes of as much as £1,000 per point. It is also more likely to take bets out of hours, but possibly not to the same size.

Guaranteed stop loss orders

Some spread betting brokers offer a *guaranteed stop loss order* or GSLO. With a GSLO, traders lock in an exit price regardless of market movements. The chart in Figure 8-2 shows a significant gap in the price. This could relate to bad company news or just general negativity in the market; whatever the case, the share price has been hit hard. If you had a stop loss order in place anywhere in the section where no trades have occurred then you'd have suffered slippage. If you'd placed a GSLO, however, you would have exited the position at your nominated price, because these don't require shares in the underlying market to trade at this price in order for the broker to execute the trade.

Figure 8-2: Gaps in the market can significantly add to your risk.

Like all things in finance, GSLOs have downsides. Here are some points to consider:

- **You need to pay a premium to place a GSLO.** This is more than fair from the perspective of the spread betting broker. The broker is taking on a large amount of risk when it comes to this type of order, so it deserves compensation. This payment may be a fixed amount or payable pro-rata based on the size of the position that you hold. Expect to pay the normal commission on the order being executed in addition to the premium that you pay for the GSLO.
- **Your spread bet position won't allow you to place a GSLO very close to the current price.** Generally, a sizeable gap needs to exist between the current price and the closest level at which you can place your GSLO – 5 per cent away from current levels is a reasonable expectation. Depending on the time frame over which you trade and your position sizes, the gap may be small or large. (You can make adjustments for any amount of risk through the sensible use of position size calculations. To find out how, see Chapter 9.)

In normal trading conditions you don't really need to use GSLOs. But no one knows when conditions will change from normal to abnormal. However, if trading using GSLOs makes you feel comfortable then spend the extra money and use them.

Most spread betting brokers only let you place a GSLO after the market opens (and you may have to do so over the phone). Whether your order is accepted or not is at the discretion of the spread betting broker – if you enquire about placing a GSLO on a company that's rumoured to be in financial difficulty, don't be surprised if the broker refuses the order.

A GSLO allows you to manage risk in a similar way to a derivative called an option because the downside is very specifically capped. The difference is that when the market reaches the stop price, the position is immediately closed out by the broker. Figure 8-3 shows that the price can rise higher in line with a rising share price, but on the downside it will go no lower than the GSLO price.

Some providers allow you to move GSLOs free of charge as the market moves higher, whereas other providers require you to cancel a standing GSLO before placing a new order (which requires you to pay the GSLO fee again). The spread betting broker's terms and conditions should spell out the details of GSLOs.

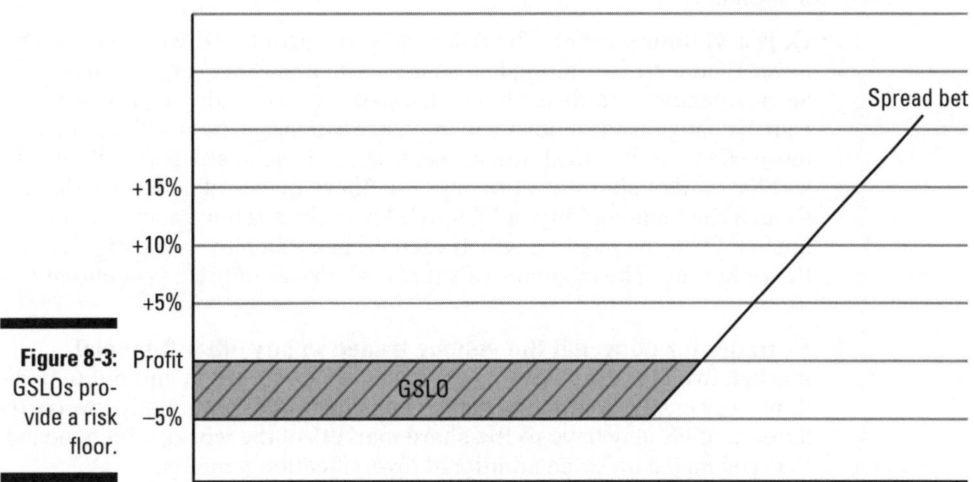

Figure 8-3: GSLOs provide a risk floor.

Reducing Risk on Foreign Exchange Spread Bets

Traders in the foreign exchange markets tend o trade in large minimum lots in the foreign exchange market, but this practice is also reflected in the spread betting market. So if you're planning on not having more than 3× leverage and have only £2,000 in your trading account then you will likely not be able to trade even the smallest amount. Even at £1 a point, you can quickly run up a sizeable loss in FX trading, and face a margin call. Here, then, you need to exercise judgement and care. Be sure to take on a position size that has you risking no more than 2 per cent of your trading capital (preferably lower, see Chapter 9), and as a part of this ensure your stop loss order is in place. Lastly, regardless of how much capital you have, start with the minimum trade size and go from there – this is a category that can really move. (For more information on trading foreign exchange, take a look at Chapter 5.)

From the perspective of managing risk, you need to take into account some very important features of spread betting FX. You can use most of the points we present here to reduce the risk of the trade you're taking:

- **Almost all FX quotes are done to four decimal places.** If you are betting at £1 per point, and the market rises or falls by one point then you'll receive a profit or loss of £1. However, your absolute exposure in the market will still be large as most forex spread bets are at 1 per cent margin only.
- **FX is a 24-hour market.** The risk of gaps occurring in the price is much lower than with something like shares, which may see large swings at the opening of trade each day. Large price swings do occur in foreign exchange trades, however, so your stop loss orders will be much more effective than in share markets. The price can still gap in times of sudden market shock or at the release of key pieces of economic data, though the high liquidity of FX spread bets does reduce some of the impact. Even the most heavily traded FX pair can move very quickly at the right time. The most active short-term driver of price is economic news.
- **FX trades far outweigh the volume traded in any other financial market.** Even in turbulent times you can generally get in and out of positions very easily. Something else to consider is the potentially low correlation that FX may have to the share markets of the world, which means that you may gain some additional diversification benefits.
- **FX spread bets generally require a margin of 1 per cent, which means that the minimum transaction size requires an initial margin of only £100.** Keep in mind that a lower margin requirement has nothing to do with keeping your risk lower.

All these points boil down to you being able to give foreign exchange some special treatment in terms of the overall leverage that you apply. However, this is reliant on you using stop losses with all your positions, which allows you to manage your downside very effectively.

Spreading the Load with Diversification

Good, old-fashioned diversification can help you manage the risk of holding your trading portfolio. Although people often think of diversification as suitable mainly for long-term investors, it also offers real benefits for spread bettors. You can have all your exposure in one or two shares, but also invest in different products and asset classes if they are available as spread bets via your provider.

Diversification offers some real benefits, even on a day-to-day basis, because it can mean that you're less exposed to the ups and downs of the share market. Of course, simply focusing on individual products like index-based spread bets is fine too – you're more likely to be able to keep a pretty close eye on the whole operation.

Some traders who focus on things such as leverage gloss over a number of very positive aspects about spread bets. The following points provide some examples of how diversification works when spread betting:

- **You can easily access myriad products and asset classes all from the same account.** Diversification primarily refers to a wide spread of different spread bets on shares, but if you're looking at diversification to reduce your overall average losses and gains through spreading your exposure around then you may be able to benefit even more by looking to different asset classes. You'll need to do more work to gain an understanding of these markets, but you can really benefit from doing this.
- **You can be very creative.** Perhaps you see a long-term correlation between the oil price and the natural gas price but believe that oil is currently overvalued. Perhaps you could go short on oil and long on natural gas. This way you're keeping your overall exposure to energy small but trading the relationship between the two. This is known as a *pairs trade*, which we look at in more depth in Chapter 12.
- **If you study the state of the global economy you can use FX trades as a means of attempting to profit from the economy.** Perhaps you think the Australian dollar will do well due to expectations of strengthening commodity demand but the Euro will fall due to weak expectations of export demand from that area of the world. Perhaps you want additional exposure to copper and oil, based on this same rationale, but want to go short on treasuries because you think upcoming interest rate changes will see prices fall.

These examples give you a good idea of the types of exposure that you can take on using spread betting. Keep in mind that you always want to be aiming to do better in terms of performance than you would be able to do by using *index funds* (funds investing in stock indices) and cash in the bank.

If you have a portfolio of share spread bets that you've leveraged, you need to monitor your performance based on unleveraged returns. For example, if you have applied an average of 3× leverage, you need to divide your returns by three to get the outcome that's down to your trading skill; otherwise, you're not deducting the effect of the leverage on your returns. Anyone can increase returns (positive or negative) by adding leverage, but the true gauge of skill comes from what you can do before you lever your exposure.

Gaining Exposure

One of the best ways of reducing risk is to balance the long and short exposure you carry in your spread betting portfolio. The difference between diversification and long or short exposure is that diversification aims to reduce volatility through spreading your money in different areas of the market, whereas the idea of long and short exposure allows you to actively pursue gains from both rising and falling share prices (for more information on long and short exposure see Chapter 3).

Diversification means spread betting on markets that have very different dynamics from each other: for example, UK shares and oil. Many pension funds still diversify their risks this way, but the difference between a trader and a pension fund is that the pension fund must be invested. A trader has a choice. Many spread bettors start off trading the FTSE 100 or S&P 500 index, and then gradually branch into other areas, like shares or commodities, as they become more comfortable with spread betting. Very experienced spread bettors also look for correlations – relationships – between markets, for example between currencies and commodities like gold and silver.

Futures contracts are one of the most important (and often misunderstood) types of derivatives. A futures contract enables traders to lock in the buy or sell price of an asset at a set price and a set date in the future. For traders who deal in shares, financial futures allow you to take exposure to a specific index. A good example is the FTSE 100 futures contract. This is a futures contract that closely tracks the value of the FTSE 100 Index. People who buy or sell this type of contract can take on broad and immediate exposure to a broad portfolio.

Recognising the Perils of Overconfidence

Overconfidence is a remarkably easy trap to fall into. We firmly believe in listening to the voice in your head that tells you not to get overexcited or overconfident about your trades. We've even said to people that we hope their first trade is a losing trade. We don't mean to be cruel, but we believe that losing trades make the best learning experiences.

'I'm better than average!'

Perhaps you are, but can you bank on it? In any given year you can expect the UK share market to rise in value by around 10 per cent on average. This means that if you have a wide spread of share investments, 10 per cent is about what you'd expect to earn. However, even the average fund manager has difficulty beating the return of the market on a consistent basis. The average fund manager usually generates an average return. Now, before you begin to mock fund managers, keep in mind that some mighty talented and skilled people work as fund managers.

'I don't need to be conservative'

We think you do. Overconfidence brought on by a few wins often leads to over-trading – placing trades for the fun of it, which is a very ineffective way of trading. Only after losing trades do you realise that being conservative and consistent in your analysis and risk management is what makes you an effective trader.

Do you remember the first trade that you ever took and how you were at pains deciding whether or not to take it? You checked your charts again and again before you decided to go for it. Whether you made money or not isn't our only point here. You were being conservative, working to a plan and doing your best to be an effective trader.

You need to develop your trading plan and your own personal discipline to the level that you can remain in control the whole time. We believe that this requires experience and learning from your mistakes (see the sidebar 'Ouch!'). Also, if you keep risk low from the outset, you can learn from your mistakes without it costing you too much in capital.

Ouch!

David can remember the best trade he ever had. It happened many years ago and was amazingly profitable – but it was nothing short of a total fluke. However, rather than simply attributing the first outcome to luck, he attributed it to his trading skills – a big mistake.

David was in his early 20s at the time and didn't really have a trading plan or much of a trading history. After his 'big win', though, he figured he was on to something and started making more trades.

After another two or three trades he had given back all of the profit and no doubt some of his original capital too. He discovered then that he needed to make a sensible plan and stick to it if he wanted to make a profit from trading.

Chapter 9

Mastering Position Sizing

In This Chapter

- Juggling position sizes and stop losses
- Using the fixed price model
- Running with the fixed percentage model
- Keeping position sizing in check
- Following the ATR indicator

Position sizing involves linking the amount that you're willing to risk with your entry point and your stop loss order; taking on a 'position' that's appropriate for these different factors. Position sizing allows you to manage your risk (for more information on the range of factors involved in risk management, and stop loss options, see Chapter 8). Models for position sizing vary, but all are based on risking a certain amount of capital in a trade and then taking on the biggest position size that you can for that amount of risk.

Position sizing based on your risk tolerance and trading capital is the best way to develop a risk management strategy when you're spread betting. The essential rule is that if you risk less on each trade then you can withstand a lot more losing trades and still survive. Yes, we know that considering the prospect of losing your capital isn't very pleasant, but the more upfront you are about the risks you face, the better you're able to assess ways to minimise them.

In this chapter, we look at the fixed price and the fixed percentage models, which are the most popular position sizing methods. When you understand these key methods, you can do your own additional research into others online if you choose. We also show you how to choose the right position sizing model for you, and how to use an average true range indicator to work out your trading range.

Looking at Basic Ways of Integrating Position Sizes and Stop Losses

When many people start trading, they begin with a way of sizing their positions so that they can apply them consistently. So they buy the same percentage worth of spread betting risk each time they trade (say 2 per cent of their total risk capital) and place different-sized stop loss orders each time, depending on the perceived risks.

Is there anything wrong with this method? Well, in short, no. Every trader has a unique way of doing things, and what's really important is understanding your own methods and being comfortable with them. However, we don't think that this method is the most efficient way to approach spread betting. If you use a different-sized stop loss each time you trade, you're taking more risk on some trades and less risk on others.

One way to solve this problem is to use the same stop loss magnitude each time you trade. When we say *stop loss magnitude*, or *stop loss size*, we're referring to the distance away from your entry point that you place your stop loss order. In this way, you're always risking the same amount on each trade that you take. However, you can run into problems sizing your position this way too, because sometimes you may be better off putting your stop loss order closer to your entry point, or even further away.

If you're dealing with a company that trades at a share price of £50 and regularly trades over a range of 50p from the high to the low on a given trading day, then putting your stop loss 20p away from your entry point isn't a good idea, because you're likely to hit your stop loss level because of normal market volatility (see Chapter 3). Conversely, if you're considering a company with a share price of £1 and you apply the same stop loss size, the closed position represents a loss of 20 per cent on the share's value – at which point you'd probably prefer not to be a shareholder in that company any more.

Keep in mind that the closer you place your stop loss, the bigger the position you can take – but you must take into account the volatility of the shares, otherwise you'll get stopped out on your trades frequently.

More often than not, you need to change your stop loss size to suit the trade. This also applies to trading methodologies when using technical analysis techniques. For example, traders who use technical analysis methods to capitalise on sudden price moves are more likely to put their stops very close to the entry point, because they can tell very quickly if the trade is going the wrong way. But a trend trader who's looking to capture bigger moves in the market is likely to give the position a lot more room to move. (For more information on trading using technical analysis techniques, see Chapter 13.)

If you're comfortable risking a specific percentage of your trading capital every time you trade, such as 2 per cent (and adjusting your stop loss size to suit the trade), then you only need to be aware that your losses, when they occur, will be limited and you won't see your trading capital fatally eroded. The best way to manage the downside using this method is to keep your exposure to the market conservative, because otherwise the losses can become very large. Another option is to apply a more robust position sizing model, like the one we cover in the following section.

Position Sizing Using the Fixed Price Model

The *fixed price model* focuses on position sizing using a measured means of risk management.

To use this model you work out a loss level (expressed as an amount in pounds, say £100) that you're comfortable with. This means that you're willing to lose £100 on each losing trade that occurs.

Using this amount as a starting point, here's how to calculate your spread betting exposure:

XYZ Ltd bet

Current price: £2.00

Stop loss placement: £1.90

Stake: £10 per point (for example)

Share price risk: 10p (£2.00 – £1.90)

Total £ risk: £100

In this case you're risking £100 on the trade.

Applying the Fixed Percentage Model

Position sizing becomes a little more sophisticated using the fixed percentage model. One of the most popular methods of position sizing, the fixed percentage model is reactive to changes in your available trading capital (the amount of money you have on deposit with the spread betting company, not the additional money it lends you to trade with).

Diverging from the 2 per cent rule

The 2 per cent rule is designed to keep you in the market for as long as possible, even with lots of losing trades. You always risk 2 per cent of your available capital with this method, and so if you have had a number of losses, you risk less because you're risking 2 per cent of a smaller amount of capital. Happily, if you have had lots of wins, your positions get bigger because your capital base has grown. Unless you're very confident and have significant statistical evidence of the strength of your methodology, don't exceed risk per trade of more than 2 per cent. Each percentage extra that you risk has a dramatic additional impact on your capital if you get stopped out on a number of positions in a row, and this makes the chances of your eventual failure that much greater.

To apply this model you work out the percentage of capital you're willing to risk on each trade. The most popular amount is 2 per cent, sometimes referred to as the 2 per cent rule (see the sidebar 'Diverging from the 2 per cent rule').

First, look at your available trading capital and then calculate what 2 per cent of it is. For example, if you have £10,000 in your account, 2 per cent is £200. Similar to the fixed price model (see the preceding section) this becomes the amount divided by your stop loss magnitude (which is the difference between your entry point and where your stop loss will be placed). If you decide that you will always limit your total loss to £200, then this will dictate how many pounds per point you will bet. If you were betting at £2 per point on the FTSE 100, you would set your stop at 100 points as an absolute maximum.

Say you're betting £10 per point at £1.90 and placing your stop loss at £1.75. In this case, your risk on the bet is 15 points or £150.

From this point on, the difference between the fixed price model and the fixed percentage model kicks in. The advantage of a fixed percentage model is that, as your available capital increases (hopefully, through a great deal of successful trading), so too do your position sizes. The percentage that you're risking remains the same at all times, but as the capital in your account grows, the percentage represents more in terms of pounds at risk.

As Figure 9-1 shows, your position sizes change when your available capital falls as well. If you suffer a string of losses and your trading account takes a beating, the fixed percentage model ensures you begin risking less per trade as a result. This method is designed to help you remain in the game.

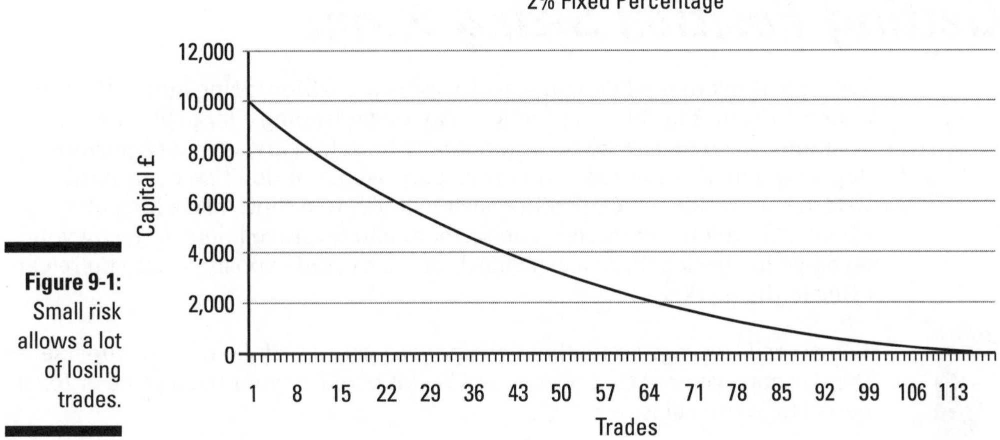

Figure 9-1: Small risk allows a lot of losing trades.

Of course, you don't have to risk 2 per cent of your capital on each trade; you may decide to risk 1.5 per cent or even 1 per cent. Take a look at the comparative graphic in Figure 9-2 to see how much extra leeway you receive by reducing your risk per trade to only 1 per cent.

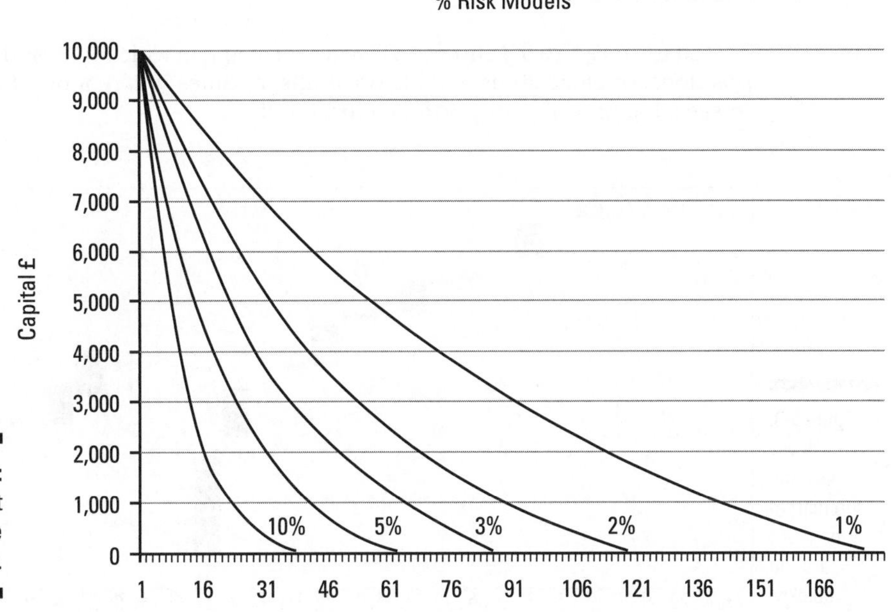

Figure 9-2: Looking at comparative risk.

Getting Position Sizing Right

You may think that when you start to apply a position sizing model (like the ones we discuss in this chapter) you can begin trading a large number of positions. In some cases you may actually be safer carrying more positions, depending on the methods you previously used, but don't go overboard. Before you decide which position sizing model to adopt, take a look at Chapter 8, which covers risk management and leverage limits. Keeping your leverage in check acts as a safeguard on the overall exposure that you're carrying in the market.

The overall leverage limits that you apply to your portfolio need to supersede the risk management that occurs as a result of either your fixed price or fixed percentage risk rules.

An unpleasant but important way of thinking about whether you can cope with all your positions is to add up what your costs would be if they were all stopped out simultaneously. Although this is unlikely, it could still happen from time to time. Take a look at the chart of the FTSE 100 Index in sharp decline in Figure 9-3 to see the kind of circumstances under which this very thing might occur. You need to be particularly careful when managing multiple open positions at the same time, as a sudden major reversal could cause substantial losses.

The chart in Figure 9-3 shows that whether you use wide stops and small positions, or close stops and big positions, at times you're more than likely to see a big part of your portfolio closed out.

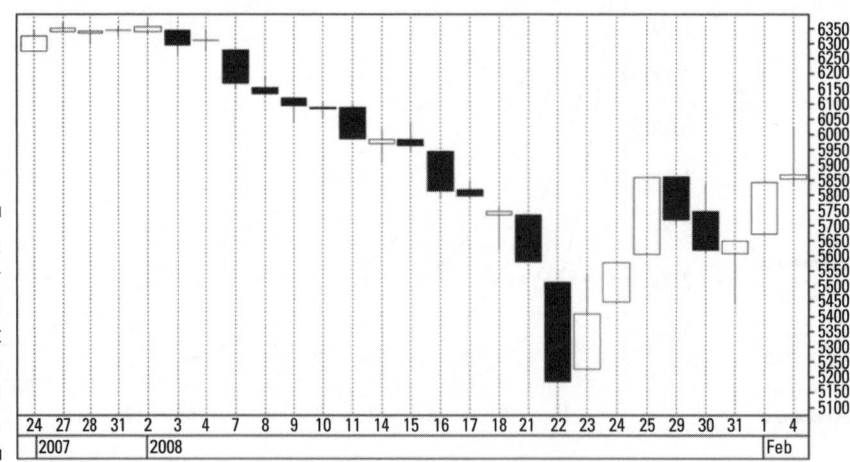

Figure 9-3: Never assume the market won't turn around quickly.

When you're using a fixed percentage model, one more decision you need to make is how quickly you change the capital amount that you use in your calculations. Some people choose to simply look at the amount of capital in their accounts at the time of the trade and then base the amount of risk on that. Others review their account size periodically (perhaps once a month) and then base their calculation on that month-end figure. We prefer working with the month-end figure to allow for more ups and downs in the market. However, if you see a significant slide in the value of your account, you may need to act more quickly than that.

You can apply the methods that we look at throughout this chapter across any type of spread betting contract. You simply need to work out where you plan to enter a trade and where you plan to place your stop loss order.

Some products, however, have a minimum position size, such as foreign exchange spread bets (refer to Chapter 5), which may require you to risk more than your chosen percentage under the fixed percentage model. If this occurs, we suggest that you simply don't make the trade – you're better off missing out than risking too much on one trade.

Working with an ATR Indicator

Sometimes you may need a slightly different way to work out your position sizes to take into account factors such as volatility in the market or a product in your own portfolio.

Analytical tools, such as volatility-based indicators, can help you decide where to place your stop losses to make your position sizes as effective as possible. The best tool for working out your trading range is the average true range (ATR) indicator. The ATR indicator adjusts itself based on an instrument's recent trading activity. See Chapter 13 for more on using this technical analysis tool.

The benefit of following this type of indicator is that it allows you to place your stops to avoid getting closed out by market volatility factors (as mentioned in 'Looking at Basic Ways of Integrating Position Sizes and Stop Losses' earlier in this chapter, and in Chapter 8). Generally, traders look at the ATR and then multiply it by two or three to ensure plenty of distance between the market and the stop loss. For example, if the ATR indicator reads 28 or £0.28 then what we call a 2ATR stop loss would be placed £0.56 away from your entry point. You are making use of the indicator to provide you with an effective gauge of where the safe point is to place your stop loss. It can also provide you with some idea as to whether this market is too volatile for you to trade safely (that is, your stops would have to be so wide that you would lose more money than you could afford if they were hit).

Working with an ATR Indicator

Part IV

Trading Strategies

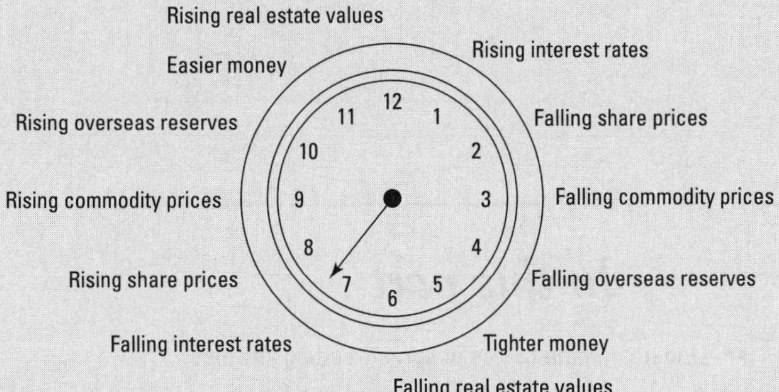
Top of the Boom
Rising real estate values
Rising interest rates
Easier money
Falling share prices
Rising overseas reserves
Rising commodity prices
Falling commodity prices
Rising share prices
Falling overseas reserves
Falling interest rates
Tighter money
Falling real estate values
Depth of Depression
12
1
2
3
4
5
6
7
8
9
10
11

web extras

In this part . . .

- Understand the basics of spread-betting strategy.
- Get into the swing of swing trading.
- Keep up to date with trend trading.
- Experience the joy of technical analysis (no, really).
- Personalise your strategy to deliver what you want.
- Go to `www.dummies.com/extras/fsbuk` for online bonus content.

Chapter 10

Making Informed Decisions Based on the Economy

In This Chapter

- Examining the economic impact of interest rates
- Taking a look at economic growth
- Exploring the link between employment figures and the economy
- Applying fundamental analysis techniques to the share market

Although many traders focus on charts for technical analysis (see Chapter 13), making informed decisions requires an understanding of what drives prices from a fundamental perspective (that is, the earnings that a company can generate or, in terms of commodities, the surplus of demand over supply). The economic factors that have an impact on the value of your spread bet are:

- Interest rates
- Inflation
- Economic growth

Economics, broadly, is the study of the allocation of scarce resources. *Economic drivers* are central to factors such as supply and demand, which affects all prices, making them go up and down (whether you're dealing in shares, commodities, foreign exchange or treasuries). When new economic information is announced, the market reacts either by increasing prices (through greater demand) or decreasing prices (through greater supply). This market correction returns the market to something close to equilibrium, where all known information is reflected in the price of relevant financial instruments. You see this type of market reaction markedly, for example, in the values of different currencies, which can move rapidly on the release of new economic data.

The interesting thing about looking to economics to determine potential drivers of prices isn't so much the figures released (which you may or may not find interesting), but rather the interconnection of money flowing from sector to sector and country to country. So much of what drives the economy boils down to the ease with which governments and companies obtain funds, and where this funding goes in the economy.

In this chapter, we look at some of the key economic releases that can impact both the short-term and longer-term prices of all financial instruments. We also look at some of the issues that traders need to consider at the time data is released, so that you can continue to manage your risk in times of uncertainty. And we give you an understanding of major economic information and also some of the key fundamental pricing considerations that you need to make to determine appropriate valuations of different financial instruments.

Understanding the Economic Impact of Interest Rates

Interest rates are an economic factor that's central to so many aspects of business, from the retail customer all the way through to corporate and government investors. Interest rates determine the cost of borrowing for investors as well as for corporations. The more expensive the cost of borrowing, the more expensive funding an expansion into new areas or funding an acquisition becomes.

Changes in interest rates are often a response to inflationary pressures on an economy. Before embarking on spread betting, you need to know what inflation is and how this measure of an economy itself is captured. *Inflation* quite simply looks at the increase in the cost of a basket of consumer goods. This measurement is the *Consumer Price Index*, or *CPI*, and it tells an important story about the cost-of-living changes that people are exposed to.

The rate of inflation – the rate at which things become progressively more expensive over time – is measured using the CPI. Movements of interest rates are frequently cited as a response to inflationary pressures. ***Note:*** A product that you buy in a shop is just like any asset – the more demand for it, the higher the price goes up. Supply constraints can also drive inflation. An example may be infrastructure constraints that have seen supplies slow down (or be bottlenecked) in some commodities, which drives up the price of what is available.

Different investments become more or less popular in times of high inflation. Possibly the most notable of these is gold, which is seen by investors as an *inflation hedge*, which means the investment often rises in value as inflation increases.

The value of currency diminishes in times of high inflation, and more stable investments like bonds and other fixed-interest products are affected in a negative way because the interest payments are now worth less due to the declining value of the currency.

You can find statistics, information about the state of play with inflation and current interest rates in the UK at the Bank of England's website (`www.bankofengland.co.uk`). If you're looking for foreign information, simply search for the relevant country's website – most of them are excellent at providing information to the public. For example, type into your favourite search engine 'US interest rates'.

Borrowing as a source of funds

Despite the recent economic meltdown doing extreme damage to the popularity of borrowing to fund company investment, it's sure to remain a major component of doing business for all companies.

Interest rates play a lead role in the monetary policy objectives that central banks implement. *Monetary policy* is the tool that central banks (like the Bank of England for the UK and the Federal Reserve in the United States) use to control the supply of money in the economy. The lower interest rates are, the easier it is to borrow, and the more entities are likely to borrow.

Borrowing isn't the only source of funds that a company can use to expand. *Listed companies* (those that are traded on a stock exchange) can issue new shares to the public. When investors buy these shares, the company can use the funds to finance new ventures.

Interest rates and inflation

Low interest rates may sound ideal, but if rates were always low then spending may start to run out of control and push prices up. Yes, the result is inflation. Higher prices reduce the value of the currency. If inflation gets too high, you end up with *hyper-inflation*, which is akin to requiring a wheelbarrow full of cash simply to buy a loaf of bread – clearly not something you want to have happen too often. Hyper-inflation can occur in all sorts of economies. Germany saw inflation of more than 20 per cent per day in the 1920s. The most recent example is Zimbabwe, where inflation got close to 100 per cent per day.

Those who manage listed companies weigh up the pros and cons of issuing shares or borrowing to fund their ventures. The downside of borrowing is that, no matter what, you need to pay the lender back – if you don't, you're in default and the whole company can then be in trouble. The upside is that you can pay back, and thereby retire, the debt. Shareholders are much more difficult to get rid of, and if they aren't happy with the way management runs a company, the shareholders can oust directors. However, unlike debt, you don't need to pay back shareholders, and in fact you can even stop paying them dividends, which adds to flexibility. Nothing is ever easy in finance.

Understanding the link between inflation and monetary policy

The concept of inflation can be kind of interesting to most people who are interested in finance. For the trader, though, inflation data is important because an analysis of it provides a view to the future.

Both the UK government and the Bank of England (the UK's central bank) play a role in controlling inflationary pressures:

- **The government:** Employs what is known as fiscal policy – for example, making changes to the level of taxation and government spending, which can make the purchasing or the deferring of purchases relatively attractive to one another. The government also sets the inflation target rate that the Bank of England has to meet. If it fails to do so, the Bank of England governor has to write a letter to the Chancellor of the Exchequer and explain why.
- **Bank of England:** Employs monetary policy. The Bank of England has a target rate of inflation (2 to 3 per cent over the economic cycle) and adjusts interest rates accordingly to keep the rate of inflation within this band as far as possible – with a view to making consumption and investment more or less attractive.

The main measure of inflation is called *core inflation*, which excludes volatile items such as petrol and fresh food. Goods and services that fall outside of those few excluded items are those that are monitored for upwards and downwards changes in price.

Keep in mind the following important relationships between inflation and monetary policy:

- Central banks around the world want to keep inflation under control because it weakens the value of money, which most impacts upon low- or no-growth investments, like savings accounts.
- Depending on inflation levels, central banks are likely to respond by raising or lowering their level of interest rates.
- High inflation equals higher interest rates, which is otherwise known as tightening monetary policy.
- Low inflation equals lower interest rates, which is otherwise known as loosening monetary policy.
- Of all the financial instruments that you can spread bet on, foreign exchange responds immediately to inflation data as it's released to the market. Ordinarily, if inflation is higher than expected, you see the currency value increase in anticipation of higher rates from the central bank. The reverse is also true.

- Traders need to consider comments that come from central banks, because this information gives hints about how aggressively the banks are likely to attack inflation and inflationary concerns.
- Like the foreign exchange market, the treasuries market adjusts to interest rate changes quickly. The bond market usually doesn't alter much if the inflation data comes out in line with expectations, because markets adjust their prices according to expectations over time. If interest rates move surprisingly high, though, the bond market expects the value of bonds to fall as a result; the converse also applies.
- Equity markets adjust to interest rates more slowly than either the foreign exchange market or the bonds market. Increasing rates (or the expectation of higher rates because of inflation data) impacts first on companies carrying large amounts of debt because they have to service a higher interest bill.
- Higher interest rates can often weigh on consumer discretionary stocks, because consumers have less money to spend on items that are not necessities (for example, a new. (You see a flow-on effect in the wider economy too, which becomes apparent in many areas of the share market.)

In the UK, if the Bank of England is going to move interest rates, it does so at its Monetary Policy Committee meetings, which happen once a month (though, of course, it doesn't always adjust interest rates). To keep on top of what the Bank of England is thinking, check out its website (`www.bankofengland.co.uk`), which is full of information that can help you to understand what's likely to drive the bank's thinking in the future.

Going bananas

When Cyclone Larry crossed the tropical north Queensland coast near Innisfail on the morning of Monday 20 March 2006, few anticipated the ensuing connection of banana price to inflation. In fact, a spike in the rate of inflation in Australia was, in large part, due to higher banana prices. The cyclone wiped out crops in Queensland, which sent the price of this Aussie fruit favourite higher (as always, you can see supply and demand at work). Though this crop is a fairly odd item to have such a profound effect on inflation, that's what happened. Hey, be glad you didn't have to report on banana-driven inflation – we did.

Turning an Eye to Economic Growth

Gross Domestic Product (or *GDP*) is a measure of the rate of growth of an economy. GDP looks at the amount of value added to the economy over a given period. GDP is calculated as the sum of private consumption, government spending, investment spending and net exports. Typically, household consumption is the biggest individual constituent of GDP. The figure itself is released by the Office for National Statistics every three months and is backwards looking (a big reason people look to forecasts).

Naturally, economists want the GDP figure to be positive – for example, a GDP above 2 per cent is considered good for a developed country, while some emerging markets are capable of posting 7 to 9 per cent growth per annum on a regular basis. However, in the same way that inflationary pressures can have a negative impact on an economy, too high a level of economic growth can also have negative impacts on the overall economy, because such growth can become very difficult to control. For example, asset prices can run at huge levels of growth, thereby driving up prices at an unsustainable rate. And a crash in share and property markets is a good example of what this out-of-control market looks like.

Instead of saying one level of economic growth is 'too high', economists look toward signals such as high inflation, which comes about due to excessive demand and which may also be fuelled by high levels of borrowing. Then the central bank controls the situation, mainly by increasing interest rates to make borrowing more expensive, and therefore less attractive.

To counteract too high a rate of economic growth, the Bank of England 'tightens' monetary supply for two reasons:

- To slow the demand for borrowing
- To make existing borrowings more expensive to service

When analysts sit down to value shares, they estimate the impact that strong economic growth is likely to have on the company. If expectations are quite high then analysts may increase their expectations of the price that the market is likely to push the share price to. Analysis doesn't stop here, though. Imagine that the GDP numbers for an economy are strengthening such that concern develops about inflation getting out of control. If such an outcome is the case, the overall market may start to increase demand for that currency in anticipation of higher interest rate payments. Even this development isn't the end. If a consensus opinion forms then you're likely to see people selling bonds (interest rate products such as gilts and bills, which are issued by the government – see Chapter 7), which in turn forces down prices and forces yields higher. The economy is highly interconnected: ordinarily, you don't see one economic factor occurring without another one being affected. It can provide the canny trader with more than just one trading idea.

Two aspects of interest rates are worth covering in a little more detail (especially if you're interested in trading different markets):

- **Higher interest rates having a positive impact on the value of a currency:** Though not the only factor, the *interest rate differential* (that is, the rate that one country pays relative to another) is one of the main influences on the value of a currency. If one country has a higher rate of interest then that country is going to attract investment, which has to be made in the country's currency. This offer of a higher interest rate creates demand from investors buying more bonds that must be paid for in that currency, which then pushes the value of that currency higher.
- **The value of the bonds:** If prices go up then yields go down. Plain and simple, but the impact isn't as bad as you may think. When a bond is issued, the issuer agrees to pay a rate of interest over the life of the bond (known as a *coupon*). When the bond is issued (usually at £100) the coupon makes up a percentage of the value of the bond. (***Note:*** A number of groups issue bonds, but spread bets are generally only available on bonds issued by governments – these being the most liquid opportunities. The most typical bonds you can spread bet on are US Treasuries, UK Gilts, German Bunds and Japanese Government Bonds.) If the coupon payments are £10 a year, then this means a 10 per cent yield. Imagine, though, that the market thought interest rates were going to fall. This scenario would see more people trying to buy existing bonds in order to lock in the higher interest rate. Because of supply and demand, this heightened interest by others may push the price up to £110. The coupon payment remains the same; however, an inverse relationship comes into play. The £10 coupon is now only a 9.1 per cent yield based on the £110 bond price. So what you see is that as bond prices rise, yields fall. If bond prices fall, then yields rise.

The Goldilocks economy

Economists use a term known as the *Goldilocks economy* when referring to the perfect economy – which, rather obviously, means an economy that is neither too hot nor too cold. You can see a perpetual balancing act going on the whole time. You want people to spend, but not so much that spending drives inflation or is fuelled by debt. You want people to save, but not so much that saving reduces spending. And so on, in a circular fashion.

Economic growth moves in cycles over time. Periods of high growth in asset prices are associated with macroeconomic factors like low interest rates and high commodity prices, contributing to higher inflation and borrowing, and in turn contributing towards the low ebb of the economy. These cycles are frequently illustrated using an *economic clock*, shown in Figure 10-1. ***Note:*** Although these illustrations of the flow of money provide a neat guide, the cycle doesn't move in such a predictable or ordered fashion as Figure 10-1 implies.

When you study economic figures, the period-to-period data can be very volatile, so we suggest you take a step back and look at the overall trend.

Top of the Boom

Rising real estate values

Easier money

Rising interest rates

Rising overseas reserves

Falling share prices

Rising commodity prices

Falling commodity prices

Rising share prices

Falling overseas reserves

Falling interest rates

Tighter money

Falling real estate values

Depth of Depression

Figure 10-1: An economic clock showing how money flows in and out of the economy over a cycle.

Looking at the Link between Employment and the Economy

A key aspect of the economic picture of a country is the level of employment or unemployment in the economy. The rate of employment in an economy influences a large number of factors, but without going into massive amounts of detail, perhaps just think about how feeling secure in your job makes you feel – hopefully (from an economic standpoint), it makes you feel the need for a new flat-screen television.

Why is making a purchase a good thing? Well, when you buy the TV, your purchase helps to keep workers at the store in their jobs, which gives them an opportunity to go and buy something else from another store, and so on and so on.

Spending in one spot can bounce around and strengthen the economy in lots of other areas. In addition to which, a very strong workforce means good levels of production, which then force up GDP (refer to the previous section) and also help government revenues (which are then either saved for a rainy day – known as a *fiscal surplus* – or, alternatively, ploughed back into the economy to help promote growth in targeted areas).

One of the ways in which economists measure the overall sentiment of consumers is with an index called (rather aptly) the *consumer confidence index* (compiled by research agency GfK NOP UK; see its website: www.gfknop.com). This survey-based methodology looks at how positive consumers feel about the UK economy over the next 12 months. You may see this sentiment reflected in areas such as retail sales, which provide another important piece of economic data. Retail sales are important for the reasons mentioned in the preceding paragraph, but also because the data helps to determine whether people are spending or saving.

Check out these websites for up-to-date employment figures:

- **Office for National Statistics (**www.ons.gov.uk**):** Government data on the domestic economy (including retail sales and unemployment).
- **US Bureau of Labor Statistics (**www.bls.gov**):** These figures are closely watched the world over because the US economy is the world's largest and can have some spectacular impacts on other financial markets.
- **Bloomberg (**www.bloomberg.com**):** Lightning-fast price movements are best illustrated with a look at the foreign exchange market, where this release of data can have some stunning and sudden effects – like a shift of more than one cent in seconds (doesn't sound like a lot, but its impact is huge). You can find economic data on the foreign exchange market on the Bloomberg website or your spread betting broker's website.

The copper connection

An example of how wide the implications of economic changes are can be felt locally: take, for example, the release of data relating to new home sales in the United States – what companies in the UK might this have an impact on? The most likely answer may be manufacturers of building products with exposure to the US market. However, if you look beyond the obvious, you can uncover other opportunities that exist outside of categories like home builders. For example, one of the biggest uses of copper is in the plumbing and wiring of new homes; so if fewer homes are being built in the United States, some of the UK mining companies are also affected. This amazing reflection of the economy leads some people to suggest that copper is the only commodity with an economics degree!

Carrying Out Fundamental Analysis

Economic information is one of the key factors that impacts on markets globally. In this section, we focus primarily on fundamental analysis of the share market and listed companies because, if you're like us, the share market is where you're going to spend much of your research time. Why? Because the implications of changes to the economic environment can reach into every product that you choose to trade or invest in, and you're likely to want to keep your understanding of the current environment up to date.

Don't worry too much about the merits of fundamental analysis versus technical analysis. Both can be very effective tools when used properly. You can very suitably employ some fundamental tools as a means of determining your shortlist of potential trades (as covered in Chapter 13) and then use charts for technical analysis to better time your entry and exits.

Exploring company earnings and forecasts

What makes share prices move? Good question. Key economic factors that can affect share price movement include:

- **Risk versus reward:** Investors look at all asset classes (such as property, shares, cash and bonds) and determine what to invest in based on the expected returns and their risk tolerance. Investors tend to seek the best investment on a *risk-adjusted basis* (they aim to invest in the best performing asset for the amount of risk they're willing to take).

- **Inflation:** As we explain in the section 'Understanding the link between inflation and monetary policy', earlier in the chapter, inflation diminishes the value of money. The higher that rate of inflation, the greater return the investor needs to generate in order to offset this figure. Returns generated minus inflation are known as *real returns*.
- **Factors of competition:** A company with the best management team, outlook and products is set to attract investor demand, which can drive share prices higher.

A company's future earnings (rather than current earnings) drive the price of shares. As a result, the market is very interested when companies update their earnings forecasts. Traders especially tune in to these forecasts of company earnings because they give them an idea of what the share price should be right now. Simply put: if expectations for growth of earnings are high, then people are willing to pay a higher price for shares.

Quarterly earnings forecasts are released and published by most companies as well as by analysts.

You can apply fundamental analysis to find out what you want to know about a listed company. In this instance, *fundamental analysis* boils down to the study of a company's future earnings and what they're worth in *today's money* (see the sidebar 'Today's money tomorrow', later in this chapter). This approach means focusing on cash flow and how much it's going to increase in the future.

The questions to ask start to get more interesting. For example, 'If I think this company is going to have growth of *x* per cent a year, then is this company the best option or is there a company with even better growth prospects in the same sector?'

The more cash the company generates, the better the overall outlook is for the company. You have to offset this benefit against the price that you're paying for the shares. If the company has good growth prospects but a very high share price then the question becomes, 'Is the growth expectation already priced into the shares; if so, are they then over-valued?'

Great questions, hey?

Analysts are people too. They can't be right all the time about the value of a company, and a lot of their expectations have to be based on forecasts. For this reason, analysts upgrade or downgrade their valuations of companies as the companies release their results, because then analysts have new, 'concrete' information to plug into their calculations.

Watch out for when a company revises its forecasts lower, because the share price reacts quickly and negatively. If a company forecasts an earning, and then tells the market it was wrong, and may make less, it will hit the share price immediately. When this earnings revision happens, you see the market revise the price that it believes the company is worth – in this case, lower. In the event of a downgrade, you're best to close out the position immediately if the price moves below your stop and then reassess the position. You're always best being on the sidelines in times of turmoil. You're not able to sell your position prior to the news, so this is just one of those dangers you have to face.

To understand how forecasts can affect a company, take a look at Figure 10-2. When analysts release new data, the impact on the company earnings is immediately reflected in the share price. For example, as soon as the market finds out the company is forecasted to earn less, the share price falls to reflect this anticipated change in future value. Sometimes, though, the market can overreact and push the price too low, after which the price may recover a little – when the market settles down again.

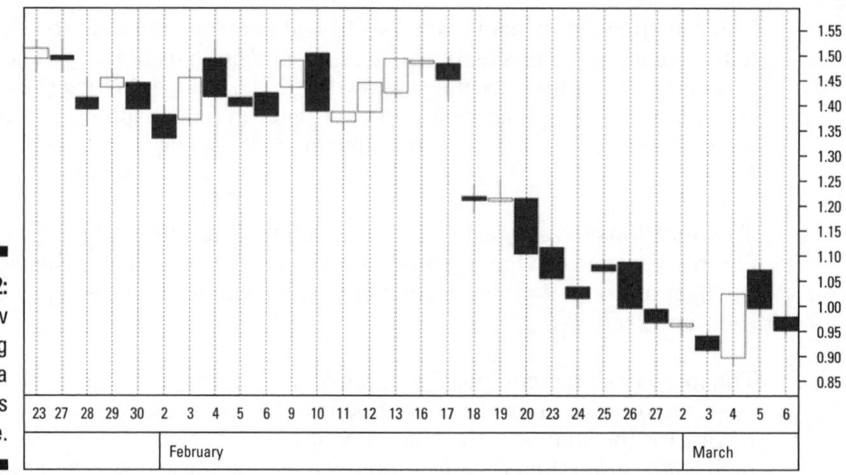

Figure 10-2: How forecasting affects a company's value.

Why is the share price falling so much and so quickly? Here are two reasons (one of which is inflexible in nature and the other flexible):

- Primarily, the market makes its assessment of a company's worth based on earnings expectations. For example, say a company is expected to earn $x for the full year. If the company then comes out and says it's going to earn only $x - 10 per cent (that is, just 90 per cent of what the market was expecting it to earn) then this figure is going to be reflected immediately in what the market now believes the shares are going to be worth. (This effect proves to be largely inflexible, because why would the market pay the same amount for a company that's going to earn less money?) The opposite of this scenario (if a company revises its earnings forecast upwards) also applies, but regardless, it always seems that companies get punished a lot more than they get rewarded.

- The general mood of the market at the time affects the company's share price. This impact is difficult to quantify, but it has a large effect. If you're in the early-to-middle stages of an aggressive bear (generally falling) market then the market is likely to treat profit downgrades very badly. However, the sell-off may not be nearly as aggressive if the same information is released in the midst of a bull (generally rising) market. You can see in Figure 10-2 how aggressive a sell-off can be when the market is very bearish. (This factor tends to be more flexible, primarily because the market doesn't always react as outlined above.)

Using some simple ratios

Even if you're itching to tackle number crunching, first you need to develop your understanding of some of the rules that go along with the use of financial ratios when dealing in shares (and spread betting on shares as a derivative of the share price – refer to Chapter 1 for more information on how derivatives work). A *financial ratio* is a mathematical means of assessing specific attributes of a company. Typically, a market analyst uses two or more components of the financial statements in a formula and compares the result to either other companies' values or to common yardstick values.

Ordinarily, a ratio on its own tells you very little. In some cases, you can apply yardsticks (such as the price–earnings ratio – see the section 'Price–earnings ratio', later in the chapter), but, mostly, ratios rely on comparisons to determine a trend by:

- Comparing the ratio of one company to another
- Comparing the ratio of one company to previous measures

Today's money tomorrow

When you say *today's money*, you're 'discounting' future earnings into what they're worth today. Consider *compound interest* (interest earned on interest over time), which accelerates the rate of growth achieved. Discounting future earnings is the opposite of this compounding interest: you work out what the end figure at some point in the future is worth today. Another key point to consider is that a pound today is worth more than that same pound tomorrow, because today you have the choice to spend or invest – but if you have to wait until tomorrow, you forfeit that choice, so you shouldn't expect the pound to be worth as much.

Market capitalisation

Market capitalisation (usually abbreviated as MarCap in financial tables) is an important financial tool by which you can accurately compare the size of one company to another. (Many traders want to deal only in the largest companies available on the market – market capitalisation is the easiest way to put these companies in order.) Though not strictly speaking a ratio, you're best getting a handle on this concept if you want to make a go of your analysis of the market.

Using market capitalisation, you can make apples-with-apples-type comparisons of, say, the size of two companies. If, for example, one company has a share price of $10 and another a share price of $1, the first company can appear to be the biggest. This assumption may well be right, but the share price doesn't tell you anything about the size of the company. This is where market capitalisation comes in – to give you the result of the share price multiplied by the number of shares on issue. To continue with the previous example: If the first company had 1 million shares on issue and the second company had 10 million shares on issue, then both companies would have a market capitalisation of $10 million. This calculation provides a much better comparative tool than just looking at the share price of both companies, which tells you only a very small part of the story.

Earnings per share

The importance of comparing like with like becomes clear when comparing the *earnings per share* (EPS) of one company to another. Calculating the EPS gives you the earning for each ordinary share, ordinarily over a 12-month period (a 6-month period is also possible, depending on the reporting period you're looking at). This ratio is a good way to accurately compare the earnings of two companies, because it removes the differences in the size of the companies by getting rid of the difference in the number of shares on issue.

Here's the EPS formula:

Earnings per share (EPS) = Net profit for ordinary shareholders/Number of ordinary shares on issue

In this case, you take the profit of the company and divide it by the number of shares. The answer is a much more relevant figure than simply assuming $10 million is a good profit – it might be, but how does it compare on a 'per share' basis?

A good exercise when working out a company's EPS ratio is to go back and look at the previous EPS figures of the company. From this information, you may also be able to get an insight into whether the company is seeing growth in its earnings and whether it has had positive earnings historically. You can find this information on:

- Your spread betting broker's website
- The website of the company in question
- A free website such as Bloomberg (`www.bloomberg.com`) or Yahoo! Finance (`http://uk.finance.yahoo.com`)

Price–earnings ratio

When you know the EPS (refer to the previous section) of the company in question, you can then go a step further and work on what's possibly the most popular of all the ratios: the price–earnings (PE) ratio. This ratio is one of the best known ratios because it allows you to quickly get an idea of the value of the company relative to its earnings. You can then easily compare this figure to the figures of other companies that you're interested in.

You calculate PE as follows:

PE = Current market price/EPS

The share price of a company isn't a good reflection of its earnings (but it is an excellent reflection of what the market thinks expected earnings are likely to be), in the same way that the share price isn't good for comparing a company's size (refer to the section 'Market capitalisation', earlier in this chapter). Say that you do this PE calculation and the result you come up with is ten. What is this number telling you? The answer is, at current market prices, you're paying a price that reflects ten years' worth of company earnings. Some analysts interpret this figure to mean that the company is likely to take ten years to repay the investment that you've made. You can very easily use this figure to compare one company to another. (***Remember:*** Ideally, companies within the same sector are the most comparable.)

Tempting though it may be, saying that the company with the lowest PE is the best value is a little too simplistic, because typically companies that the market is expecting strong growth from are going to be trading at a higher PE.

PE ratios can be based on both historical and future earnings expectations; the latter is the most common. So, always keep in mind that when you're considering what the company is likely to earn, you're contemplating the future, not the past.

If you buy into companies at high PE levels, you want to be very confident that the growth is going to be there to support this very high level, because if the market loses confidence and starts selling the shares of the high PE companies and buying lower (potentially better value) PE companies, the share price is going to fall.

Sitting pretty

During very strong bull markets, analysts focus on those companies with what people refer to as 'lazy balance sheets'; that is, those companies carrying little debt and, perhaps, not a great amount of growth prospects either. These companies often come under great pressure from the market to lever the balance sheet (borrow) and try to make the company grow faster. This pressure is often down to buying out another company or expanding existing divisions of the company. The market and analysts may use the argument that if the company has no need for the cash it holds then it should return the cash to shareholders. This is because investors would rather invest their own cash than have a listed company do it for them.

It was interesting to see the 'love' these companies got during the global financial crisis as the market turned on any company carrying significant levels of debt and rushed towards those that had very sustainable models and faced less impact during the crisis. However, when the market is bullish, it loves debt and can tolerate heaps of it. You have to pay the price, though, if the economy slows down, which is why you need to look more deeply into the story – and your financial ratios can give you quite a bit of help with this scenario too.

Debt ratios

Dozens of ratios are available to you, but the amount of debt that the company is carrying has to be an important factor in your decision making. When you look into the way a company finances itself, you're best considering how much debt it carries because . . . drum roll . . . the company always has to pay back the debt.

Here are two important debt ratios:

- *Debt to equity ratio* (which shows how much a company is financed by debt):

  Total debt/Shareholders' equity

- *Debt to assets ratio* (which shows how much debt the company has taken on in comparison to the assets it has – just like with your personal debts, which you don't want to outweigh your assets):

  Total debt/Total assets

Both of these ratios provide an insight into what a company is built on and how high its level of debt is. You may think that you want the company to have no debt, but this approach is a little too simplistic. Debt, when used sensibly, can greatly enhance the growth prospects of the company. However, too much can be a destabilising influence and can become dangerously difficult to service, especially during a market downturn (see the sidebar 'Sitting pretty').

Net tangible assets

Calculate a company's *net tangible assets* (NTA) to look at what the company is actually worth if it were to sell all of its assets and pay off its debts. You calculate NTA as follows:

NTA = (Ordinary shareholders' equity – Intangibles)/Number of ordinary shares

The outcome of this equation gives you the worth of the company on a per share basis after repayment of debts.

Chapter 11

Understanding Trading Methods

In This Chapter

- Fine-tuning your trading techniques
- Working with the trading time frame that's right for you
- Searching out short-term trading methods
- Looking at longer-term trading methods
- Identifying different trends

One of the biggest attractions of trading on the stock market is having a large degree of freedom to find your own way and to make your own decisions. This freedom means that the difficulties for anyone trying to catalogue the vast array of methodologies for spread betting – over different time frames – are the same for a seasoned trader as well as a novice. However, no matter what sort of time frame you're using and how you choose to approach the market, you're best incorporating good risk management strategies into the equation.

In this chapter, we take you through several of the more popular trading methods you may come across, and we look at how you can apply these methods while employing risk management strategies to limit the downside of your positions when you lose.

Trading Methods and You

When you look back in years to come at the ways in which you approached your trading and, with hindsight, realise how your methods altered along the way, you're going to have a better understanding of two things:

- The kind of methods that most specifically appeal to you
- How these methods developed into a model that you refined specifically for your own preferences

Realistically, don't be disappointed with the outcomes of your first trading strategies. Knowing how trading methods are going to perform in real time is very difficult, no matter how carefully you test your strategies. Until you mix in a good dose of psychology (read 'greed' and 'fear'), you're not going to know where a particular methodology is really going to take you.

Trading Over Different Time Frames

Before making any assessment of the benefits or otherwise of short-term (ten minutes to a few weeks) and longer-term (three months to a year) spread betting trading methods, it is essential to understand one of the key implications of the marked-to-market settlement system (see Chapter 1 for more on this).

Marked-to-market means that at the end of every trading session (meaning when the market closes for the day), all profits and losses are settled and every trader starts the next day with a clean slate. For the most part, this process doesn't make any difference to traders. However, one key implication is relevant – a trader doesn't have to sell a position (the spread bets that he currently holds) in order to benefit from a rise in its value. For example, if the value of that position rises £100 in a day, the trader is immediately able to put this money towards new positions or indeed withdraw it as cash from his account. The opposite also occurs if the value of the position falls: the £100 is immediately debited from the trader's account.

A key point to remember about spread bets is that, unlike most investments, you don't have to sell a position to receive the advantage of a beneficial price movement.

Choosing between short- and longer-term trading methodologies needn't be simply about which one allows you to get cash in hand more quickly (because the marked-to-market system takes care of that) but should be about the one that's most suitable for you.

In any case, you have to work out the balancing act of benefits versus disadvantages that exist for short- and longer-term trading. The pros and cons of each include the following:

- **Short-term trading benefit:** You're able to lock in profits more quickly.
- **Short-term trading disadvantages:** You have to deal with narrower risk and reward margins, and your cost of dealing (as a result of spread costs) is higher.
- **Longer-term trading benefit:** Your profit potential on a per trade basis can be substantially higher.

- **Longer-term trading disadvantages:** Your financing costs and potential for adverse price moves due to factors such as gapping can be much greater. (Where there are 'gaps' in the price – the point where no trades occur – this can lead to slippage on your stop losses too. A *stop loss* is the point at which you exit the position if you make the wrong decision. See Chapter 8 on managing risk.)

No matter whether your approach to trading is short-term or longer-term, for each benefit you gain, you're likely to have to give one up.

Understanding Short-Term Trading

A variety of trading methodologies is available to help you decide how best to take advantage of short-term trading. For most of these options, you need to look at a number of different time frames before making your decision to enter a position.

Moving average crossover

A method of analysis known as a *moving average crossover* can determine the relative position of price across a range of different time frames. A moving average crossover occurs when a shorter-term moving average crosses over a longer-term moving average (see the section 'Moving averages', later in this chapter) on each of the different charts, which not only determines direction of price movement but also helps you to time your entry into the position (see Figure 11-1).

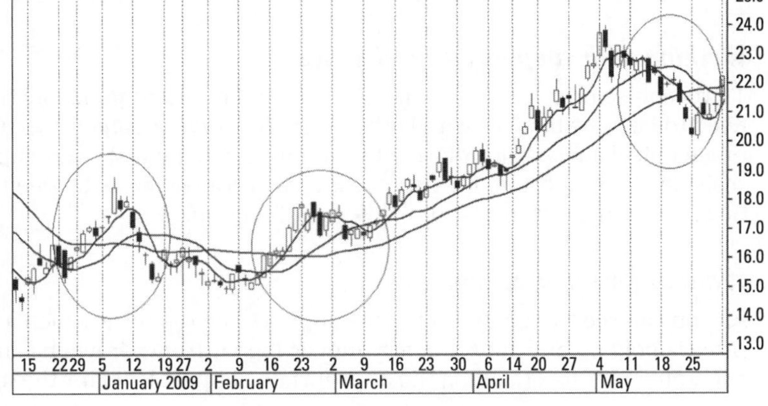

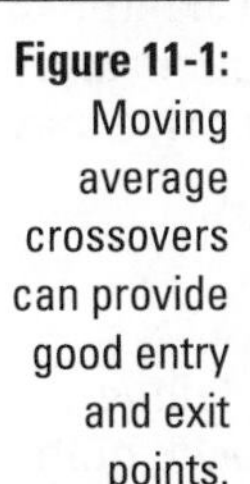

Figure 11-1: Moving average crossovers can provide good entry and exit points.

If you're trading based on a 10-minute chart (see Chapter 13 on technical analysis if you need more info) then you're likely to analyse or scan the 30-minute and the hourly charts as well, before making your decision.

For instance, if you're looking for a trending move in the value of a currency and you want to trade using the 10-minute chart, you may first look for the 10-minute, the 30-minute and the hourly charts to all point in the same direction – that is, show the same trend line. When you start to look at different time frames in this way, you can see that the same instrument can look like it's pointing in all sorts of different directions. If this is the case, you may want to look for instruments that are moving the same way in each of the different time frames.

Using swing techniques and price patterns

A popular trading method for short-term trading is *swing techniques*. This category of trading is quite broad – so much so that you can use a range of methods including the employment of algorithms and indicators to look for points at which an instrument may be entering a new upswing or a new downswing. Another way in which traders can look to find swings in the market is through the use of price patterns. *Price patterns* allow you to trade using specific rules about when to enter and exit the instrument at both a profit and a loss.

We're quite big fans of price patterns as pointers because they don't require the use of any specific indicators or other technical analysis tools beyond being able to recognise important price occurrences (or patterns). We look at how to apply these pointers in a short-term trading situation in the following section on support and resistance. (Because this trading method covers a wide-reaching area of trading, we suggest you check out Chapter 13 for more information on technical analysis.)

Working with support and resistance

To recognise price patterns, one of the most important concepts that you need to become familiar with is that of *support and resistance* (see Chapter 13 on technical analysis for more information on what constitutes support and resistance). Support and resistance give you some idea as to when price may be starting to move in a wholly different direction.

Waiting for the breakout

As you can see from Figure 11-2, the support line (a line at which a falling price is held up and subsequently moves higher from) drawn has been quite accurate in terms of finding the appropriate support level for the movements in price. You can see, though, that some minor breaches of support failed to turn into major price moves. This scenario means that you have a choice as a trader. You can either:

- Take the trade immediately after support is broken and place your stop nice and close below the previous support line or above the previous resistance line.
- Wait for extra confirmation. Waiting for extra confirmation may mean you either:
- Wait for a move of a certain size past the breakout point (when the price moves beyond the resistance /support level).
- Wait for the price to retrace towards the breakout line (established resistance/support level) before entering.

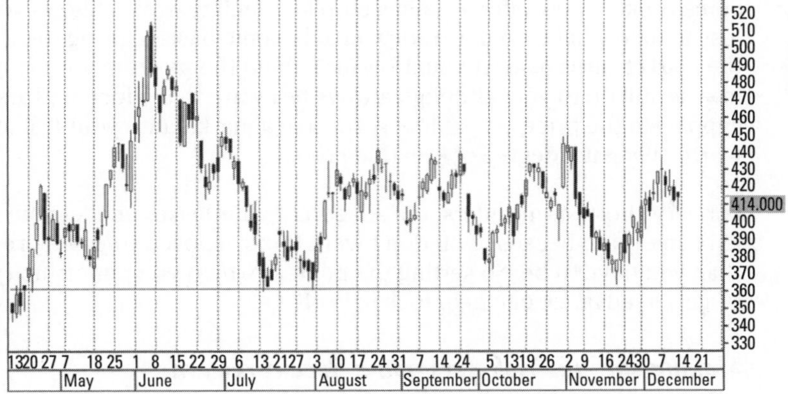

Figure 11-2: Notice the price finding support repeatedly at the same level.

If you don't wait for confirmation that the breakout is going to hold then you're less likely to have a successful trade. However, on trades that are successful, you're able to generate a greater amount of profit if you act quickly. As you can see, sometimes this strategy is effective and other times this strategy fails. Unfortunately, you can't tell which is which until after you complete the trade.

We've seen some arguments in the past about the validity of support and resistance when it's so easily recognised by all market participants – when this happens en masse, people may place a large order just on the other side of a support/resistance line in order to take advantage of larger volume when the level is broken. We agree that sometimes this does occur with the result that you get a failed breakout – at other times, however, the breakout through the price level works perfectly. Sadly, you can't know which scenario will happen until after it occurs. But all isn't lost because you can apply risk management techniques (see Chapter 8). On average, your aim is to lose significantly less on losing trades than you gain on winning trades. Over time this result can still leave you well ahead overall.

As a general rule, waiting for extra confirmation that the breakout is going to hold makes life less frustrating, so wait for this additional clue.

Getting out with a profit target

When you approach the problem of how to deal with your short-term set-ups, you may want to give thought to setting yourself some sensible profit targets and using them as part of a disciplined approach. Alternatively, if you're able to watch the market closely then you may be able to employ a method that locks in profit as soon as the market starts to move against you after a positive run. The second of these options is clearly superior but it requires that you watch the market at all times, which isn't feasible for most people.

Some brokers now offer a trailing stop loss facility, which allows your stop loss to follow behind your trades on a dynamic basis, closing the trade once the market turns against you. How far behind the position your stop loss follows is still up to you, although always be aware that widening spreads and gapping in the price can suddenly reverse a market into your trailing stop. It's worth giving it a degree of breathing room.

For very short-term traders, the adage 'cut your losses and let your profits run' isn't an option because you don't want to be exposed to any more volatility than you have to be. So setting the point at which you jump ship (your profit target) in advance can help lock in profits.

Making sure the risk gets you a decent reward

You need to consider what you're risking compared to the reward that you're getting. If you're getting on average a much bigger reward than you're risking, you can afford to be wrong more often than someone whose profits are about the same size as his losses. This assessment may sound obvious, but you don't want to fall into the trap of letting profits burn a hole in your pocket the moment they appear while letting your losses receive the benefit of the doubt all the time.

Generally, you need to look for a risk-to-reward ratio of around 1 to 3 as a minimum (and you want to capture even bigger moves when you can), because otherwise the onus of being right becomes too much of a hardship.

Figure 11-3 shows the price oscillating between the lower support level and the upper resistance level.

Figure 11-3: Support and resistance can interact repeatedly with one another.

We cover two ways to approach this situation from the short-term trader's perspective. First, assume that the support/resistance line is going to hold and that the price is going to reverse away from it. You can approach this setup in two basic ways:

- The most aggressive approach is to wait until the price moves very close to the support/resistance line and then take on the trade while anticipating a reversal. This way means that you go short if the trade is approaching resistance or long if it's approaching a support line.

  The principal drawback here is that if the price move continues and breaches the support/resistance line, then you need to exit in a hurry – that is, move to the sidelines and preserve your capital.

- The less aggressive (and also likely more prudent) approach to enter this type of position is to wait for some additional confirmation that the price is respecting the support/resistance line. If, for instance, you're using a daily candle chart (a chart that shows a new candle with the high and low price for each day), you may wait for the price to close above the high of the candle that touches the support/resistance line (as Figure 11-4 shows).

One of the main benefits of either of these approaches is that you can place your stop loss nice and close to the price, which helps keep your potential risk-to-reward ratio high.

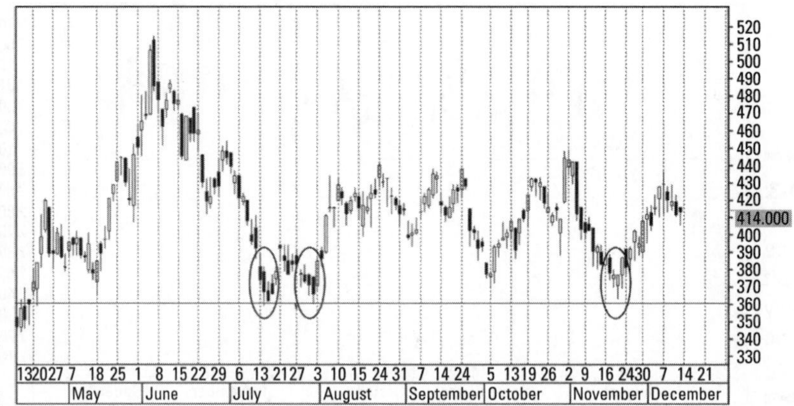

Figure 11-4: The circled areas shown can be good entry points based on support levels.

Although you may wish to put your stop loss order very close to where you enter the position, don't put it so close that short-term volatility can knock you out of the position. If you don't have a risk-to-reward ratio that you're happy with when you place the stop at the price you think is the most sensible, then you simply decide not to take the trade. You're best not to risk capital on a bad trade when much better ones are potentially just around the corner.

The second short-term method comes from reading about a trader named John Carter. His methodology is fascinating because it looks for turning points in trends in a way that allows you to place your stop loss nice and close to the price of the market. Carter refers to HOLP (High Of the Low Period) and LOHP (Low Of the High Period). Figure 11-5 shows basic examples of these patterns.

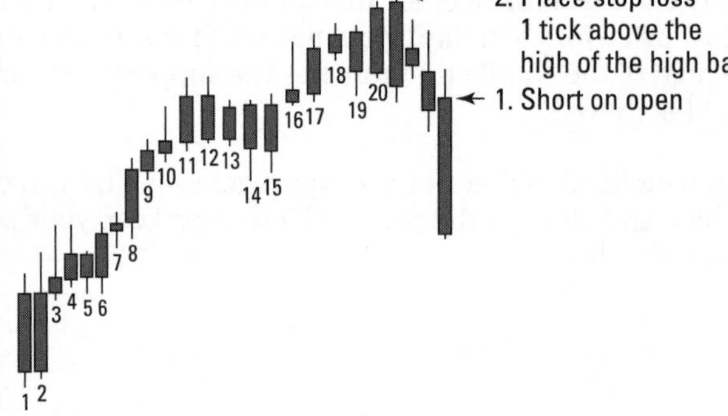

Figure 11-5: The method shown here can help you identify and trade turning trends.

Essentially, what you're looking for is a position that shows a consistent trend and, after you've found this, a price point at which you have evidence of the trend beginning to break down. When hunting for a consistent trend, Carter recommends waiting for at least a 20-period high or low as part of a definitive trending movement (see Chapter 13 for more on trends). In an uptrend, the reversal pattern looks for a price level on an individual bar or candle that closes below the lowest point at the bottom of the highest candle in the trend. These rules are reversed for a price that's in a downtrend.

The real benefit here is that you place your stop just above the high of the highest candle (see Chapter 13 for more on technical analysis) so you're accomplishing two things:

- Entering the trade based on the earliest evidence of a trend breaking down
- Placing the stop such that you get out as soon as you know you're wrong about the trade

A lot of the time you may read about placing your stop one tick (the smallest price movement that can occur in the particular market you're trading) above the previous high or something similar – this information is telling you to get out as soon as the price action moves against you in a confirmed fashion. Watch out for a trap here. If you're trading an instrument such as foreign exchange with a spread of, say, three ticks then you need to take the spread into account as well as the previous high/low (or other price indicator you are using). So if you want to get out at one tick higher than the previous high then you need to take the spread (the difference between the buy price and the sell price) into account. Essentially, you should place your stop loss at one tick plus the spread above the high. Otherwise, you get out of the position before you even meant to.

The other brilliant factor in Carter's methodology is that the stop is easy to trail up (or down if you're short) in line with the price movements. The basic idea is that as soon as the price moves in your favour for two time periods (say hours), you begin to trail the stop loss in your favour. The advantage of doing this is that you can gradually lock in your profits in line with the movements of the price. The method calls for you to close out the position only when the price closes below the candle that is two candles back from the current close. If you can't be in front of the trading screen then you may have to place the stop at this level and be closed out automatically. Sometimes this different stop methodology can work for you and sometimes against you (see Figure 11-6).

If you can be in front of the screen (how often you need to be depends on whether you use a five-minute, hourly or daily chart and so on) you can also keep in mind that you don't move the stop if it moves to a level where you would immediately close out the position. This situation can occur if, during the time period that you're watching, the price moves lower (if you're long) but doesn't close below the stop level; which means you're still in the trade but you don't move the stop loss until the trend resumes. If this occurs, you're likely going to guess that something is amiss.

Using this rule, you only close positions at the end of a time period and not the beginning.

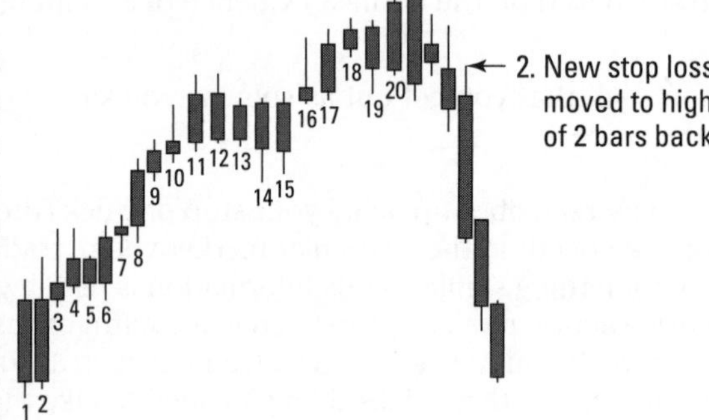

Figure 11-6: Trailing the stop can help you capture profits and not give too much back.

Carter's style of methodology can work across a range of different time frames so it doesn't necessarily fit into the short-term methodology only.

The shorter the time frame you deal over, the smaller the profits are likely to be, as are the risks. However, the costs of doing business (through the cost of the spread, which occurs when you have to pay more through your provider than in the underlying market) can take up a greater portion of your profits. So you need to remember that the benefit of locking in profits quickly balances with the disadvantage of profits being smaller in size, as well as the trade more frequently incurring costs.

Looking at Longer-Term Trading

Spread betting is more about the longer-term than the long-term. 'A case of semantics?' you ask. The common definition of *long term* (around five years or more) doesn't adequately apply in the spread betting world. Generally, in the world of trading, three months is around the longest traders are going to hold on to positions – that is, longer than short term (refer to the section 'Understanding Short-Term Trading', earlier in this chapter). (However, just to keep you on your trading twinkle toes, and because nothing is a given when making trades, a trader may choose to hold for longer than this time frame as well.)

When spread betting, one of the main reasons traders are unwilling to carry positions for an extended period (past the longer term of three months, for example) is that they have to pay financing charges (refer to Chapters 3and 4 for more information). So long as a position moves consistently in your favour, the gains comprehensively outweigh the cost of the financing charges. For this reason, closing out a good position just because you've been holding it for a while can be unwise. Instead, be a prudent trader and let the market price be your gauge as to when you exit the position.

When you begin to look at choosing between using short-term trading methods and longer-term methods, you need to consider:

- Defining which way the instrument is moving in general terms – is it trending higher or lower?
- Whether or not now is a good time to enter a position.
- What methods you're going to use to refine and define the decision to enter a position.

You need to look across different time frames (in the same way as when engaging in short-term trading) to make decisions for the longer term, but in this case the weekly, daily and, possibly, the hourly charts are those you need to be most concerned with.

No single indicator or methodology is going to be universally successful when spread betting, but when applied sensibly and consistently, they can help you develop a more measured approach to your trading.

Making Friends with Trends

Pretty much every longer-term trading methodology revolves in one way or another around finding and capitalising on trending movements. The key for a lot of traders is to be able to spot a movement in a trend early and then to run with it for as long as they possibly can. However, the question remains: how does a trader identify a trend movement in the first place? This section looks at some of the indicators that can help you identify trend movements and use them to your trading advantage.

Moving averages

The *moving average* (the average value of a security over a defined period of time) is one of the favoured weapons of traders in the trend-following arsenal. It emphasises the prevailing direction of a trend by smoothing out fluctuations of price and volume that might otherwise easily confuse a trader's interpretation of events. You can find out more about the moving average in Chapter 13, but for now we look at some of the ways you can employ this indicator to help you better find and then follow the trend.

Although you can calculate a moving average easily, it suffers from the same flaw as all indicators – that is, it lags the price movements, meaning the longer the term of the moving average, the more it lags. So accurately pinpointing a trend movement becomes more difficult and you can potentially miss out on large profits.

As an exercise, we suggest you start with the weekly chart and refine your direction from there. (At the opposite end of this analysis spectrum is the 200-week moving average. Although the application of this broader moving average may give you an excellent idea of the broader trend of any instrument, it lags so far behind the instrument that it offers little in the way of actual timing benefits.) From there, you can start to apply some different moving averages to begin the trade timing process – that is, how to time a trade.

Begin the process with a shorter time frame for your moving average and then add more – not just one extra time frame but perhaps as many as three, for comparison purposes, because as you take on longer time frame moving averages you get an idea of the broader trend. The shorter-term ones (which track the price more closely) can give you a good idea of when the price trend may be changing direction.

One of the favoured methodologies for using moving averages is the *crossover method.* This system signals an entry point or an alert of a shift in direction when a shorter-length moving average crosses from below to above a longer-term moving average (for longer-term trading) or from above to below (for short-term trading).

You're likely to see a wide range of differing opinions related to selecting the most appropriate length of your moving averages to use. Some traders suggest days in the week, days in the month or trading days in the month, for example. The difference of one increment in the length of time over which you calculate a moving average is unlikely to make a vast amount of difference. As soon as you're content with the concepts, you can start refining the numbers. ***Note:*** While a moving average filters out the 'noise' of the market, the more noise filtered (by making the moving average longer), the more the price lags.

To start with, we recommend you use a simple 5-, 15- and 30-period moving average on the weekly chart. The most useful for the timing is likely to be the 5 crossing over the 15. Having a longer-term moving average on the chart provides an excellent reference point and can often demonstrate the speed and the angle of the trend that you're following after it starts to form.

As soon as you get these moving averages set on the chart, you can begin to use them as a scan for potential trending positions. For example, you may want to look at the close of each trading week for the charts that show a 5-week and a 15-week moving average crossover and then use this analysis as the basis of your shortlist of potential trades for the following week of trading.

The challenge now is how to refine this scanning process further to the point where you can actually execute a trade.

1. **Look for the daily chart to show the spread bet price to be rising away from a trend line (see the next section) or moving average (or at least not falling), which shows that momentum is on the rise. A market deviating from trend represents a profit opportunity.**

   Note that sometimes a chart can easily rise on the weekly and fall on the daily.

2. **Wait for the price to be rising on the weekly chart.**

   For this weekly scan, you may want to reference the daily chart against a moving average, such as the 30-period, to see whether the spread bet price is above or below it.

3. **Wait for the price to be rising on the daily chart.**

   If the price is above the 30-period moving average on the daily chart then it's quite bullish (positive for the price), and if it's below then it's quite bearish (negative for the price).

4. **Execute a trade.**

   As soon as you confirm that the price is moving higher on the weekly chart and that on the daily chart you have probabilities much more in your favour, this moment may be the start of a trade or at least a means of adding to your shortlist. In any case, don't forget your stop loss.

When you're scanning the market using moving averages you sometimes find a crossover occurring on a share price that largely seems to be moving sideways. You can ignore these crossovers because they don't show a shift in trending behaviour. Instead, they reveal an oscillation that's simply part of a sideways movement. You're best served to wait until the price starts trading at a higher or lower level than the current range before examining them again.

Using trend lines

You draw *trend lines* under troughs in the price (uptrend) or above the peaks (downtrend) to determine the prevailing direction of the instrument you're watching.

You may find that a lot of the time when you see an obvious trending movement, you can actually draw a trend line under the price you see on the chart (see Chapter 13 for more detail). When you go to make a trade, in many cases, you're going to want to buy as close to the trend line as possible. Though some may argue, for example, that buying at this trend line level is 'cheap', that's not the best reason for doing so. Rather, getting a trade in close to the trend line is an effective approach because it allows you to place your stop loss close to your entry, which means that it can become a very good risk–reward trade for you to take on (that is, for each pound you risk, you may be able to generate three or more pounds in profit).

You can opt to use trend lines in two main ways:

- **Wait until the price moves back and touches the trend line (or nearly touches) and then make your entry.**

  This option is aggressive because you're not getting any confirmation that the price is respecting the trend line (that is, the price has only moved back to the trend line and touched it), which is the whole reason that you're making the trade in the first place. However, this is the time that you're closest to your stop loss point so you have a good chance of making a decent risk–reward trade out of it.

- **Wait for the instrument price to bounce away from the trend line and then make your entry.**

  You may want to wait for a certain percentage movement or a specific period of time holding above the line as your threshold decision point. This approach may give you a lesser risk–reward trade, but at least you get extra confirmation that the trend is still in force, which should increase the probability of a successful trade.

When using trend lines as a tool to help you decide when to make a trade, you need to consider the trade-offs. Either you can have an early entry, which is a lower probability trade, or a later entry with a potentially reduced risk–reward opportunity.

Scaling and pyramiding

A prudent trader neither enters his full position all at once nor gets out of a profitable trade all at once. This approach is known as *scaling in* and *scaling out* of a position.

Pyramiding is similar in many ways to scaling, but may be something that you do over a longer time frame. Pyramiding is a process whereby you add to your position (invest more in the trade) as the price runs in your favour.

You may sometimes hear traders say that they make 90 per cent of their money from 10 per cent of their trades. For this scenario to be the case, pyramiding needs to be part of their trading approach. When you have a trade that runs for an extended period of time in your favour, you're really taking the fullest advantage of the situation. So rather than just taking a single, you're looking for extra runs.

Here's how to use scaling in and scaling out of positions:

- **Scaling in to a position:** If you're scaling in, you can respond to trend line touches by both trading immediately and waiting for confirmation. For instance, you may choose to put in one-half of your position at the touch of the trend line and then the other half as soon as the position rises for two days subsequent to the trend line touch.
- **Scaling out of a position:** Consider aiming for three times your risk as a trading strategy (3R). What you may wish to do is take one-third of your profits at 3R, take maybe another third at 4R and then leave the remaining third and see what happens – perhaps closing it out if profits slip back to 2R or 3R. ***Note:*** Although losing money is irritating (but part and parcel of the business), closing out a position only to see it continue on its merry way can be really infuriating. By following an idea like this, you can take some profits but leave some money on the table with a view to seeing how far it goes.

Here's how to use pyramiding to your advantage:

- **Adding to a trade:** Pyramiding (see Figure 11-7) is similar to scaling but revolves less around spreading the entry point and more towards really hammering those winning positions home. You have a large number of alternatives for timing your entry to each phase of a pyramid. In essence, you're likely to be looking for setups that stand on their own as separate trades when you pyramid. This may mean that you add to a trade each time that a trending position retraces to the trend line.

- **Adopting a sensible strategy:** You need to follow some rules in order to keep your pyramid strategy sensible.

  The first thing to consider is where the pyramid strategy gets its name from – not surprisingly, the shape of a pyramid. But how does this shape apply to positions? Well, each position should be smaller than the one before it. This means that you put the biggest position on first and then, subsequently, you put on smaller (or at least no bigger) trades thereafter (see Figure 11-8). You may ask why each trade has to be smaller when surely the right thing to do is to buy more as the trend continues. The problem with going about using a pyramid strategy in this way is that when the position eventually turns against you and the final additional trade is the biggest position, it can eat up all the profits from your previous trades.

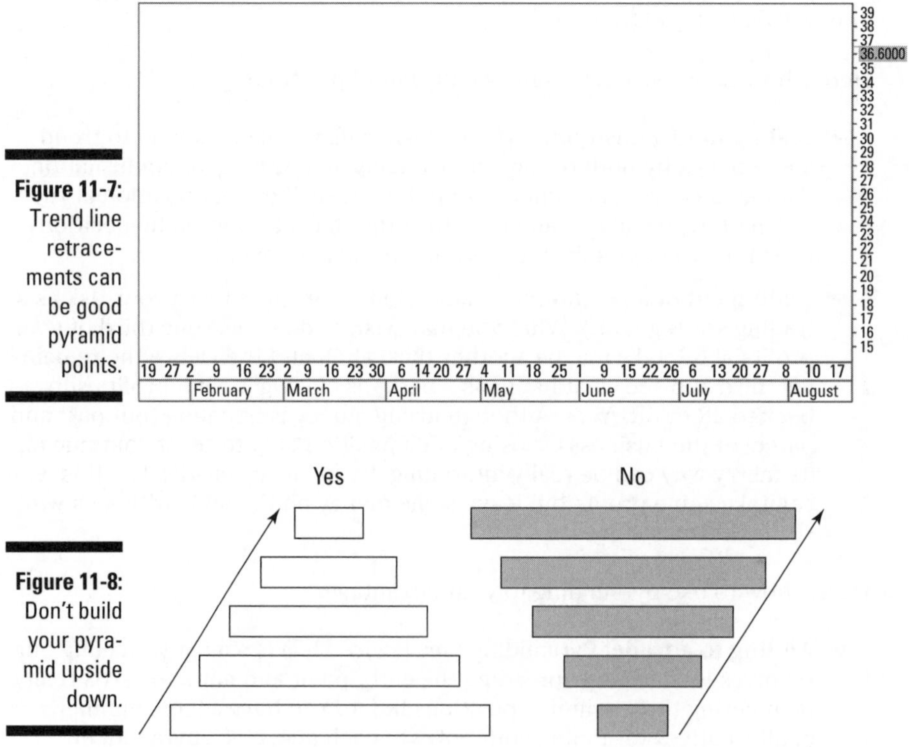

Figure 11-7: Trend line retracements can be good pyramid points.

Figure 11-8: Don't build your pyramid upside down.

You need to be sensible with your money management. Take on a new/additional position only if the subsequent position is in a decent winning position. Ordinarily, you're likely to add one position at a time, but when the time comes to close out you sell them all at once. Accordingly, when you make your first pyramid you should have enough profit in the first position so that if you get stopped out you end up no worse off than at break-even. After your second and subsequent pyramid trades, you want to be locked in to a profit if you get stopped out of the trade.

When you pyramid into a trade, you're more likely to have to give up the profits you've already made if the position reverses direction on you. This result is likely because if the second tranche (the first trade that you added to your initial position) reverses, the losses that it makes eat quickly into your existing profits. In order for a pyramid trade to be worth your while, you need to take the fullest advantage possible of the positions that do move strongly in your favour.

Trading ain't gambling: Here's why . . .

Some people consider gambling and trading to be one and the same, but that assessment isn't really the case – or at least not in the way that many people think. Although financial spread betting is treated as gambling for tax purposes, it is very different from gambling when it comes to outcomes and probabilities.

Gambling means that you're risking money on an uncertain outcome (for example, whether you're at the casino, trading, investing in shares or investing in property, the outcome isn't assured). When you gamble at a casino the odds are always against you because the casino has to make the odds in its favour – it certainly doesn't want to lose money over time and it's the casino's house. Trading has some similar elements, in that aspects such as spreads tilt the game against you and make it harder for you to win over time. Compared to casino gambling, though, a trader has some real advantages:

- If the trade you're making is going against you, you can close it out. Yes, you lose some money, but at least you can preserve the majority of it – try asking the blackjack dealer for some of your money back after a losing hand. (We should point out that some games like poker do allow you to 'fold' if you don't like the cards you get dealt, but most gambling games don't offer this option.)
- You can add to a trade moving in your favour (which you can't normally do when you're gambling – although, again, poker is one of the exceptions). This advantage means that you can alter your exposure as the trade unfolds so that in the end your losses can be small when things go poorly and can be large when things go well.
- Most casino gambling places no value on skill – with the vast majority of outcomes being down to luck. If you keep playing long enough at the casino, the house always wins – the odds are certain. However, a hardworking and disciplined trader can make the odds work for him over time, thus taking the winnings beyond short-term luck. This point of difference is what allows the trader to be profitable over time where the casino gambler just can't be.

Chapter 12

Taking Lessons from Hedge Funds

In This Chapter

- Checking out the traditional approach of hedge funds
- Understanding the long/short balance when trading hedge funds
- Incorporating different asset classes across different time frames
- Looking at advanced strategy concepts

As we became more interested in spread betting, it occurred to us that retail traders have a lot of trading choices and opportunities that simply wouldn't exist were it not for hedge funds. The good news is you can, to a very large extent, run your own hedge fund if you're so inclined (that is, if you're prepared to put in the time).

Hedge funds use a variety of different methods in an attempt to generate strong returns, which may include trading on both the long and the short side of the market as well as incorporating leverage. One of the aims for many hedge funds is to generate positive returns whether or not the market they're dealing in is rising or falling.

In this chapter, you discover some of the principles of hedge funds and some of the ways in which you can work out how to develop and then apply this investment strategy to your own portfolio.

Hedge Funds: The Traditional Approach

One of the main things that a hedge fund trader traditionally does is to take on *hedged exposure* – this approach means the trader devises a low-risk strategy and then employs large amounts of leverage (that is, increasing the amount of market exposure that the fund carries primarily through borrowing and the use of derivatives – refer to Chapter 3) in order to make the hedge fund profitable.

Although many spread bettors focus their energy on employing leverage, the more savvy traders focus their energy on clever market exposure; that is, not tying themselves to all long or all short portfolios, and not having exposure to only a single market (for more information on dealing on the long and the short side of the market, refer to Chapter 3).

Hedge fund strategies offer you the power of combining a long portfolio with a short portfolio and allow you to spread your exposure throughout different markets.

Adopting a Long/Short Balance

Most traders show a predisposition towards focusing their energy, initially, on the long side of the market. Why? Because the first words that most traders hear when it comes to share investing relate to 'buy and hold', and 'buy low and sell high'. However, while these adages may be solid, an approach that includes just investing in the long side of the market doesn't really take into account the product qualities and benefits on offer when it comes to spread bets.

Many traders ask the question: but what if I'm perfectly happy dealing in spread bets on share prices on the long side? Looking at some statistics helps to illustrate why this fairly one-sided approach may not be the best way to go (we know, we know – stats . . . but before you roll your eyes out of their sockets, wait, these are good figures to consider). Between 2000 and 2013 the UK benchmark FTSE 100 index traded anywhere between 3,800 and 6,800 going through two prolonged upward and two downward trends. Surely this presents evidence that the short side of the market gives you a lot of possibility too. In fact, if these figures are anything to go by, you may need to be thinking about having roughly one-half of your share market exposure on the long side and the other half on the short side of the market.

Before spread betting (for most traders), the options were pretty much either be long or be out of the market. Since spread betting, tools such as the charts of shares (or any investment product) allow you to look at a trade entirely on its merits to decide whether you believe you're best going long, short or doing nothing with it at all. (Chapter 13 gives you more information about how charts can help you to develop your trading method.)

Wising up to weighting

Looking into the concept of long/short portfolios in more depth, you need to realise one simple fact – on a day when the market falls, having short exposure doesn't necessarily protect you from the losses on your long positions. If market analysis were that easy then everyone would be a trader – sadly, working out that balancing act is far from easy because such a trade isn't just about taking on half long exposure and half short exposure.

In hedge fund terms, a fund that is closely balanced in long and short exposure is referred to as *market neutral*. The idea here is that you're not too worried about the rises and falls of the underlying market because you're evenly weighted to benefit from these rises and falls in the short term. But hang on, the downside is that you're unlikely to get returns as good as a rising market nor as bad as a falling market, which means you're giving up your equity return profile to some extent.

You need to develop a portfolio that can carry long and short exposure but one that's also weighted by the ebbs and flows of the market – a *weighted* portfolio. You can consider one of two strategies:

- **Make a judgement of the strength and direction of the market.** For instance, if the FTSE 100 Index is above its 200-day moving average then you're generally trading bullish (you assume that the market will move higher), and if the index is below then you're ordinarily bearish (you assume that the market is moving lower).

  However, this approach is a lagging methodology and so doesn't allow for much in the way of protection from a sudden shift lower in the prices of shares.

- **Scan the market for both long-side and short-side exposure at the same time.** If your basic scan of the market is to look for something like the 5-week moving average crossing the 14-week moving average (to try to determine a trend. See Chapter 11 for definition of moving average crossing) then start your scan by looking for the 5 crossing from below to above the 14 for long-side position and the 5 crossing from above to below the 14 for the short-side exposure. You can see then that this charting methodology isn't a matter of what the market is doing, but instead what the individual shares are doing; that is, you're trading your portfolio based on the direction as determined by your scan of the charts.

Scan the man . . . and correlation

Scanning charts is a strategy that works well for the share market, but you can easily incorporate similar scans into different markets, including spread bets, and apply similar rules each time – if something is trending down then you go long, and if something is trending up then you go short.

Easy? Not quite. You need to be aware of the correlation that your portfolio has in terms of its different constituents. For example, if you hold spread bets over three different gold stocks and you buy some gold bullion spread bets, you're not diversifying your portfolio – you're simply adding to the amount of exposure that your portfolio has to the gold price.

Using beta

Another way to consider your market exposure is by looking at your *beta*. Beta is a statistical measure that gives you an idea of how much the share price of a company is going to move in relation to the underlying market.

If a company has a beta of 1.05, you can expect it to be 5 per cent more volatile than the underlying market. If a company has a beta of 0.95 then you can expect it to be 5 per cent less volatile than the market.

You can also determine the expected volatility of your portfolio using your beta measure. You can work out your portfolio beta by multiplying the beta number by the percentage that the individual holding makes of your portfolio. You can sum this calculation and get an idea of how wider market moves impact your portfolio.

Beta numbers are available from your spread betting broker, or you can visit a free news website such as Bloomberg (`www.bloomberg.com`).

If you're short a given position then its beta number becomes a negative. You still sum all the figures together in the same way, but depending on the coverage of your portfolio, you may actually end up with a portfolio beta of zero. This result means that movements of the market at large cancel out (at least on a statistical expectation basis).

You don't need to aim for a particular beta number, but by having awareness of these figures you can get an idea of how your portfolio may behave.

Beta figures aren't a guarantee of share price movement. They're a look at how the individual shares move relative to the market historically. This glimpse means then that over a period of weeks, for instance, the beta expectation may be very accurate, but day by day you end up with all sorts of anomalies.

Incorporating Different Asset Classes

Hedge funds offer traders opportunities across a range of different asset classes in order to generate profits. One of the most exciting aspects of spread betting is your ability to incorporate different strategies to join different asset classes together as part of a working trading portfolio in much the same way. One of the most interesting aspects of this approach is the fact that you can feasibly integrate different methodologies across different time frames to take advantage of different market movements that you see.

The greater the variety of asset classes in the spreads you trade and the more methodologies that you apply, the more time you spend consuming the research and monitoring your portfolio.

Throughout different trading cycles, conditions can change very quickly, so you need to be aware of the risk that you're exposed to at any given point in time. (Be sure to check out Chapter 8, which considers risk management, because you're best not to over-leverage your trading account no matter how well diversified it is.) This section looks at some methodologies that you can consider when building a portfolio of different asset classes into a reality.

When you're scanning for trades and making decisions about whether or not to hold on to them, one tool you have available is to look at methodologies that include different time frames.

Looking at short-term time frames

Two of the most popular areas of the spread betting world for short-term trading are foreign exchange and indices. Depending on the time frame in which you're looking, you may want to set up your trading method so that you have a stop loss order linked to a take profit order (known as an OCO or One-Cancels-Other). This way you're working out ahead of time the complete parameters within which you wish to trade and you're moving in the market accordingly.

In the short-term time frame, you're best having a profit target in mind and then putting the order in to close the trade as soon as you reach this target level. If you're trading in this way, the downside is that if you look away from the screen for a little while, you may miss out on a successfully closed trade. To counter this disadvantage, and depending on the spread betting broker you're using, you may be able to set up your orders well in advance so that your entry order and your profit and loss exit orders are placed automatically.

Even in a short-term trading situation – for example, where you're trading on a chart such as the hourly (refer to Chapter 13) – you may want to plan ahead as far as you can. This option is a good short-term time frame because you don't have to watch constantly, which means you can plan the trade further in advance. Keep in mind, though, that some trade set-ups may take hours (or even days) to establish, so be ready for them when they occur – which gives you even more reason to place your entry trades in the market so they're automatically triggered.

Using longer-term time frames

On a longer-term time scale, you may want to look at trend following of spread bets on shares (and, potentially, on other instruments like foreign exchange), if you believe that the share price is going to trend consistently and you're willing to deal with the volatility attached to trading it.

The benefit that you can potentially derive by trading longer-term is one associated with diversification not only of products but also time frames. Here's why:

- You can take advantage of trending movements that require you to ride some ups and downs of the market – with the benefit of capturing some potentially large market movements.
- You can capture some short-term movements in the market and then move to the sidelines. The upside of this type of strategy isn't going to be as great as that seen from a trending move, but at least you can lock in the profit that you make and then move on to the next position.

Advanced Strategy Concepts

Traders who manage hedge funds are particularly defensive of the way in which they make their trading decisions. Unlike most conventional managed funds traders, who are reasonably detailed when outlining their strategy, the hedge fund traders remain very tight-lipped about the details of how they do business. Hedge fund traders fit into some broad categories (such as macro-economic and trend following) and stick to that approach for the most part. Other methods such as pairs trading (see the next section) are now quite well known as well.

Some hedge fund traders have been around for a while and can provide a really great education for you regarding creative and in-depth ways to use spread betting in a more advanced fashion. Naturally, you don't have to go into this depth, but you may use some details to develop new ideas and then create something unique of your own.

Understanding pairs trading

Pairs trading is about looking for two instruments that are highly correlated with one another over the longer-term (see Figure 12-1 for an example of this).

Pairs trading is probably the most commonly discussed of the hedge fund strategies because it covers all the things that you like to see in a hedge fund:

- Use of correlations
- Minimal market exposure (though potentially large sterling exposure)
- Exploitation of a perceived market mispricing

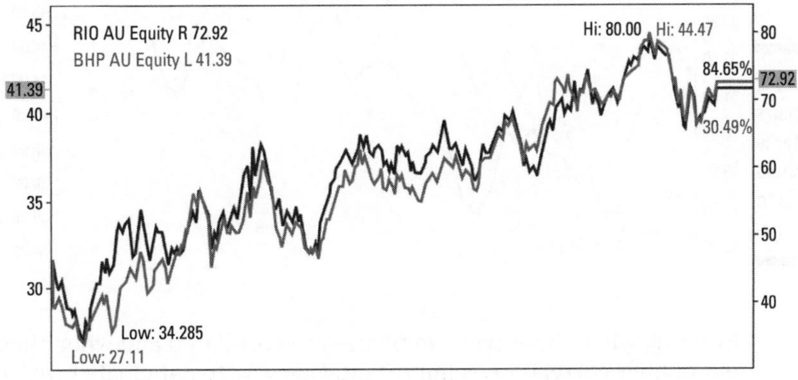

Figure 12-1: High correlation levels are key to making good pairs trades.

Here's how to identify your pair of instruments:

1. **Look at companies from a very homogenous sector – often the banking sector is a good example.**
2. **Look for a breakdown of their correlation (the relationship between two companies' share prices, where they tend to trade closely to each other in terms of price pattern) where one company is trading relatively expensively to the other.**

Anticipate that the prices of the two companies are going to converge once more and that the longer-term correlation is set to begin again. This means that you go short the relatively higher priced company and long the relatively underpriced company. The expectation is that you're going to see a convergence in price but be largely protected from market movements by the high level of correlation. You can see the convergence occurring in Figure 12-2.

The word *relative* is important. Whether the company has a higher or lower share price has nothing to do with a company's relativity. Instead, you're looking for companies that have broken out of their correlation. You tend to take a short and long position of the same sterling value.

The idea is that, on top of the convergence, while the trade is on, you have limited exposure to the market because the positions generally offset each other to a large extent. What you may also tend to do is monitor the two positions as one because you're interested in their relative combined movements and not the individual movement of the companies.

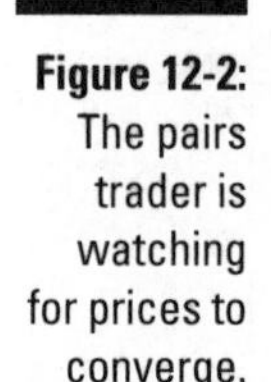

Figure 12-2: The pairs trader is watching for prices to converge.

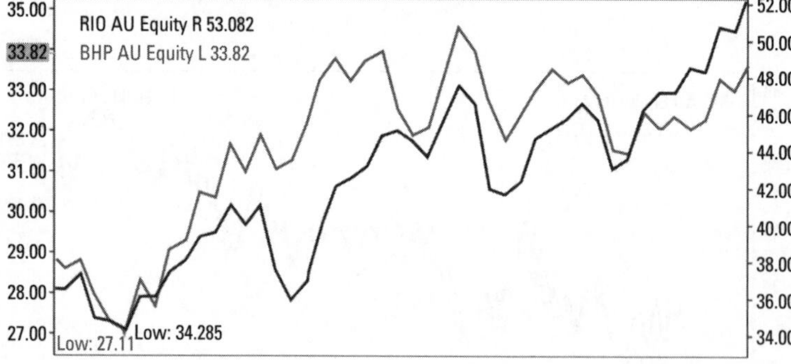

Knowing when these two companies are correlated and when they break out of their correlation is important. One way to anticipate break-outs is to overlay the charts of the two companies on the same scale, but this is a fairly poor method. You're best getting the raw price data, placing it in a spreadsheet and running a correlation formula over it – this way you know for sure how tightly correlated the companies have been.

There is no set correlation formula. Here is just one example: `www.statisticshowto.com/articles/how-to-compute-pearsons-correlation-coefficients/`

The next thing to look at is how far apart the prices have moved and whether they're stretched to the point where they're likely to move back together for you.

To help your analysis of price movement you can examine some historical measurement, but the better way is to head back to your spreadsheets and analyse, historically, how far the companies have been apart. You can then calculate standard deviations of price spread. You may find that, historically, every time the spread goes beyond two standard deviations, the prices converge quickly after that. To help with this calculation, check out the Investopedia website (`www.investopedia.com`) and type into the search box *standard deviation*. ***Tip:*** Use a spreadsheet, like Microsoft Excel, to do the calculation itself.

Don't be surprised if only one of the 'legs' of the pairs trade is a winner. As long as it makes more than the other side of the pair loses, you're going to be ahead overall.

Correlations that don't work have been the undoing of some very smart traders in the markets, so don't assume that a correlation must be respected, because such an approach isn't always going to make the grade.

You don't want to be holding a pairs trade forever. Having one long and one short position helps to offset the financing somewhat, but the tendency to take on larger positions can mean that you end up with a hefty finance bill, so be mindful of that possible outcome in your planning.

Tapping into index stripping

Index spread bets (spread bets that track an entire index like the FTSE 100) are a very popular hedge fund product because they give you exposure to a wide range of the market, which allows you to benefit from broad market moves. However, if your plan is to carry this exposure for some time and you believe a certain market sector isn't going to be a great performer, you may not want to carry as much exposure in that sector. The strategy here is called *index stripping*. The methodology includes removing this underperforming component of your exposure so that you have only exactly the portfolio you want.

Example: Say you're bullish on the wider market but you think the finance sector is going to be something of a lead weight on the performance of the overall index. If you're long on a UK share index spread bet then you're going to likely shed this weight and remove it from your portfolio. Here's how:

1. **Work out how much exposure you have to the market with your long index position.**

   If you bought a spread bet on an index at 5,000 points with a £5 a point stake, then you have £25,000 exposure to the market.

2. **Work out exactly how much exposure the financial sector makes up of the index.**

   If you say this exposure is 20 per cent (check the website of an index provider such as Standard & Poor's – `www.standardandpoors.com` – or with your spread betting broker) then you need to gain short exposure worth £5,000 on the finance sector.

   Depending on your spread betting broker you may be able to use a *sector bet* (a spread bet that tracks an individual sector of the market such as the mining sector or the finance sector) here. Alternatively, you have to go short the finance sector stocks. Ordinarily, you need worry about going short only on the companies that make up a significant weighting in the sector – smaller companies have very small weightings and have an almost negligible effect. If you're dealing in small amounts, you may worry about going short only on the top three or four constituents, which likely gives you a quite similar overall effect.

If you choose your weightings correctly, you can see that you aren't really taking a short position in the finance sector – in fact, you're taking no position at all. Why? Because you're long the sector in the index exposure that you have and short the sector using the short share or sector spread betting position that you have. This strategy, in effect, leaves you net neutral to the finance sector. This means you're hoping that the finance sector indeed underperforms and your index position is going to do better overall due to not having exposure to that particular sector. This tactic is sometimes referred to as index stripping, and can be used with individual shares as well as sectors.

Myriad strategies are available to spread bettors. You need a bit of creativity to come up with them, but the main point to take on board is to work hard on the testing of your strategies before applying them in real-life trading. By looking at ways to apply both short-term and longer-term exposure to the market (and not necessarily one market but potentially several), you can consistently direct your exposure such that you generate positive results.

Chapter 13

Ah! Technical Analysis

In This Chapter

- Predicting patterns
- Identifying trends
- Looking at some useful indicators
- Understanding the benefits of swing trading
- Clarifying some technical stop loss points
- Analysing software options

Technical analysis has gone from being seen as something akin to tea-leaf reading to an essential tool that all short-term traders are familiar with. Even for longer-term investors, technical analysis can provide an important bridge between making a fundamental determination about the underlying quality of an investment and actually making the trade based on sensible timing factors.

Like any type of method that you choose to employ to determine what positions to trade, technical analysis isn't foolproof, and nor is it 100 per cent accurate. Technical analysis tools, or charts, give you the opportunity to get on the right side of the price movements occurring at a point in time and, specifically, allow you to isolate points where you can safely say you're wrong about the trade that you're making and exit while the losses are minimal.

In this chapter, we describe some of the key technical methods that you have at your disposal as a trader.

Using Technical Analysis to Predict Patterns

Technical analysis is based on the premise that price change is determined not only by new information, but also by how humans respond to news and are influenced by fashion and 'herd' behaviour. Why? Because these human responses form repeatable patterns that you can predict through analysis of price.

A range of technical analysis tools (in three broad categories) is available to the trader:

- **Trend indicators:** Indicators and methods that look to determine whether an instrument is trending, which you can then use to decide on the strength of the trend and whether or not it's likely to continue. This type of methodology can also help determine whether your timing (to enter the market) is good or not. Trend indicators include items such as moving averages, the lowest low value (LLV), the parabolic stop-and-reverse (PSAR) and the average true range (ATR). (For each of these methods, see the section 'Applying Useful Indicators', later in this chapter.)
- **Chart pattern analysis (which may also fall under broader swing trading):** Involves looking for patterns that occur within price movements over time, such as rectangles, triangles, breakout patterns and symmetrical triangles. Through study of past prices, traders know specific ways in which to trade instruments that have a price chart that falls into these types of patterns. (For each of these methods, see the section 'Getting into Swing Trading', later in this chapter.)
- **Momentum oscillators:** Attempt to give the trader a view as to whether an instrument is overbought or oversold (where a price has moved too fast or too far in either direction). By analysing how the market ebbs and flows, this method allows the trader to better determine whether it may be a good time to buy or sell. This category of technical analysis tools includes indicators such as the Relative Strength Index (RSI) – see Chapter 14.

Identifying Trends

One of the core ideals that underlie technical analysis is that the market (and individual instruments such as a spread bet on a listed company) moves in trends, and trends persist. An instrument in a trend is more likely to remain in that trend than it is to break down and move in the opposite direction.

Although sticking with a trend for its entire duration isn't for everyone, identifying the direction of a trend and then following it can help you to determine when's best to get into a trade (or out of one).

Identifying three kinds of trend directions can get you started:

- **Uptrend:** Where price is moving in a generally upwards direction.
- **Sideways trend (or trading range):** Where price is moving in a generally sideways direction between two levels (*support and resistance* – lines where the price has repeatedly been unable to move above or below).
- **Downtrend:** Where price is moving in a generally downwards direction (that is, the opposite of an uptrend).

A trend can show plenty of upwards and downwards movements and still quite clearly highlight whether the instrument is trending or not. The most common approach taken by traders that highlights this movement is (for an uptrend) to take the time to trace a straight edge trend line underneath the prices that are shown on the chart, as shown in Figure 13-1 (and, of course, the opposite for a downtrend).

If you're drawing a 'dictionary definition' uptrend, you need to be able to draw a straight line that connects three price troughs together; for a downtrend, this should be three price peaks. If the price breaks through the uptrend line, it may be a good time to sell. On the other hand if the price touches this level and then starts to move in the other direction, you may have unearthed a good time to buy (or sell / go short in a downtrend).

Figure 13-1: An uptrend line, making you really, really rich.

The drawing of a straight edge trend line is one of those simple and under-appreciated skills of technical analysis. Not only does this trend line help to define the broad direction of the instrument, but the line itself serves as a good point of reference to help you with your buying decisions (refer to Chapter 11 for more information on trading methods). You're best strengthening your ability in this effective type of charting before making forays into other more complex methods.

Being able to draw the trend line as neatly as in Figure 13-1 is great, but it doesn't have to appear like this in order for there to be a trend in place. More specifically than the trend line, you're actually looking for a series of higher peaks and higher troughs (see Figure 13-2) in order for a trend to be in place.

In some cases, you can also draw a second line parallel to the trend line above the price action and engulf the price in a channel, as shown in Figure 13-3. A channel can be quite useful in determining when a price may have extended to the maximum away from the trend line. The only downside of relying purely on neat channels is the relative rarity with which you're able to neatly fit a channel around the price action.

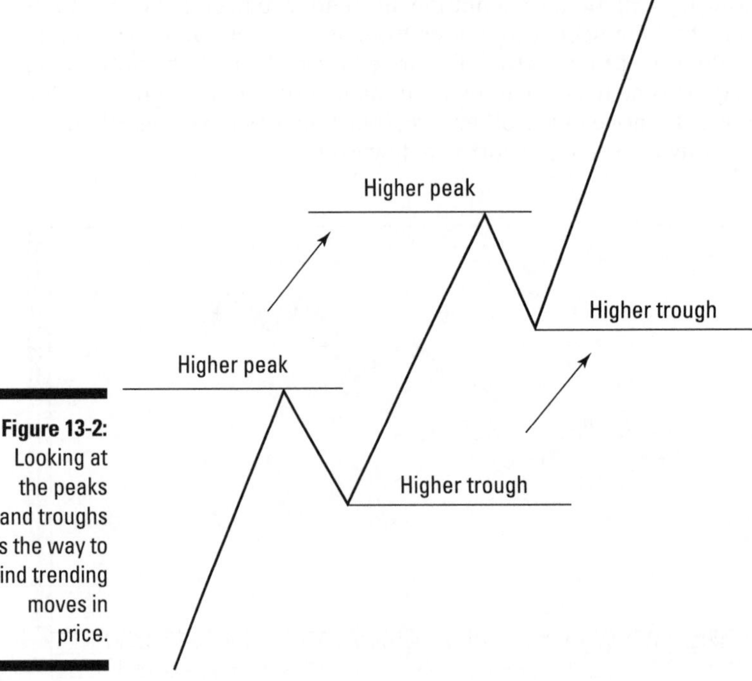

Figure 13-2: Looking at the peaks and troughs is the way to find trending moves in price.

Figure 13-3: A channel trend line, showing rising support and resistance.

Applying Useful Indicators

Indicators are another tool in the trader's arsenal of methodology with which to decide market entry and exit points. For the most part, indicators involve applying a mathematical formula to the recent trading price of the instrument that you're trading to give you information about where the price is, relative to where it has been.

Determining overbought and oversold levels can be one of the great strengths of using indicators, but these levels can lead new traders to ruin because they are deceptively simple to use.

In this section, we look at some of the key considerations that traders need to be aware of for stop loss order placement.

Always approach new technical analysis tools with great caution because nothing, especially tracking price movement trends, is ever as easy as it seems.

Getting the most from moving averages

The *moving average* is the first mathematical-based indicator that most traders come into contact with. Like the trend line, this simple indicator can go a long way to helping you determine likely entry points on any instrument that you choose to trade.

Here's how to calculate the moving average:

1. **Take the average closing price value over a certain number of time periods – for example, 30 days.**
2. **The next day, add the next time period and remove the first – in this case, add day 31 and remove the first day.**
3. **Recalculate the average.**
4. **Repeat Steps 1 through 3 for every time period from then on.**

This process makes a moving average. This type of calculation results in a line that follows the price of the instrument but has some of the *market noise* (meaning volatility – the daily ups and downs) removed. The longer the period over which you calculate the moving average, the more market noise you remove (see Figure 13-4).

You may find that using a moving average (say a 21-day average) is a good way of determining which way the price is trending. If the price is above the line then it's trending up; if it's below then it's trending down.

Traders often use moving averages to determine an entry point. The method traders most commonly use is referred to as the *crossover*, which occurs when a shorter-length moving average crosses over a longer one: for example, a 5-day moving average crossing a 15-day moving average, as shown in Figure 13-5. A combination of shorter-term and longer-term moving averages allows the trader to reduce the noise of the market while continuing to see changes in trends quite quickly.

The downside of a long moving average is that the direction of the average becomes less responsive to changes in price.

Marking the lowest price

A useful indicator for placing a stop loss is the lowest low value (LLV). The *lowest low value* is an excellent tool for trend following because it allows the trend to give a good sign of a breakdown before you exit the position and it's a means of trailing your stop upwards as you move further into profit. The LLV marks the lowest value that the price has traded at in the last *x* number of periods. You can then place your stop loss on the other side of this value and, hopefully, watch your profits climb. Have a look at Figure 13-6 and you can see the way in which the LLV trails the price, which gives you a good place to put your stop loss orders. (***Note:*** Like most things in spread betting you can look at this issue from the flipside too – traders on the short side of the market are able to use the *highest high value* (HHV) as a means of managing positions they hold.)

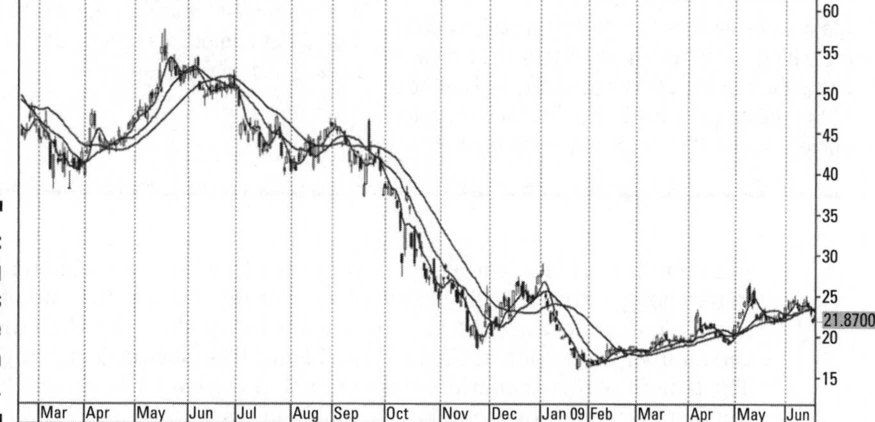

Figure 13-4: Moving averages show the market with less 'noise'.

Figure 13-5: Shorter-term and longer-term moving averages at crossover.

You can adjust the number of periods over which you calculate the LLV depending on your needs, but for the most part you're best choosing a value between 5 and 20. If the charting application you're using doesn't have this adjustment available, your option is to draw one by hand. You can work out where the LLV goes simply by counting back the relevant number of time periods.

Weekly, daily, hourly

A trend on the weekly chart trumps a trend on the daily chart. And this in turn trumps a trend on an hourly chart. Strange, isn't it?

Many short-term traders neglect weekly charts, reasoning that they're too long term to be of any use to them. However, they can be highly effective at pointing out the broad direction of companies (or any other tradeable instruments).

Looking for a moving average crossover (of prices) on a weekly chart is usually an excellent scanning tool. These weekly trends can bolster your trading methods, helping you to identify a shortlist of companies to look at more closely on daily and hourly charts.

Although the LLV indicator seems very easy to follow, keep in mind that you're going to have to give some of your profits back at the end of the trending movement because the LLV always sits below the price. And the larger the number of periods in the LLV, the bigger this give-back is going to be. The benefit of this scenario, however, is that the trader has a much better opportunity to let the trend keep running in his favour rather than cutting it off short.

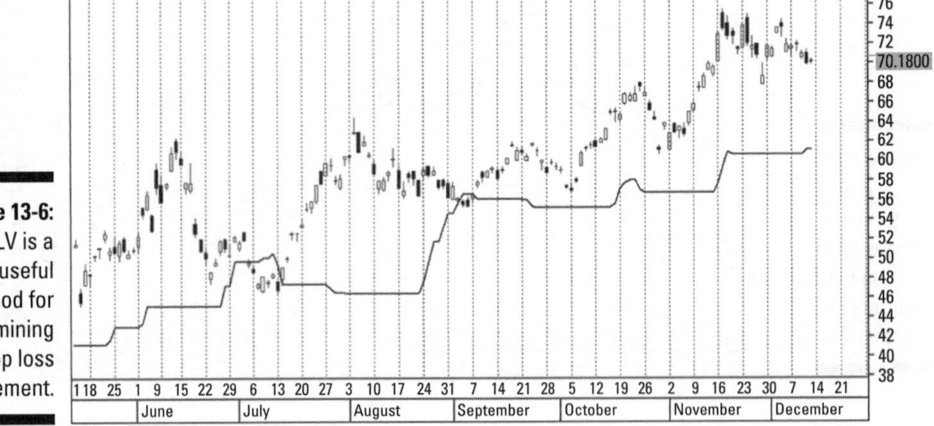

Figure 13-6: The LLV is a very useful method for determining stop loss placement.

Stopping and reversing a trade

The *parabolic stop and reverse* (PSAR) is designed for use only in trending markets as a means of looking for turns in price for entries, and even more for exits.

When price moves from below to above the PSAR, this movement is considered a bullish (or buy) signal – the opposite of this applies too (that is, when prices move from above to below the PSAR, this movement is a bearish, or sell, signal).

The PSAR allows a level of automation that is like music to a trader's ears. Why? Because for each time period, this charting application adjusts itself and moves closer to the price. The PSAR can do this because it contains an *acceleration factor* – the longer the price keeps moving higher (or lower), the faster the value of the PSAR changes, thereby moving the stop closer and closer to the current price, which means that when price eventually reverses you're quickly stopped out and hopefully have locked in a large profit. Figure 13-7 shows how this indicator generates potential entry and exit signals for the trader depending on the prevailing direction of the market.

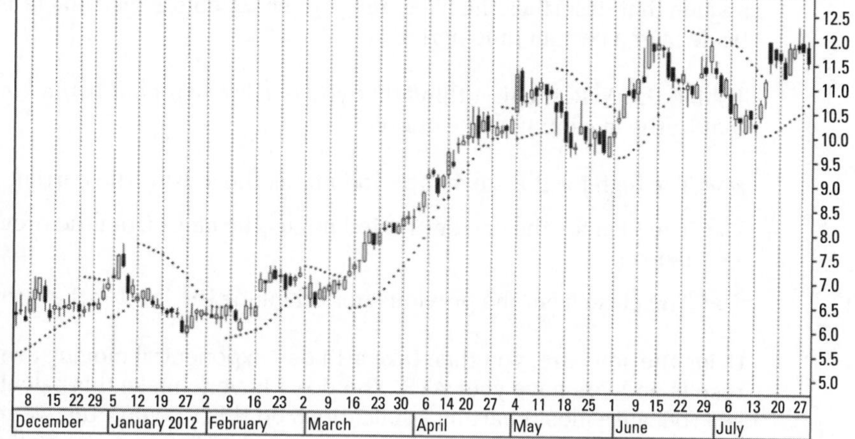

Figure 13-7: The PSAR helps the trader identify shifting trends in the market.

This PSAR indicator was created (by renowned technical analyst J. Welles Wilder) to enable a trader to respond to being stopped out of a position – to reverse the trade and continue. The problem with this approach, though, is that eventually you end up holding a long or a short position in everything. In this case, when we say 'everything' we mean that literally, because if you use the PSAR as your only indicator, it tells you to either buy or sell on every chart that you look at. To counter this effect, you need to filter the indicator more carefully. For example, why not look for a trending instrument (that is, something that's moving consistently higher or lower in price) and then test the behaviour of the PSAR as a trailing stop loss indicator.

Although you can change the settings of the PSAR on your charting application, the creator of this indicator was clear that it should be left programmed to its default settings.

Spotting the average range

The *average true range* (ATR) – also developed by technical analyst J. Welles Wilder – uses volatility in the movement of an individual instrument as a means of working out potential stop loss points.

Like the moving average (see 'Getting the most from moving averages', earlier in this chapter), the ATR allows you to look at price in a different way. The ATR looks at the trading behaviour of an instrument and expresses it as a value that describes the likely range over which the instrument is going to trade over a certain time period.

To find the ATR, the first thing that you need to work out is the *true range*; that is, the maximum value out of:

- The high for the current period minus the low for the current period
- The high for the current period minus the close from the previous period
- The close from the previous period minus the low for the current period

Using the software, you then take a 14-day exponential moving average of the results and you have your ATR. You don't have to make this calculation yourself (because most charting applications do this for you), but we recommend that you do, so that you understand exactly what the numbers all mean. You can see that the value of the ATR rises and falls in line with the volatility of the instrument's price in Figure 13-8.

To enable you to absorb more than the recent amount of instrument price volatility in your placement of a stop loss, you can employ a multiple of the ATR as your stop loss placement level – for example, 2× ATR. The logic behind this approach is that you're waiting until the price moves outside of a reasonable range (determined by the ATR) before closing out your position. This helps you avoid getting closed out unnecessarily.

The ATR (or multiple of it) can be an ideal stop loss placement solution when other options such as using support or resistance levels (horizontal lines where the price has repeatedly been unable to move above or below) may not be available.

Figure 13-8: The ATR tells you a lot about the trading behaviour of any instrument.

Getting into Swing Trading

Swing trading is a methodology that allows you to look for patterns in share price charts (which can include rectangles, triangles, breakout patterns and symmetrical triangles) that point towards a certain type of outcome being probable. This form of trading gives you opportunities to take measured approaches to your trades with precise rules for the placement of stop loss orders as well as take profit orders. The idea of the swing is that you're getting in at the start of a new upswing and getting out (or maybe going short) at the start of a downswing. Like everything trading related, though, saying is much easier than doing.

Much of what swing trading is about falls into the category of what traders refer to as *breakout trading* – where you're looking for some type of support or resistance to build up, at which point you make the trade when the price breaks out, or when the pattern of support or resistance breaks.

When swing trading, one of the main skills that you need is *pattern recognition* (although you can use this skill in other forms of trading too), which considers the way in which an instrument is trading and then isolates how you can deal with it (based on your trading rules or parameters). (***Remember:*** Moving averages are also very useful for helping you to find changes in prevailing price direction.)

One of the key benefits of this type of trading is the option it gives you to apply it across a range of different time frames without changing the rules that you use.

For example, the chart in Figure 13-9 shows a formation referred to as a *rectangle*, which is a continuation pattern. You can identify this pattern by the price being arrested in its movement – that is, by the price moving in a sideways movement between a support and a resistance level. Typically, you're looking for two peaks hitting the resistance line and two troughs hitting the support line before you call it a confirmed rectangle. The pattern is eventually confirmed by the price breaking out and continuing in its previous direction, which is what the trader is waiting for before entering a new position. This chart is a daily time frame.

Figure 13-9: Rectangles show a wonderful interaction between support and resistance.

A popular and powerful swing trading pattern is the *ascending triangle* (see Figure 13-10). This pattern is intuitive in the way it unfolds, so much so that you can see the market psychology lying behind it.

Figure 13-10 shows the price striking a resistance point and then being repelled to lower levels as heavy selling greets the rally. Each time the price falls, though, it's supported at a progressively higher price level – which is what gives the pattern its distinctive shape.

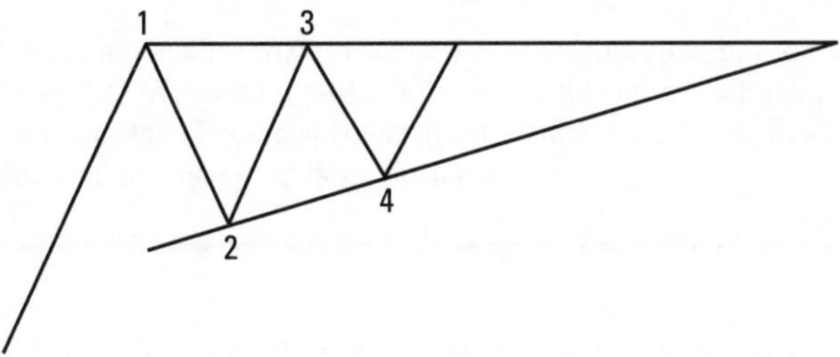

Figure 13-10: Triangles show prices being squeezed between two trading levels.

The way that you approach this trade from an entry point is to buy as soon as the price resistance level shows signs of breaching. Then you can place your stop below the resistance level, because if the price slides below this level, you're not likely to want to hold the position anyway.

You can see on the ascending triangle chart (Figure 13-10) that you measure the target for the price breakout by the height of the triangle in the build-up phase. The fact that you have a price target (a common feature of most swing trading methods) means you can be very clear from the outset where you're likely to sell out for a profit – if you have a successful trade.

Another important trading pattern is the *symmetrical triangle* (see Figure 13-11).

Figure 13-11 shows the price movement moving closer and closer, together with the peaks becoming lower and the troughs becoming higher – which is something of a sign of uncertainty for the market.

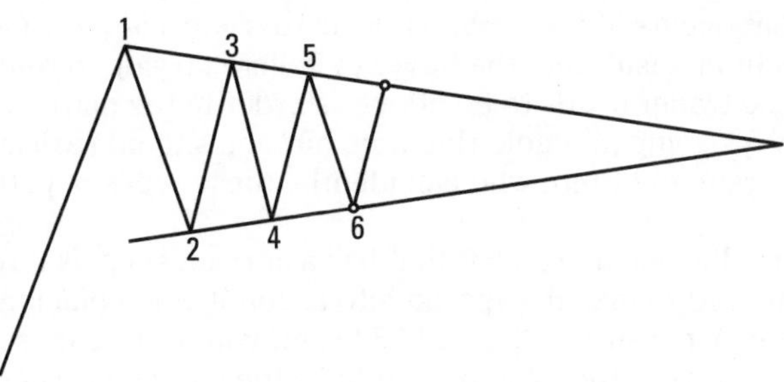

Figure 13-11: The symmetrical triangle has rising support lines and falling resistance lines.

Minimising losers

No matter what sort of methodology you're using, make sure that the reward you anticipate making is likely to be significantly greater than the risk you're taking.

A 1:3 risk–reward ratio is the ideal minimum to aim for. Otherwise you're in a position where you have to have significantly more winners than losers in order to remain profitable over time.

Like the case with the ascending triangle chart (refer to Figure 13-10), you can see in Figure 13-11 that the symmetrical triangle chart measures to the height of the pattern and then extrapolates this measurement forwards as the target for anyone buying in.

If a swing trading pattern begins to fail in the build-up phase, consider it void and ignore the pattern.

Understanding General Rules on Technical Stop Loss Points

When you see a support and resistance level in the price chart, you can be sure that the rest of the market can see it too. So remember that if you're placing your stop loss points just on the other side of these levels, you may be disappointed with the result that occurs if the price trades at this level.

If you're looking at a foreign exchange chart for instance, and the price breaks through a level and continues briefly in that direction and then quickly reverses, you're best assuming that a big buyer or seller is using the momentum that occurs at the breakout level to trade a large amount in the opposite direction. It isn't that the buyer or seller is trying to ruin everyone's fun, but that the trader needs to position his order in the market. This scenario isn't always going to unfold this way, but you should realise that you're not the only person out there who can identify these types of patterns.

When you're trading an instrument that has a spread, such as foreign exchange, you need to take the spread into account when placing your stops. So if the price is between 1.2345 and 1.2348 and you want to close the position if it reaches 1.2320, then you need to take the spread into account. If you simply place your stop at 1.2320, you're going to be stopped out as soon as the bid price touches this level – not the offer. So if you want to be sure that the price has indeed broken this level then you place the stop at 1.2316. This is one pip below the nominated stop level, plus the spread. In this way, you're sure that the level of your stop is properly breached.

Stirring the Software Pot

These days, you can't flex your technical analysis wings without software . . . charting software.

Your spread bet broker is likely to supply you with basic software, usually free of charge. At the other end of the spectrum are charting applications that allow you to create original indicators completely from scratch. If you want this type of advanced functionality, you have to pay for it.

Advanced functionality doesn't improve trading capabilities, however. Little correlation exists between the quality of different types of charting software and the traders who use them: if you're a new trader and spend £3,000 on a charting application, you're still likely to be less successful than an experienced trader who's using a £100 piece of charting software.

Regarding your choice of charting software, start your journey with something cheap and then upgrade as your ability begins to expand beyond the limitations of that software. Don't buy the software with the expectation of one day using all of its tools. The most advanced software allows you to program your own indicators and scans (which may look across entire markets for instruments that satisfy a number of technical criteria), but this functionality isn't very useful for beginners.

In addition, many spread betting firms now offer relatively sophisticated charting packages as part of their proprietary trading platforms. These also allow you to open and close bets off the chart, bringing you a much higher level of interactivity. They are also free to use, so worth trying before you spend money on third party software.

Also, don't forget that with spread betting, you are trading the price quoted to you by your broker, not the price quoted to you by a software provider. You may find there are small differences. Hence, it can be easier to use your broker's charting functions if they offer them.

For more information on charting software, see Chapter 14.

Chapter 14

Charting Spread Bets with Software

In This Chapter

- Charting software – what's around
- Choosing the right charting software for your experience
- Adding indicators to the mix
- Creating your own indicators
- Scanning the spread betting market effectively

Technical analysis, or charting, is the core method that traders use to determine when to open positions and close positions, and to explore ways to manage risk.

A large range of charting software (with varying functionality) is on the market. The range in price and features available (and, in some cases, the options in terms of customisation, scanning and program indicators based on your requirements) can be mindboggling. Ordinarily, though, for each new feature that you do need, you're going to find lots more that you don't need, so you're best being sure of exactly what you're after before spending your money.

Remember, spending heaps of money on software doesn't make the process of improving your trading ability any easier. You're best assessing the different software based on your requirements and then determining whether the price is fair for you. Your first charting software purchase should cost you very little – you work up from there. If you make your trades based on fundamental factors (see Chapter 10), you're likely to need only reasonably basic software, but if you use only technical analysis then you may find making an extra investment well worth your while.

In this chapter, we look at some of the key considerations to take into account when looking at charting software. We also describe particular pieces of software that are available.

Introducing Charting Software

Some of the problems that traders face when choosing software are:

- How to decide what charting software tools are the most effective for them
- How extensive a set of charting software tools needs to be to meet their trading goals; for example:
    - How powerful it needs to be
    - Whether a particular charting software's functionality is, in fact, the most suitable for their experience level

This section takes a look at the progressive functionality available to traders – from the most basic of charting software to the top of the pops.

Before we get into a large amount of depth in the world of available software, we want to point out that any list of available software that we give in this book is far from exhaustive due to the fact that a great many options are available.

You can get access to charting software applications from:

- **Your broker:** Generally, the most basic charting software is available online and offered by your broker. The great advantage is the cost to you – nothing! When Internet trading was developing, you had access to free charts but they were quite rudimentary. Now, however, traders are a more demanding lot and they want brokers to offer things like live streaming charts for free as well, which in turn means lots of competition between providers that eventually gives them and you more of the fancy stuff. Be aware, though, that you get what you pay for (or not, so to speak).
- **Search engines:** Interactive charts are available from websites like Google Finance, Big Charts or Yahoo!7 Finance. The only downside for this category of online software resources is that they often don't provide charts on some of the indices and commodities that you may be interested in.

- **Hybrid installed software:** The first step that you may make into more advanced charting software is to use hybrid software installed on your computer. First, you install a program on your computer, and then you go online to use it. The good thing about this kind of software is that it allows you to save all your work so that all your analysis is there waiting for you next time.
- **Offline/standalone:** This is the point where the expense starts to get interesting – remembering, of course, that no automatic correlation exists between the expense of the software and its success. Basically, the more expensive the software, the more flexibility you have to make the software do exactly what you need by doing things such as modifying, combining and creating technical indicators. In addition, you can have the software scan the market for many more criteria. (You can even take it further – custom indicators allow you to scan based on a combination of criteria built into a single indicator.) Sounds great – and it is – but there's a downside too. You need to pay a data provider for the data that the software needs to run, and to get into advanced scanning you need to learn a programming language. This is far from impossible to do but additional data costs are something you need to keep in mind. (See the section 'Exploring Top Ways to Scan', later in this chapter, for more on scanning.)

  Another thing that sets high-end software aside from cheaper options is the ability to backtest. *Backtesting* involves programming a set of criteria for entry, exit and risk management and then testing how your trading plan would have performed over time. Although it's a wonderful feature, the programming can be very time consuming and the more advanced pieces require you to learn a programming language in order to use them.

  A lot of programs have basic backtesting functionality built in, but you may have to buy an add-on for the really fancy stuff. For instance, Sierra Chart (`www.sierrachart.com`) costs you around $12 to $40 per month, depending on the features you need – naturally, the more expensive, the more complex the work the add-on can do.

The extra features offered by standalone software are very important to some people but totally irrelevant to others, so you're wasting your money unless you're planning to do quite specialist work. Not only does specialist software require significant effort but you need to do a lot of extra learning to properly understand the test results that this type of software generates.

Picking up where you left off with hybrid software

Sometimes you can look at a chart and make an assessment about where you think stop losses should go, the likely direction of the trade and where you think you might take profits. If you leave the chart unmarked and come back to it in a couple of days, you may make a totally different assessment of what's going on. Things such as changes to prevailing market conditions and even your own mood can influence this new assessment. More importantly, you can end up missing important patterns that may otherwise have been very plain to you on a different day.

Installing hybrid charting software allows you to get around the problem of missing evolving chart formations by allowing you to:

- Draw all the points that you can identify when you see them at first glance. Even if the pattern isn't complete, you lay the groundwork for identifying a more complete pattern in the future. If you mark up charts as you go, you can see many tradeable formations occurring over time.
- Regularly mark all the interesting points that you see.
- Write notes on your charts to remind yourself of why certain trends and patterns are of interest.

Choosing the Charting Software That's Right for You

This section looks at some specific attributes that you can consider when choosing charting software options. Unfortunately, too many software options exist for us to cover them all individually – otherwise the title of the book would be *Charting Software For Dummies*. However, we include some examples of software here.

Ordinarily, one software application is more appealing than another kind because of its:

- **Availability of charts:** Once upon a time (when dial-up Internet was the norm) it was a real pain to have to connect to the Internet in order to get access to charts. For the majority of people, though, those days are long gone, so connectivity isn't the issue that it once was. Unless you have a laptop and you're planning to do a lot of analysis on the go, having to connect isn't really a problem. The one thing that can sometimes be a bit of an issue is that each chart has to load individually; this adds only a second or two of waiting time, but it's something to be aware of.

One of the real benefits of using your broker's charts is that these facilities will likely provide real-time intra-day charts, which can help with short-term timing of the market. These charts can be quite expensive when you're paying for them yourself. It's interesting that in the time that online trading has been available (not much more than ten years) traders have gone from being happy with any old charts to demanding free streaming charts – which goes to show the benefits of competition for consumers.

With free and hybrid software, up-to-date charts are available as soon as you go online.

With standalone software you'll have to download data – generally daily – so that your charts remain up to date. This extra downloading isn't a big drama because the software that comes from your data provider generally prompts you to do it all with just a few clicks of the mouse.

- **Features:** The free charting software offered by your broker isn't going to be the best software in the world, but it should offer a good range of different charts such as line, bar and candle – if it doesn't, your analysis will be pretty limited. Many programs offer more specialist types of charts too, such as 'point and figure' and 'renko' charts, so for no money you do get a lot. Most also offer drawing tools (straight lines) for trends and support/resistance marking, as well as a number of indicators such as moving averages, the parabolic stop and reverse and the average true range (see Chapter 13 for more information on indicators). And it's not unusual for the program to offer a reasonable amount of price history, going back at least a few years, that's viewable over intra-day, daily, weekly and monthly time frames.

  Depending on the provider, the free software offered may or may not include volume on the charts. It also rarely saves your chart settings automatically, and some won't allow you to save your chart settings at all. Check with your provider to find out whether the software your provider supplies offers this feature.

  Hybrid software can offer all the above features, with the added feature that you can save the settings, marks and comments you've added to the charts.

  Offline or standalone software can also provide all the above features – and a whole lot more. With this software you can do things such as modify, combine and create technical indicators, and scan market data based on defined criteria. A lot of these types of programs also allow you to backtest your trading strategy (for very advanced testing you often need add-on software). See the section 'Introducing Charting Software', earlier in this chapter, for more on the features of offline or standalone charting software.

- **Functionality:** This is a bit tricky to define based on the type of software because we've seen really cheap software that does things better than really expensive software – so you don't always get what you pay for. However, you want to look for more flexibility the further along you go.

  Software at any level should allow you to modify the indicators that are available, making the software useful in a wide range of different situations.

  Any software type should also allow you to scan the market for different criteria. Free software may only offer basic scanning, like looking for share prices that are hitting their 52-week high. Standalone software should allow you to do things like combining several different indicators and finding the bets that fit all the criteria that you need.

  More advanced software also allows you to custom-write your own indicators, so your only limit is your ability to write the program code to tell the software what to do.

- **Price:** The price for software can differ enormously. To give you an idea, we've included examples for each level of software, and what you'd expect to pay. (Naturally, we don't need to talk a lot about the cost of free software so we've started with hybrid software.)

  - **Hybrid software:** One of the better pieces of software in the hybrid software category comes from Incredible Charts (www.incrediblecharts.com). At the time of writing, this software cost £18 per month and offered a wide range of features for the price, with charts available for London Stock Exchange shares and with additional fees for shares from a number of foreign markets. The software saves any drawings and indicators you add to the charts for the next time you view the charts and also offers some decent scanning options.

    Some data providers allow you to pay less if you access the data only after specific times – for example, after midnight of each trading session. You need to consider what's appropriate for you, but if you only look at your charts in the morning before the start of each day's trade then this discount may be just what you need.

  - **Standalone software:** The price for a mid-range product is about £400. A good example in this range is EzyChart (`www.ezychart.com`), which at the time of writing cost $429.50. The good thing about this software is that it's easy to use – the average Windows user can get the software under control in 30 minutes.

  - **Metastock:** One of the better options in the higher echelons of software is Metastock, which is US-based software that you can purchase directly from Equis (`www.metastock.com`). The reason that we mention buying directly from the programmer is that, depending on the exchange rate, in doing so you can sometimes save a lot of money – just make sure that you check out the alternatives first. Several other packages are out there for around the same sort of money. By the time you want to buy this type of software you'll have a decent idea of what you're looking for, so keep your requirements in mind when comparing products. Metastock's end-of-day software, Metastock Pro, costs around £350.

- **Advanced software:** For the really enthusiastic. The software in the preceding bullets has end-of-day data, but you can also purchase software that provides real-time charts. Of course, these added features come at a price. There's an easy rule to remember, and to illustrate we quote from one of our favourite films, *Lock, Stock and Two Smoking Barrels*: 'It comes with a gold-plated Rolls Royce . . . as long as you pay for it.' The same goes for charting software. Metastock's real-time version (Metastock Pro) costs around £1,000 for the software, with Metastock selling annual data for the Europe / Middle East region for £1,000 per annum on top of that (`www.metastock.com`) – quite a bit of money, so be sure you need the software! You can also look at alternatives like Bull Charts (`www.bullcharts.com`) or something extra-flash in the form of Trade Station (`www.tradestation.com`).
- **Specialty software:** This looks for very specific features in the technical analysis environment. Programs can run to several thousand dollars and we don't cover them in this book – by the time you need them you'll be able to find them on your own.

Before making any investment in software be sure that enough support and education is available to help you learn how to use it effectively – if it's complex, you may need quite a bit of help! Some providers offer standalone packs that go with the software and they may have a helpline that you can call. Also, check online to see whether you can find any forums on the software you're interested in – these can be invaluable because people on these forums are often keen to give advice.

Incorporating Indicators

These days, most technical analysis software has a pretty comprehensive suite of indicators available, so this level of functionality isn't going to be a factor when deciding which software package to buy. The ways in which you can apply indicators and use them to find trading opportunities, though, vary from package to package.

Technical indicators are available in technical analysis software to scan the markets, and these are likely to make up a decent portion of your overall set-up. The times you're most likely to look at more advanced options on the indicator front is when you want to program your own or combine several indicators into one, which requires some decent software.

Although overlaying several different indicators at the one time is easy in terms of the functionality of most software options, being able to do so doesn't mean the indicators are going to be more effective. For example, indicators that fall into the oscillator category (a type of non-trending chart that fluctuates above and below a central line, such as the Relative Strength Indicator and the Stochastic Oscillator) may give quite similar results at similar times to one another. So, rather than overlaying several similar indicators that are going to give you roughly the same signal, you're best looking outside of that family of indicators when determining your scan.

Imagine how difficult it is to prepare a scan that uses five different indicators; trying to then manually reconcile the result gets even harder. Instead, a good starting point for putting together tests that you can more easily debug is to use the moving averages indicator (which helps you determine likely entry points to a trade). For lots of traders, using moving averages is appropriate because they're looking to trade trends anyway. The reason moving average indicators may be particularly useful is because you can easily see where trends such as moving average crossovers are occurring on the chart, which means you can work with your scan to ensure the results are those that you're looking for. (See Chapter 13 for more on moving averages.)

Writing Your Own Indicators

If you type 'J. Welles Wilder' into a search engine, you can read about a technical analyst who's responsible for coming up with many of the most popular technical indicators that traders use today. You can also enjoy the rationale he applied to create them, which may just bring on a flurry of creativity of your own – hopefully enough to develop some of your own indicators (see the sidebar 'Building your own bit of genius'). Before you get too excited about designing your own indicators, though, you need to realise that the new skill-set you're about to learn is going to take plenty of patience and perseverance because it's going to take more than one attempt to get the process right.

Here's one possible method for creating your own indicator:

1. **Take a selection of indicators you like.**

   For instance, you may like trading based on companies that have a certain value RSI (Check out Chapter 13 for more on this) and maybe a crossover of two moving averages.

2. **Join them together as one big indicator.**

   This step may sound complex, but ordinarily it isn't too much of a drama in terms of the overall interpretation. The single indicator usually takes on the form of a binary indicator, which means you get a yes (that is, all the criteria are in place) or a no (that is, one or more of the criteria is missing) answer. You can only do this using more advanced stand-alone software, but it can be very useful as a means of finding instruments that fit the characteristics that you're looking for in a trade.

3. **Check that all the criteria you're looking for are in place.**

   If so, your custom indicator tells you to buy, and if not, it tells you to do nothing at all.

4. **Start your trade.**

   When you're satisfied that the time is right to trade, go ahead – just don't forget your risk management and your position-sizing rules (see Chapters 8 and 9).

Building your own bit of genius

J. Welles Wilder's work allows you to look at the Relative Strength Indicator as an example of the kind of equation you may be looking at when planning to build your own indicator.

The Relative Strength Indicator is built with the following:

- UPS = (Sum of gains over N periods) / N
- DOWNS = (Sum of losses over N periods) / N
- RS = UPS/DOWNS
- RSI = 100 – (100/(1 + RS))

This indicator can then have a *smoothing average* (a mathematical technique for getting rid of extraneous data) applied to it to reduce visible market noise.

Although the overall equation isn't too taxing, it doesn't mean that developing the idea from scratch for what *you* want to examine is going to be easy, so be very mindful of the complexity of what you're taking on. Once you've figured this out, all you have to do is work out what the result is telling you and how you can apply the indicator in order to make better trading decisions.

Exploring Top Ways to Scan

Scanning is informative; scanning is fun (at least for some people). You discover all sorts of information about what's happening on a given day. The following roundup offers some great ways to scan the market using charting software.

- **Price and volume:** If you're a new trader, start with price and volume scans. You're likely to want to look for shares that have turnovers well in excess of one million shares a day. On the price front, you might want to look for prices that are at the highest level they've been at in the last 52 weeks. Alternatively, you may want to look for prices that have increased more than a certain percentage (a figure determined by you) in the last week.

  The general rule when it comes to using software to scan share markets is the more volume (amount traded over a given period), the better, because you can get in and out of a trade more easily.

  Foreign exchange (the value of two currencies, or the exchange rate) doesn't have volume displayed because no official market exists for it – the rate is simply determined by the prices banks are paying one another for currency at any given point in time. So you can't scan foreign exchange markets using volume as a criterion.

- **Price breakouts:** A very popular way to scan charts. When you look at charts from the swing trader perspective, you're looking for price breakouts in price patterns such as the ascending triangle (refer to Chapter 13 for more on swing trading patterns).

  You can look for price breakouts that take the form of a *highest high value* (or *lowest low*). This kind of scan looks for a chart that reaches the highest or lowest level seen in *x* number of periods. You can use this scan as part of an entry or exit set-up or as a means of short-listing trading opportunities on the long side (52-week high) or the short side (52-week low).

When looking at the results of your scanning, also consider:

- **Number of trades a day:** As you develop your scanning, you quickly come to the conclusion that you need to balance your desire to scan with your need to create scanning results that don't present you with too great a number of opportunities. As a trader you're naturally going to want as many returns as possible from your scans, but this approach isn't a very efficient way of trading. Why? Because every time you trade you're up for trading costs. Plus the simple fact is that not every trade is going to be a winner.

If, for instance, you're holding positions for several weeks trying to capture trending movements, you don't want your scanning software results telling you to take on 30 new positions a day – you end up with so many that you're unlikely to have sufficient capital to carry them all, let alone carry the risk tolerance. Really, then, taking on one or two positions a day is the likely maximum you're able to tolerate.

If you get one or two of the good trades a day, you're doing okay, and if you're getting 10 or 12 then they're probably not that great a prospect – or if they are, you're putting yourself up for a win for the Nobel Prize somewhere down the track!

- **High-probability bets:** Certainly, trading on a shorter time frame enables you to carry more positions for a shorter period of time, but you need to be able to balance out the equation of length of trade and number of positions realistically. More important is the quality of the scan that you come up with, because you only want to be entering into trades that you consider to be 'high probability'. These are bets that you're very confident are going to turn into successful trades. You don't want to waste your time (and more importantly, your capital) on trades that you don't feel confident about.

On the hunt for market momentum

A good way to shortlist share bets for trading is to scan for those that are making new 52-week highs. The reason for this approach is that you at least know that the company has some market momentum on its side. As a trader, you want to resist the temptation to look for companies that are trading at very low levels (and are trending down), thinking they represent good value. Always be aware that value is a relative interpretation and that shares may be very cheap for a very good reason. Ordinarily, you're best looking for a share that's heading in the direction that you want to trade in.

Part V
Knowing Where You're Going

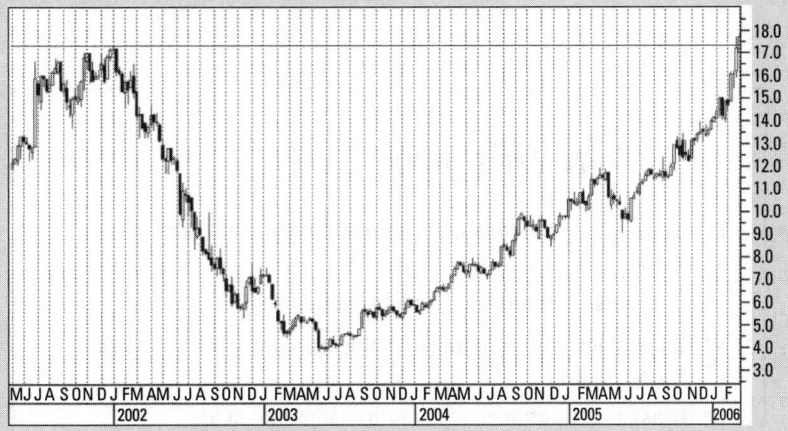

For Dummies can help you get started with a huge range of subjects. Visit `www.dummies.com` to learn more and do more with *For Dummies*.

In this part . . .

- Learn how to put together a spread-betting plan – and stick to it.
- Get yourself an effective trading methodology.
- Understand your own trading behaviour, and work out whether it's working.
- Grasp the importance of accurate record-keeping.
- Keep a firm grip on your spread-betting progress.
- Go to `www.dummies.com/extras/fsbuk` for online bonus content.

Chapter 15

Analysing Your Trading Behaviour

In This Chapter

- Steering clear of mental trading traps
- Assessing whether you're suited to part- or full-time trading
- Dealing with the fear of losing

You need to keep analysing and assessing your approach to trading and take responsibility for the outcomes that you generate from the market. The study of trading behaviour has revealed that an individual's natural tendencies actually work against successful outcomes. People who make rational decisions in everyday life start acting strangely when money's on the line!

In this chapter, we talk about the way you behave as a trader. Who's responsible for your gains? Who's responsible for your losses? You are, of course. You also need to ask yourself how much time you want to spend trading. Giving up your day job to go full time may not be the wisest move when you're just starting out.

We discuss how to recognise the problems common to traders, such as making decisions because you're afraid to lose money, which helps you manage the mental side of trading; and consider how frequently assessing your trading behaviour helps ensure your success as a trader.

Avoiding Common Trading Pitfalls

At least half the battle of trading goes on in your mind. Your self-esteem can plummet after you've lost money, compared your own failures to someone else's successful trading or sold a position in profit too early because you were afraid of it reversing (even though doing so was contrary to your trading plan). Do you sometimes think of the market as an entity that's out to get you? Why do you stop thinking about the losing trade but not the winning trade? Why do you follow your trading plan when you're winning but abandon it when you're losing? Well, you're only human . . .

Being aware of the mental traps traders can fall into can help you stop and assess your trading behaviour and stay on top of the game. The following sections consider pitfalls you might encounter on your trading journey, with tips on how to avoid them.

Personalising the market

A dangerous trap that people fall into is treating the market almost like a person, sometimes one who's out to get you! Some people take this further and say that a certain stock owes them money; they might say, for example, 'I lost £500 trading XYZ and I'm going to keep trading this company until I get my money back.' If you've ever felt this way or actually focused on a company or instrument in order to exact your 'revenge trade' then it's time to move on. The company itself extracts money from shareholders when it lists (and during corporate capital raisings), but other than that the ups and downs of the share price don't make the company directly wealthier or poorer. And there certainly isn't a vault over at the company's headquarters labelled 'Gains from unwary shareholders'.

The market doesn't feel that you're a good trader or a bad trader whether you lose money or make money. It doesn't feel anything. In the UK, the share market isn't even run by a person; it's just a computer that matches buyers and sellers with one another. This means that the sad reality is that you aren't going to get praise or acceptance from the market – you need to find this within yourself.

Hoping and waiting instead of taking action

Like most people, you're probably not particularly good at taking losses. Through a combination of hope or plain old denial many traders let a position run against them for a long time before eventually doing something about it.

Have you ever heard or used the phrase 'I'll wait until it gets back to break-even and then sell it'? Just how long are you willing to wait for this to happen? You can see from the chart shown in Figure 15-1 that you may be waiting an awfully long time. And your decision to wait is based on the assumption that a stock moving lower will bounce and return to its former glory, which unfortunately isn't always the case.

By waiting, you're creating a goal that potentially risks a lot of money in order to give you the satisfaction of not having a losing trade.

Make a decision and act to clip the loss early and then move on to the next trade. This way you're at least taking active control over your positions rather than simply hoping that they'll come good for you at some stage in the future.

Figure 15-1: Long-term price movement back to break-even.

Exploring prospect theory

Lots has been written about *behavioural finance* – the study of the psychology of trader behaviour and the resulting effects on the money market – because it helps explain why and how markets operate.

A major concept of economics, *rationality*, says that people will act in such a way as to make the best choices – about consumption, saving, and so on. But it seems that many people don't make rational decisions when they're trading on the share market.

Prospect theory looks at how people make different types of decisions when faced with risky situations. Research has found that people give different answers to the same or similar questions depending on how the questions are framed, whether the outcome was a loss or profit they had to take immediately, and depending on what was going to happen next. Here are some examples of trading behaviour that defy rational thinking:

- A willingness to take a risk to get back to break-even, even when the alternative is an even greater loss if the risk doesn't pay off.
- A willingness to lock in a profit rather than take a risk to gain an even bigger profit.
- An aversion to loss that makes traders employ strategies and defences to avoid losing money that actually *prevent* success.

You've probably heard the expression 'cut your losses and let your profits run' – behavioural finance studies have found that people may be pre-programmed to do just the opposite.

Starting from scratch instead of adjusting

Some traders are quick to throw their hands in the air, tear up their trading plan, sulk for a while and then decide to start from scratch every time they have a string of losing trades.

Trading has the potential to be an extremely frustrating activity because you're trying to predict movements of prices that are very difficult to predict. Having said that, your experience is one of the best assets you have and you only develop it through actual trading. You can test using old data all you like, but when you actually start trading you learn things that you never thought of before. If you start from scratch every time something goes wrong, you aren't using your experience to the fullest because you're going down entirely different paths again and again.

You need to keep modifying your trading plan, strategies and methodology – making fine adjustments and moving closer and closer to the ideal method for you. (We discuss developing your trading plan in Chapter 16.)

Forgetting to monitor what you already have

A common problem for traders is focusing too much energy on finding the next trade and less on monitoring what they have already. New trades are exciting and full of potential, but remember that your prime determinant of profit isn't your entry but your exit. You need to spend more time thinking about the optimal exit strategy for what you already have instead of thinking about what you might do next, because the positions that you already have represent genuine capital at risk: potential new trades don't. We discuss managing your existing trades in Chapter 17.

Keeping your own counsel

You need to learn to trust your own judgement and trading plan and be wary of other people's advice. One of the most damaging things to your self-esteem is hearing how well someone else is trading when you're having a bad run of it. It doesn't cost other people anything to tell you how wildly successful they are with their trading, but it could cost you plenty. People can tell you they haven't had a losing trade in a year. You may think, 'Wow! I haven't done anywhere near that well.' But maybe they haven't closed any paper losses and are deluding themselves, or maybe they're flat-out lying to you (and themselves, we might add). We advise you to wish them well and get back to your own planning. You should feel lucky if you get one or two people in your life with whom you can talk shop and believe that what they're telling you is a pretty close version to reality.

Closing out too early

When a position has moved in your favour for a good period of time you'll probably start feeling edgy and want to close out. But you only want to get out when your trading plan tells you that it's time to, not just because the profit is burning a hole in your pocket.

If you get out too early, you might regret your decision when the price rallies higher. This will happen, in the same way that sometimes you'll get stopped out on a trade only to see it rally. Have a look at the average true range indicator in Chapter 13 for more help with dealing with this problem. You can't blame anyone in these circumstances; it's just one of those things.

Your trading diary (see Chapter 17) can be really useful for tracking whether you're getting out of positions too early on a regular basis. If you can see that this happens regularly, you can then make a modification to your trading strategy.

Don't drive yourself nuts over making mistakes like closing out too early, though, because annoying things like this will happen all the time over the course of your trading career. Remember that sometimes the market goes in your favour too, so don't chop and change your methods all the time to try to catch lucky moves.

Asking Yourself Whether Working at Home Is for You

One of the best (and scariest) aspects of trading is that you don't need anyone's permission and you can approach your trading in any way you like. How much you trade and whether you do well or not is up to you.

A lot of advertisements for trading courses and the like push the idea that people can give up their day job and trade full time. You know, telling the boss to shove it and getting out of bed late and then spending your days in a bathrobe. But do you really want to give up the social aspects of your job to sit by yourself in front of a computer screen all day?

You may need to make some shifts in your wider life in order to adapt too. Although you may not have thought of it, going to work each day provides you with a large amount of social interaction. If you trade from home, you have no clients and no co-workers to keep you company. You may not think this sounds like a big deal, but it's probably worth thinking about how you can replace this interaction in another way, rather than trying to cut yourself off from the world altogether.

If your mind is not properly focused on your trading strategy, you may be tempted to trade for amusement rather than follow your carefully formulated trading plan (see Chapter 16). You could trade 24 hours a day with your broker, but you need to be disciplined and stick to your trading plan, otherwise you aren't trading, you're gambling – without even the spectacle of the horse racing to amuse you.

We suggest you keep your full-time job and trade part time, especially when you're first starting out. Imagine the extra mental pressure that you put on yourself if you have to earn a living from trading alone; each trade you make will help to determine the sustainability of your newly chosen profession. However, if your regular pay cheque is still rolling in then you're under less pressure to perform.

Perhaps further down the track you can consider full-time trading if you have a long history of consistent profitability and your job is actually interfering with your ability to go to the next level.

Fighting the Fear of Losing

Fear is something that you'd probably like to remove entirely from your emotional repertoire, but you do need it. Fear reminds you to stick to your trading plan: Manage the downside, keep your positions small and employ stop losses on your trades.

One of the negative aspects of fear is hesitating to make a trade when the opportunity arises, but this is a relatively minor problem. The biggest problem is when the fear of losing allows you to deem a losing trade to be acceptable because there's a chance that it will come good at some stage in the future.

Some traders, though, may have a very good reason to be afraid of losing – if you're carrying positions that are too large for you based on your available capital then you might be risking all or more of your capital in a single trade, which is very dangerous. This type of behaviour may arise as you become emboldened after a string of winning trades – but what you aren't considering is the fact that one loss on a highly leveraged trade can be your undoing. Good risk-management strategies should help you avoid terminal losses even in the worst of circumstances, and they can help remove a lot of the fear element from trading and let you take a big step towards success. See Chapter 8 for more on managing risk. With a lot of the fear removed, the whole decision-making process becomes more clinical and objective and your trading more enjoyable.

Accept the fact that you're going to lose sometimes and fight against the fear of losing. When the position has moved outside the parameters of your trading rules then you have to give it the chop, rather than finding ways to justify holding on to it a little while longer.

Remove the expression *paper loss* from your vocabulary. This term refers to a position that you hold that's worth less than you bought it for but that may come back to profit. This is just a way of thinking that everything will be okay if you just hang on long enough. Be clear in your own mind about what the risk is before you place the trade.

A sure sign that you're feeling the fear too much is sitting and staring all day at the trading screen. We call this the 'intra-day stares'. You feel that if you keep a very close eye on the market then nothing bad can happen. The opposite is in fact the case, because the more you stare at the market, the more you can convince yourself that the market is at its top or at its bottom, or that you have to sell out because it's as high as it can go. The fearful side of your personality whispers lies in your ear. Be clear on your plan and be sure to stick to it.

Every trade that you take is a risk, and no matter how clever you are, you aren't going to know the outcome before you place the trade. Giving in to fear and getting stressed while carrying the position isn't going to help you. The best you can do is to follow your risk-management rules. Ask yourself:

- Is my position size based on an appropriate amount of risk for my capital?
- Do I know where my stop loss will go?
- Am I sure that the position fits my entry criteria?

If you can answer yes to all these questions then you are as in control of the trading process as it is possible to be. The market will rise and fall, but not because you hope that it will. See Chapter 16 for more on developing your trading plan.

You'll overcome your fear when you grow comfortable with your method and when the actual process of trading becomes quite mundane because you're simply following the rules you've set for yourself. Over time you may have a success rate of little better (or indeed worse) than 50 per cent, but as long as your average win is bigger than your average loss, you're still doing okay.

Chapter 16

Developing a Trading Plan

In This Chapter

- Looking at a trading plan's key components
- Understanding why a trading plan will help you
- Knowing how you want to trade and how to set goals
- Testing your trading plan
- Keeping your risk levels down

Some people say that 'failing to plan is planning to fail'. Nobody plans to fail, but many people don't put nearly as much work into their trading plan as they should.

Financial spread betting offers you a vast world of trading opportunity. However, without a trading plan you subject yourself to not understanding what you're doing right and what you're doing wrong. Your trading plan helps you to better understand yourself as a trader.

In this chapter, we show you why time spent on planning is never wasted. Answering some simple questions about your motives goes a long way in determining what you want from your trading, which you can then incorporate into your plan. Whether your goal is to generate extra income for yourself or to trade full time, you can craft this into your trading plan. When you put your plan into practice, you can then start to fine-tune it because real-world experience helps you better understand the world of spread betting.

Putting First Things First

In order to take full advantage of the flexibility of spread betting and to create a trading plan that works, you need to be able to answer these questions:

- **What type of markets are you going to trade?** This may include domestic share and index bets with a small portion of foreign exchange. Or you may focus your energy on international shares and commodities.
- **What time frame are you interested in?** This can be anything from intra-day trading through to trading over several weeks (medium-term trading) or months (longer-term trading). No best answer exists, but whichever time frame you choose requires a specific skill-set. Remember that the shorter the time frame, the more time you need to dedicate to watching the market.
- **What set of conditions will you use to determine when you enter and exit a position?** For example, you can choose to wait for a specific technical analysis formation to help you best time when to open and close your trades.
- **How much are you planning to risk on each trade you make?** You only want to risk a small percentage of your overall capital. A good rule is to never risk more than 2 per cent of your capital on any trade.

These are the key components that make up a trading plan. If you can't answer each question then you're leaving the world of trading and getting results that might as well be generated by the flip of a coin. You need to know how you'll respond to a range of market conditions and not leave outcomes to chance.

To make a success of your trading you need to keep moving your capital into positions that are moving in your favour, and quickly dispense with those that are moving against you. Your strategy and the market conditions determine how long you hold positions.

Getting Started

When you start developing your trading plan, you need to sit down with a piece of paper and decide how you're going to approach the situation. Write down the reasons you want to trade as well so you're clear on what you want to achieve.

The key thing you want to work on initially is deciding how you plan to enter the trade and, in particular, the way in which you plan to exit the trade.

When we talk about exiting a trade, we mean quitting a trade after making either a profit or a small loss. We've heard people say (when talking about a losing trade) that they get out when they feel the position has moved far enough against them. This type of behaviour isn't based on a plan. This reaction is simply following gut feeling, and it won't help you become more consistent with your approach to trading.

When you know where you want to get into a trade and where you'll want to get out, you can then work out your position sizing very easily (for a rundown on position sizing, refer to Chapter 9).

Evaluating an example plan

In order to better understand what your plan should look like, you need to be able to define the key characteristics, such as time frame, entry and exit rules, and your risk management methods.

Dave is a medium-term trader aiming for a holding period of between two and three weeks and he likes to follow trends. He's a conservative trader, so if he's carrying more than 3× leverage (the amount of money borrowed from his broker is more than three times his own cash risked), he takes a new trade only when he's moved the stop loss on the previous trade to break-even value or higher, or it has closed out at a small loss. Here's the outline of Dave's trading plan:

> I'm going to bet on shares on the opening of trade after the five-day simple moving average crosses the 30-day simple moving average. I will confirm the strength of the trend with an average directional index indicator. This indicator measures the strength of a trend on a scale between 0 and a 100; if the reading is between 0 and 25 there is no clear trend and the share is trading in a narrow range. I will look for a minimum threshold value of 30. I will risk 2 per cent of my trading capital. I will close out my position when the share price falls below the 20-day moving average, or trades below its lowest value in the last five days. I will place my stop loss with my broker. If I'm carrying more than 3× leverage on my account, I will not take on any new positions until I've closed another one out.

In this example of a trading plan you can see that Dave isn't taking any new positions until the stop orders on his old positions are at break-even or better, or until the previous position is closed out for a small loss. This is a good idea because it helps prevent Dave from making 'boredom' trades, which can occur when your portfolio hasn't done much in a little while. Also, this strategy ensures you're preserving your capital as best you can, and not adding losing position after losing position to your trading portfolio. (We describe all the technical indicators we mention here in much greater detail in Chapter 13. See Chapter 8 for more on keeping leverage under control.) By using this method, you generally won't have more than one losing position at a time.

These points are important and answer the major questions we list in the section 'Putting First Things First', earlier in this chapter, and that you as a trader need to ask yourself when determining your trading plan. In the example, Dave knows exactly when he'll enter and exit his trades, and he's kept his risk nice and conservative. You want to do the same with the trading plan you develop.

Understanding why you need a trading plan

A trading plan separates average traders from great traders. That's because those with a trading plan know where they're going and those without one, don't. (In Chapter 15 we provide some helpful guidance on understanding some of the mental challenges that trading places upon you.)

The main reason you need to trade with a plan that you follow to the letter is so that you can easily work out what you're doing wrong. Don't believe that the first trading plan you come up with is going to be completely successful and remain unchanged over the course of your trading career. You'll need to fine-tune your plan over time and consider doing so to be part of the process (we show you how in 'Fine-Tuning Your Trading Plan', later in this chapter). When you get into trouble is when you trade without a plan, because then you have no way of knowing what you're doing right – or wrong.

When you become interested in trading, you're inundated with different possibilities. These possibilities include using methods such as:

- Trading price breakouts
- Using oscillators and moving average crossovers
- Trading based on company and market-related news

You can find these terms in Chapters 10 and 13, which relate to fundamental and technical analysis.

These are just a few of the different methods people use to trade – none of the methods are right or wrong, but you're spoiled for choice, that's for sure. The trouble starts when you try to take the sampler option, and have a bit of a go at all of them. The problem with doing this is that sometimes you'll win and sometimes you'll lose; because you've chosen methods largely at random, you won't know whether a win was good management or good luck. The best traders are consistent with their methods and also consistently profitable. This is what is required if traders want to make a living from their trading or indeed make a worthwhile improvement to their incomes.

To see how charting software works (see Chapter 14, which contains a section on software selection), you can take different indicators and use them over different time frames, simply by changing their calculation values. We suggest that you spend time in front of your charts and try out the different functions that are available. After you see how long the different values will keep you in trades, and how much you'll need to risk, you have a much better idea of the methods that suit you.

Keeping things in check

How many indicators should you use? Well, hundreds of different technical analysis indicators are available, but don't try to use them all. Start with two or three and become comfortable with them. Adding more doesn't always increase your chances of success, but it does make your life more complicated. We like the envelope analogy: if you can't fit it all on the back of an envelope, it's too complex!

What you always need to keep in mind is that creating the plan is relatively easy, but *sticking to it* takes an incredible amount of discipline. There is always a temptation when trading in a live market to ignore your trading plan, but it rarely ends well.

Looking at Your Individual Needs

We mention throughout this book that there's no ideal way to spread bet, but whichever way you choose must suit you. Regardless of your requirements, even making small amounts of extra regular income can make a huge difference to your overall financial position over a long period of time.

One of the best places to put extra income is into your mortgage. You may not think that an extra £100 a week would make a lot of difference, but if you put this amount on a mortgage that charges 8 per cent per annum over ten years, it adds up to almost £80,000. So don't believe that small amounts of income won't help your financial position.

Working out what you want from your trading

The scale of reward that you hope to generate from your trading guides the amount of effort that you need to put into developing your trading plan. For example, if you're looking to generate some extra income then you need a trading plan that allows you to review your trading portfolio less regularly than people who get all their income from their trading. This also means that you need to aim to hold positions for a longer duration to help keep the time commitment down (Chapter 13 contains a guide to short- and long-term trading methods).

When you begin trading, we suggest that you start with trend following. You can look at several different markets, including share-based spread bets (both domestic and international), and even foreign exchange and commodities if you have a higher risk tolerance and you're interested in day trading. To track these higher risk products, you want to focus on daily and weekly price charts, and indicators like the Relative Strength Index (RSI) and moving averages, which you may find helpful (see Chapters 13 and 14 for more information on trend following, price charts and indicators).

Don't fall into the trap of thinking that the faster you turn your portfolio over, the more money you make. Trend following involves holding your positions for a longer period of time, but the rewards can also be significantly greater, so be sure not to disregard a method just because it doesn't sound exciting. In addition, even though spread betting is usually commission free, the hidden drag of the spread you pay with each trade still adds up if you're turning your portfolio over frequently.

The person who makes the most frequent trades is the *day trader*. Day traders open and close all their positions on the same day, which means they carry no overnight exposure. If day trading is something you have time for then you need to focus your energy on products that have high degrees of volume and volatility. A real favourite in this area is foreign exchange (which has the greatest volume of any market). You can also consider share spread bets and commodities (though the big markets of the United States are probably the best for this, so you may need to be prepared for some evening trading). With day trading, you focus more of your analysis towards the hourly, 30-minute and even 5-minute charts. Also, in most cases you start to add indicators to better time your trades (for more information on these indicators, see Chapter 13).

If you're planning to trade full time then look at a minimum of a three-year time frame in order to build up your skills and experience. When you're starting out, work on methods that fit in with your current career path, rather than ones that try to replace it.

The advantage of part-time trading is that you don't face additional pressure due to trading being your sole source of income. We believe that you only need to consider going full time if your current job is hindering your trading from moving up to the next level. See Chapter 15 for more on deciding whether trading part time or full time suits you best.

Taking trend following to its heights

One of the world's foremost traders and an advocate of trend following is Ed Seykota. He was also a pioneer of computerised trading in the 1970s. Some people may consider trend following to be dull, but Seykota has been able to grow his wealth to such an extent using trend following that he's been able to pursue other passions in life, which have extended to things such as challenging generally accepted concepts in science. Although trend following certainly isn't for everyone, we believe Seykota's success highlights what the real attraction in trading should be – being able to achieve your own goals.

You don't want to consider any type of trading a hobby or something that you do for a bit of fun, because the effort and time commitment required and the potential financial risk are too great for that to be an effective way of dealing with your trading. You're making a serious commitment, so you need to be looking for some decent reward.

Nearly all spread betting firms allow you to place stop orders so that your position can be closed out automatically after a price target is reached. This means that you don't have to sit and stare at the computer screen all day. The only people who need to do this are very active intra-day traders.

Setting realistic goals

In the preceding section we state how important it is to consider trading a money-making exercise and not a hobby, but the question remains: how much should you be aiming to make?

Some people are very *goal-oriented* and need to have a specific target that they're always aiming towards. Others are more *absolute* (or unrestricted) in their nature and are simply looking to take the fullest advantage of whatever opportunities come their way. Your 'style' is a very personal decision and something that you can only determine for yourself.

If you're aiming towards a specific income target, such as £1,000 a month of income, you'll have times when you can't achieve this because no trading opportunities are available to you. When you've made your trading plan you only make a trade when it satisfies your rules, otherwise you have to sit on the sidelines. You need to follow your rules rather than make your target.

One of the most common spread betting markets people deal in is share-based bets, which are spread bets that follow the price of listed companies. With share bets, your absolute minimum return (that you'll be targeting as a return in a one-year period) is to match the return of the underlying share index. In the UK, the main index is the FTSE 100. This is your minimum because it's a return that you could achieve with no effort on your part whatsoever (by dealing in an index fund). By buying a FTSE index tracker, you can generate the same performance as the index, so if those returns are enough for you then index trackers like ETFs (Exchange Traded Funds) are where you want to put your money. Then you don't have to lift a finger. Ironically, some firms allow you to spread bet on ETF prices, with the additional benefit of leverage.

An *index fund* is a managed investment that attempts to replicate the returns of an underlying index, such as the S&P 500 in the United States and the FTSE 100 in the UK. These index funds are attractive to investors because they have relatively low management fees, low capital gains tax (due to low holding turnover) and long-term growth potential. Probably the best known funds manager in this category is Vanguard.

Trading with spread bets enables you to far exceed the returns that are generated by the index, but you need to remember that the more leverage you apply, the more risk you're taking to achieve these returns. (For more information on managing risk when employing leverage in your trading strategy, refer to Chapters 1 and 8.)

The other big question that you need to ask yourself when setting goals relates to what time frame you plan to trade over. Traders employ methods that can see them holding spread bet positions anywhere from a few minutes to more than a year, although it starts to get expensive to hold positions for more than a month. We provide more information on some of the methods traders use in Chapter 11, but here it's important to understand the broad issues related to trading using different time frames.

For example, the idea of very short-term trading is often attractive to people as they embark on their trading journey. This isn't surprising, because the idea of opening a position in the morning and closing it in the afternoon for a nice profit is very appealing. But remember, this type of trading is the most difficult to master, because you're relying on relatively small moves in your favour from the market in order to capture a winning trade, so your losing trades on average have to be smaller still.

Although *trending movements* (followed in trend trading, covered in Chapter 13) take longer to unfold, they can be very profitable for you. Trend trading requires you to absorb more market volatility, but it also means that you save money on commissions. If a position is running in your favour, you should take full advantage of it – let the market do the work for you.

In your first year of serious spread betting, a reasonable goal would be to break even. We know that this sounds less exciting than making a fortune, but you need to be realistic. If you keep yourself steady, you'll gain a lot of experience and you won't lose any of your precious capital, which will make your next year of trading a lot easier.

If you want to set a profit target for yourself, you can get started with something moderate, like £100 per week. Depending on your account size, this may be more or less than the index rate of return, but it's a nice round figure to work with. This doesn't mean, though, that you should stop trading for the week once you've made your weekly target, because you always want to do the best that you can over any given period of time.

Another goal that we particularly like is to avoid experiencing losing months. This means not putting a target on your profits, but simply aiming to do the best that you can.

Avoid making daily goals for yourself. Some days the market isn't going to move in your favour at all, which means that you have no chance of making your target. Subsequently, you have added pressure the next day to earn even bigger returns simply to catch up.

A lot of traders find that the vast majority of their profits come from a small percentage of their trades (say 90 per cent of profits from 10 per cent of trades). You might want to aim for an annual profit target instead. This way you can allow for a lot of ups and downs in your trading, but still focus on coming out ahead in the end and being consistent in the medium to long term.

Using your individual needs to create your trading plan

In the financial markets, the level of risk that a person is able to tolerate is frequently attached to her age and the number of years left until retirement. Younger people are seen as more able to tolerate risk because they have more working years ahead of them to recover any losses they make. This is reasonable to an extent when looking at spread bets; however, because the average time frame of investment in spread bets is usually quite small, the time factor is less relevant. In any case, the amount of your total assets that you expose to spread bets should be only a small percentage – for example, less than 5 per cent.

A trading plan helps to further reduce your exposure to risk. But remember that you need to stick to it.

Time factors and amounts invested aside, your trading plan needs to help you determine *your* individual level of risk. Most new traders put all their focus on the upside, and put little or no focus on what happens when things go the wrong way. Make sure you know when you'll exit a trade if it doesn't move in your favour. You should also know how much it will cost you to exit the trade at a loss. Remember that any losing trade should cost you only a small percentage of your total capital.

Most position sizing methodologies (see Chapter 9) require you to know the placement of your stop loss in order to properly work out the position size. Determining your stops this way also ensures that you focus on controlling losses at a time when you have no money at risk (that is, before the opening trade is executed), so you're likely to be at your most sensible and rational.

For more information on managing your individual needs, see 'Balancing Risks with Your Goals', later in this chapter.

Fine-Tuning Your Trading Plan

As you begin your spread betting journey you're likely to find that your plan needs to change. This is normal, but generally you want to keep changes minor and not make frequent overhauls.

Effective ways of taking a detailed look at your trading methodologies can help you fine-tune your trading plan. In the following section we outline two of the most useful methods, which are backtesting and paper trading.

The major difference between backtesting and paper trading is that backtesting looks at the past, while you do paper trading in real time – so it's forward looking.

Backtesting

Backtesting is a means of making a very deep analysis of a trading strategy by looking at each and every trade that a set of trading rules would have made, based on past data, and then looking at the outcomes it would have generated. Backtesting tests a strategy in a comprehensive manner by considering not only how profitable the strategy would have been, but also its rate of wins and losses and other information, like the longest string of winning and losing trades.

Non-discretionary or system traders use this type of method very heavily. Backtesting, though it sounds rather simple, also involves dealing with a unique set of emotional challenges. As a wise academic once said, 'When it comes to finance, if you think you have found a risk-free trade, you have done something wrong.'

Whether you backtest on paper or on computer, the process requires you to spend vast amounts of time looking at historical data and considering ways that you can exploit the information to your advantage. The data that you generate from your backtesting allows you to probe your trading plan for weaknesses.

After you've completed your backtesting, don't be put off if your first trading plan fails to be profitable. Discovering this early is always better because you don't have any capital riding on the outcome. You should be relieved that you found out when you did that you were heading down the wrong path.

You judge trading by one thing – your profitability. Backtesting is a great way to test a trading methodology; however, it won't help you improve your methods if you can't be completely honest and thorough in your testing, so you must record all the profits as well as the losses.

These days, you do backtesting primarily on a computer and doing so generates large amounts of data.

Paper trading

The most common first step that any trader or investor takes when she gets involved with the markets is to undertake *paper trading*. This simply involves determining what positions you 'would' have bought and then monitoring their progress on paper, checking to see whether your strategy would have been a successful one.

To make the most of your paper trading, the main thing you need to do is be honest with yourself (just as you need to be when backtesting, which we describe in the preceding section). If you look back on a losing paper trade and then come up with a reason you wouldn't have taken it, you're ruining a potentially valuable lesson about your method. A good rule to follow is this: if you have more than 80 per cent winning trades on paper then you're not properly monitoring your methods, because this would be unlikely in real-life trading.

Paper trading is usually the final step you take before putting a trading plan into action with real capital on the line. You're simply following your method in real time to test the outcomes. It's very important to have clearly defined your method already and then follow it to the letter. By doing this you can highlight some of the negative and positive aspects in your plan that you may not have thought of otherwise.

Either on paper or in a spreadsheet, keep a list of all the positions that you would have taken had you been following your plan. Don't forget to include all spreads and financing charges, because these can make a big difference to your bottom line, particularly if you're trading frequently (most broker platforms include the spread cost in your profit and loss anyway). You need to monitor this list for several weeks or more to get an accurate assessment of how your plan is behaving.

After you complete the test phase you can then digest the data that you've recorded. Ask yourself questions about the size of the losses of your test trading, and the number of losses you record in a row. Consider these points:

- Are you comfortable with these losses?
- Could you make changes to minimise these losses?
- Are you letting your profits run to a reasonable level?
- Could you change your stop loss levels?
- Are your commissions taking up a huge percentage of profits? If so, would you be better off with a plan that gives you trade signals less often?

When you answer these questions honestly and you're happy with the results, you can proceed knowing that you've given yourself the best chance at a successful start to your spread betting. Although it's very tempting to simply 'have a go', without paper trading (or backtesting), rushing right in only sours the experience that you could have in spread betting.

Paper trading, when done diligently, provides an illustration of how a set of trading rules might behave in real time. The process is informative if you carry it out honestly and accurately. However, paper trading isn't a means of building prowess as a trader and it's in no way a replacement for real-life trading experience.

Balancing Risks with Your Goals

If you've read the rest of this chapter, it should be plain to you by now that no matter how you approach your spread betting, you're in for a lot of work. The main thing to remember is that you need to focus your energies first and foremost on keeping your risk level low. This means that whatever your trading plan, it should feature small position sizes and the continuous use of stop losses. Chapter 8 goes into detail on managing risk when you're spread betting.

No matter what you do, you're going to make a lot of trades that are losers. This doesn't mean you can't be profitable, but you won't make any money at all if the size of the losses on average begins to outweigh the gains. Having losing trades is just part and parcel of the business that you're getting involved in, and the real difference between a winning trader and a losing trader is how you deal with these losses.

We've seen a number of trader surveys in our time, and one thing we find most unnerving is the number of traders who say that their trading strategy is based on gut feeling. If you wonder why people seem to have difficulty trading then this factor is a likely reason.

Begin your endeavour by trying to find a combination that signals when a trend is in existence and then when the trend is beginning to break down. In the early stages, focus your energy on the daily and even the weekly chart. These time frames determine the dominant direction of the price movement.

Even if you plan to trade over a very short time frame, know the direction of this dominant trending movement and plan to trade only in the direction of this prevailing trend.

Chapter 17

Tracking Your Progress

In This Chapter

- Managing existing trades – time well spent
- Staying focused on making a profit
- Keeping records of your trades

If you don't plan your journey, how will you know when you've arrived? People in trading circles often ask this question, and for you it means that if you don't keep track of your trading, you can't measure your success (or failure!).

In this chapter, we discuss how spending time watching the trades you already have is wiser than becoming obsessed with finding the next trade. You need to stay focused on what you have and make sure that you're making money; here, we show you how to set financial goals and measure your profits.

Keeping good records of your trades can give you a much better understanding of your own performance – and not just the pounds and pence. Making daily notes can be tedious and dreary, but doing so gives you an insight into your performance in the market. You can start to look at things like your trading behaviour, your win–loss ratio and the value of your winning and losing trades. We cover what to include in daily entries in your trading diary, how to analyse the data and then how to act on it.

Monitoring Your Existing Trades

Managing the trades you hold is an important part of tracking your progress. As you become more experienced with your own trading behaviour you'll start to know how many positions you can manage.

If you're dealing in share-based spread bets and not trading full time then you can likely manage eight to ten positions (and probably less) at any one time.

You might think you can manage more, and maybe you can, but remember that for each position you have you need to monitor the charts, amend the stops regularly and exit the position when required. Spread bets are not a set-and-forget investment, so you need to set aside plenty of time to monitor your positions.

In Chapter 14 we look at different ways that software can assist you with managing trades. The more automated your methods become, the more positions you can carry. The ability to automate your trading, though, comes with trust in your method, and you can only build trust over time and with experience.

Try to spend as much time monitoring your trades as you do finding new ones (for more information on monitoring, see Chapters 13 and 14). Every day you need to decide whether you want to keep a particular position or replace it with something else. Follow your trading rules carefully because you need to keep your portfolio moving forward as best you can.

If you don't keep a close eye on your positions, leaving them in your trading portfolio but outside of your direct focus, you can very easily end up in a position where you take a significant loss on a trade that could have been avoided with some active monitoring on your part. Don't let the first thing you hear about it be your broker demanding more money as part of a *margin call* (a request to deposit more money to support a losing trade).

When you're building your trading plan, you may want to consider the idea of a *time stop*, which is put in place to get rid of positions that aren't going down but aren't going up either. Even if a position isn't falling, it's tying up precious capital, so you're better off replacing it with something that's got some wind in its sails. And even if a trade isn't losing value, you opened it because you thought it was going to move higher in value, so it's not doing what you thought it would.

Relying on a trading robot

In the trading world, and particularly in foreign exchange, there's growing interest in 'robot' software. This software scans the market using set criteria, opening and closing positions automatically based on rules that have been programmed into it in advance.

We don't know many people who could tolerate giving over control of their trading to a piece of software, but this would be the ultimate test of confidence in your method.

Perhaps you could add this to your list of things to do when setting a trading method: 'I must have enough confidence in my rules that I would let a robot trade for me.'

Measuring Your Financial Success

You need to keep tabs on whether you're making a profit trading, because basically if you're not making money, there's no point trading – you can find lots more fun things to spend your time and money on! You need to focus on measuring your success simply in monetary terms.

Determining how much profit you want to make trading, and focusing on achieving that goal, ensures you're not drifting on the trading sea without a rudder. Setting realistic goals to achieve in a certain time frame helps you keep track of your trading progress. A good way to establish financial goals is to follow the **SMART** rules. Goals need to be:

- **Specific:** Establish a goal that you can clearly define. You might decide that your goal is to become a full-time trader. You could also say that you plan to design a foreign exchange trading strategy that you expect to win on 60 per cent of trades that you make.
- **Measurable:** Make your goals measurable. 'I want to get rich trading' isn't a measurable goal. Here's a measurable goal: 'My goal is to make £200 a week from my spread betting.'
- **Attainable:** As in the previous example, a goal of £200 per week will likely work for most people if they put together a reasonable plan and have a decent capital base. To become a millionaire in your first year with starting capital of £1,000 is on the low end of the attainable scale.
- **Realistic:** Set a realistic goal, like £100 profit per month, and then ratchet things up from there. Avoid setting a goal of £1 million in your first year (although we seem to remember Martin Schwartz making his first million in his second year . . .). Just try to be profitable at first and go from there.
- **Timely:** Set a deadline for when you want to achieve your goals.

Remember to keep adjusting and adapting your goals as you gain confidence and experience in trading. You can set progressively higher goals for yourself when you have your methods and trading plan down pat.

If you're trading index or foreign exchange markets, you may want to set goals in terms of point movements; for example, 50 points a day. The amount of money that you make is just a multiple of the number of points you make times the size of the position you take. If you have a small trading account it may be £50 a day on average (50 points @ £1 per point, although some brokers offer smaller amounts per point if you're truly risk averse) or it could be £500 or more. So you can see that the pounds you make are only a multiple of how many points you can make.

Focusing on the bottom line

The reason behind your trading must be to make money; you must be in it to win it. If you're looking for an interesting hobby or pastime, you should probably go with model building or stamp collecting because at least they won't gobble up your money and leave you with nothing.

If you're lucky enough to find trading a mentally challenging activity, that's fantastic because it will make the arduous and tedious times more rewarding. But finding the whole trading business exciting can be dangerous. You may want to keep reliving the heady excitement and adrenaline of that first successful trade, which was a trip into the unknown. The way you conquer this urge is by following a carefully constructed and tested trading plan (Chapter 16 shows you how). Step outside of the rules of your plan and you're back in the realms of chance.

As boring as it sounds, you'll experience the best outcomes when each trade is as dull and unexciting as the last, because if you get to this stage you know that, win or lose, you're sticking to your plan and managing the trade as best you can.

Keeping a Trading Diary

Keeping a trading diary sounds simple but it can be difficult to keep up – you may need to exercise some good, old-fashioned discipline to maintain it. You need to write down all your potential trades, your actual trades, any thoughts that you have about the market at that point in time and the decisions you made. Do this every day so that you have a record of the thought process behind each trade you've taken as well as the profit and loss.

You can then go back and check on the decisions that you've made. You may find regular recordings of 'placed my stop order too close' or 'too quick to take profits' – if so, you can take steps to modify your trading plan (refer to Chapter 16). Traders can talk at length about their best trade and their worst trade, but probably not in much detail about the vast majority that lie somewhere in between the two.

Filling in your trading diary is hard to do for an extended period of time, especially if you're doing badly. When the market is moving consistently in your favour it's a great pleasure to write the fine details of your success and reflect on what a brilliant trader you are – you could do this for years on end. But you deserve a huge pat on the back if you can write in your diary every day for a week after ten losing trades in a row and still record the events in vivid detail.

Table 17-1 shows a basic template for what your trading diary may include. You can put whatever you like in your own diary, but be sure that the contents are relevant. Every month go through and see whether there are things that are consistently going right and consistently going wrong – then do more of the former and less of the latter.

Table 17-1 A basic trading diary

Date	Code	Entry	Stop Loss	Exit	Units	PL £	PL %	Reason
17/5/12	Company A	457	442	531	1200	888.00	16.19%	The share price broke resistance at 450, which confirmed an ascending triangle formation. The trade was held and closed out as soon as the projected profit target of 531 was reached. I risked £0.15 and made £0.74, giving me a risk–reward ratio of just under 1:5, which I am very happy with.
18/5/12	Company B	610	580	580	1000	–300	–4.9%	This was an inverse head and shoulders trade that I had followed for a while waiting for the correct set-up. Unfortunately, it didn't continue higher after the breakout and was quickly stopped out.
21/5/12	Company C	998	953		250			I have entered this trade based on a breakout from a rectangle. It is quite a wide range, which means I have a large stop loss placement and a small position size.

You need to account for all the costs of financial spread to make it profitable and to give you an accurate picture of exactly where you stand. You also need to be able to extract certain details from your recorded data:

- **Profit and loss:** You can use a spreadsheet to calculate this simply by working out the start value (entry price × £ per point staked) and deducting it from the exit value (exit price × £ per point staked). You make only a small modification to turn this into a percentage calculation.
- **Financing charges:** You can calculate these by using your broker's formula for financing and applying this to your spreadsheet.

Making the most of spreadsheets

You *can* keep handwritten records, but in this section we focus on using your computer and how you can increase its functionality in regards to your trading. We don't want to limit your flexibility by giving you specific formulas to use in your spreadsheets. In the help section of modern spreadsheet software you find examples of all you ever need for a trading diary, so if you aren't familiar with spreadsheets then make this your first stop.

Using a spreadsheet is the best way to record your trading data because you can use formulas to automate commissions, monitor financing, calculate win–loss ratio averages on days a position is held, track your accounting costs and easily work out your average profit and loss. You may need to invest in a book to help you. For Microsoft Excel, we recommend *Excel 2010 For Dummies* by Greg Harvey (Wiley).

Set up your file so that it includes all the entries that we specify earlier in the chapter in 'Keeping a Trading Diary', then record away. Yes, you still need to manually enter all the details of trades, but think about the upside of doing this – you're forced to keep thinking about the open positions you have at any given point in time, which is good because losing sight of leveraged positions is financial Russian roulette.

Microsoft Excel makes life easier because with one press of a button you can activate a formula list. Here you can search for what you need to do and then you either just plug in the numbers or, better yet, refer the formula to the cells that contain individual details of your trades, such as the number of pounds per point and entry price, which you use in your calculation. Use these formulas to:

- **Count winners and losers.** To do this, create a formula that looks for whether the profit and loss is positive or negative and returns a 1 or a 0 (or, indeed, a blank cell if you like) depending on what you're looking for. Then all you need to do is count the results up to find out what your winning and losing trades are.

- **Keep track of the financing (the account costs of spread betting).** You can create your own formula or you can choose to add the charge each day from your broker's daily statement. This latter option takes more time, but at least you're always on the same page as your provider. Check your broker's terms and conditions for how they calculate their financing so that you can replicate their formula.
- **Note where you placed your initial stop losses.** Then you can work out your average return for each pound that you risk, known as *expectancy*, which is useful for working out how strong your trading is. Seeing at a glance where your stop losses are helps ensure that you're getting out when you planned to, and if you aren't, you need to work out why.
- **Total the profit and loss for all your positions in a gross and net form.** This way you can see what the effect of costs is on your overall profitability, and find out your average profit, average loss and your win–loss ratio.

If you don't have Microsoft Excel, you can always download Open Office, which includes a very respectable spreadsheet program that contains most of the same functions as Excel. You can also buy Excel-based spreadsheet software designed specifically for use with spread bets; have a hunt around on the Internet to see what you can find. Just make sure you don't end up using a sports spread betting template by mistake!

Using off-the-shelf software

Even though spread bets are relatively new in the financial world, savvy programmers have already developed record-keeping software that can calculate all the things that you can do in a spreadsheet in a much simpler to use and pleasing-to-the-eye set-up. These programs are either custom made for spread bets or have functions to help with them. You may also find that some brokers provide you with this facility. Proprietary spread betting platforms are becoming increasingly friendly in this respect, making it much easier to keep track of the total cost of your trading.

Before buying a program, make sure the software works out your financing and commissions for you and that it provides a statistical breakdown of your trading activity. You don't want something that's designed for share investors and has been lightly modified to adapt to spread betting, so don't be afraid to email the provider of the software and ask questions. Also, make sure that the software firm keeps it up to date – the best financial software remains in continual development to reflect changes in the user base and the market it serves.

This software is really good for beginners because it sets you up in the right frame of mind for recording and analysing the trades that you make. We strongly suggest, though, that you spend no more than £200 on spread betting-specific software and that you search for the program that best suits your needs.

Like any software, it should be easy to use and come with good instructions as well as some form of support if you need it. The program itself should work out things like number of winners and losers, average gain and loss, and total gain and loss, and it should also help you determine where you're doing well and where you're doing poorly so you know what you need to work on. In the end, there isn't much that software like this can do that a diligent Excel user can't, but it comes down to what you prefer and what you are willing to spend.

Keep in mind that simply spending big money on record-keeping software won't do the work for you. You still need to be disciplined and spend a lot of time looking at how you trade; only that way will you understand your strengths and weaknesses as a trader.

Part VI

The Part of Tens

the
part of
tens

For Dummies can help you get started with a huge range of subjects. Visit www.dummies.com to learn more and do more with *For Dummies*.

In this part . . .

- Avoid ten common spread-betting pitfalls.
- Learn ten lessons for dealing with the risks and rewards of leverage.
- Pick up ten top tips for planning your trades effectively.
- Go to `www.dummies.com/extras/fsbuk` for online bonus content.

Chapter 18

Ten Common Mistakes Beginners Make When Spread Betting

In This Chapter

- Underestimating the power of leverage
- Failing to make proper plans
- Taking your eye off the market

In this chapter, we look at some of the most common issues that people fail to fully comprehend when spread betting. One of the recurring problems is the way in which most people approach the problem of trading and then add fuel to the fire with leverage. Many of the major issues people have when trading relate to a lack of contingency planning for unforeseen events. When you're dealing with a leveraged product like spread bets you need to focus a lot of your energy on working out how you'll deal with negative outcomes as they arise. You must be prepared with a solution if a problem arises.

Being Unfamiliar with the Product

Being unfamiliar with spread betting can cause problems when trading. Spread bets are powerful and highly leveraged trading instruments. They have the ability to let retail traders get closer to running their own hedge fund. Spread bets allow you to access the markets of the world from a single trading platform, and allow this access very cheaply in terms of your commission, which is very low compared to dealing in products such as shares. Spread bets also enable you to lose more than your initial investment, which is your margin payment. You can also lose more money than you have in your account, which means you have to come up with the rest.

Pay close attention to the terms and conditions of your financial spread betting account. Although all spread bets work the same in principle, the management of leverage and trades by each broker differs from firm to firm. Terms and conditions establish the rules of the game with a particular broker, covering how the broker prices bets and extends and manages leverage.

Being Careless When Executing Trades

All spread betting providers have differing software through which you execute your trades. The software may even let you deal with only a single click of the mouse, which means that you can deal quickly but also increases your opportunities to make a mistake. For this reason, we suggest that you act like a stockbroker and read your order back to yourself before you execute it. It's worth an extra few seconds.

We've heard stories of kids in the house jumping onto a live dealing platform and having a costly play around. You're still responsible for the trade even if you didn't mean to make it, so be sure to lock the computer when you're away from it.

At some stage you're likely to make a trade in error – going long when you meant to go short, buying too many or selling too many. We suggest that when you trade in error, you close out the position and start again. You still need to pay the spread on the trade, but you shouldn't be thinking about the spread at this stage – you didn't want this trade and didn't mean to be in it, so why would you stick with it?

Forgetting about Outstanding Orders

When you place a stop order or a limit order (both of which are often referred to as *pending orders*) over a position you have open, that order may remain in place even if you close the position that you put it over in the first place. This means that if the price subsequently falls or rises to that order level, you're left with a new position that you didn't want. Regularly check outstanding orders and be sure that you don't have any in place that you no longer want. Repeat this procedure whenever you manually close out a position.

Opening a Position without a Stop Order

Sure, you want to be right all the time, but the reality is that you won't be – and this is especially true when it comes to trading. You should know in advance of opening a position when you're going to get out of a position. One of the best ways to be sure that you get out of a position is by placing a stop order with your broker. This means that as soon as the price where you know you're wrong is reached, the position is closed out straightaway. It's better to be wrong and preserve the vast majority of your capital than to be wrong and lose a lot more money.

Never move stop orders away from the direction you want the position to move in; that is, if you're long, stops only go up, and if you're short, stops only go down. A stop is worth something only if you allow it to be executed, because cancelling and leaving the position open means you're flying totally blind.

Trading Too Often

You can trade all you like, but be sure that you're trading because your plan says to do so, not just for entertainment value. Every trade costs money in spreads. Keep costs to a minimum because they're another impediment between you and profitable trading.

On this same note, people often feel that the more often they trade, the more money they can make. We think that, realistically, trying to capture trending moves of decent size is more profitable because your costs are kept significantly lower.

Failing to Keep an Eye on the Market

Spread bets are by no means a set-and-forget product. By spread betting you are making a huge commitment in time and effort because you need to regularly watch the performance of your positions. Using stop losses can go a long way to reducing the requirement to watch the market like a hawk, but you need to be mindful of movements that are occurring all the time. We're talking here much more about defending the downside and not so much about cashing in on the upside.

The advent of mobile trading apps for phones and tablets means it's now much easier to keep tabs on live trades than it used to be. Most of the leading brokers now offer mobile trading for no extra cost.

Don't let a winning trade turn into a losing trade. When you've managed to make some good gains in the market don't give them back because you're not spending enough time watching the market.

Trying to Be Too Big Too Fast

Lots of people prefer to know how they're performing compared to others and whether they're doing well. Should you be trading bigger sizes?

Just being profitable is something that should please you. You may hear about someone making £10,000 on a single trade and think that you'd like to do the same. However, keep in mind that for a person to make a large profit she must also be willing to risk several thousand pounds in the same time frame.

Nothing in the market is going to be given to you easily. There's always a risk-and-reward trade-off, so unless you're willing to risk thousands in a day then you aren't likely to make thousands in a day. Don't believe that someone else is applying some sort of risk-free method to the market, because such a method doesn't exist.

Be very careful who you accept counsel from when it comes to trading. Keep away from most public discussions on the market because you'll end up feeling that you should be doing something differently, better or not at all, which doesn't help you with your trading.

Failing to Preserve Your Capital

However you approach the market, you need to be very focused on keeping as much of your capital intact as you can. Always remember how many hours have to go into earning £1,000 and you'll be less likely to risk the money lightly. Of course, you can't make money trading without risking some of your money, but this doesn't mean you want to give your money away through carelessness.

Also, remember not to add to losing positions. It can be tempting to add to positions that have fallen in value so that you can get a lower overall average entry price. This is called *averaging down*, or even worse, *doubling up*. Averaging down puts you in a position where you're risking more capital on a position that's done the opposite to what you'd anticipated. Averaging down is a dangerous strategy and encourages a dangerous mindset because it can empty your account very quickly. Save the capital for adding to positions that are moving in your favour.

Confusing Paper Trading with Real Trading

Most people do some paper trading before they start to trade for real. Interestingly enough, nearly everyone does very well as a paper trader because almost everything that's difficult about trading disappears when you're dealing only on paper. You can also conveniently leave out whatever results you don't like the look of.

When you trade for real all the challenges come back into the equation, making things a lot more difficult. Paper trading can be very effective for final testing of a carefully constructed strategy, but it isn't a substitute for actual trading experience.

Blaming Someone Else for Risky Trades Gone Bad

When you lose money on a trade (and you will) there's a great temptation to try to push the blame onto another party rather than look inward for responsibility. Sometimes the market moves against you just enough that you're stopped out (you hit your stop loss) and then it goes back the other way. A lot of people want to blame their provider, but this type of market movement is one of those annoying things that happen. We suggest that for your own self-development you look to yourself for responsibility before pointing the finger at someone else.

By the same token, having a losing trade doesn't mean you should feel bad. You'll have lots of losing trades. You can't win all the time, so don't crush yourself with self-criticism every time you have a loss.

On rare occasions, your broker may quote you a bad price and this can hopefully be rectified with a call to your broker. The broker can resolve problems for you the fastest, so make the broker your first stop if something does go wrong. Program the number for your broker's dealing desk into your phone, and be sure you know your account number and any passwords that you need to deal.

Chapter 19

Ten Lessons for Dealing with Leverage

In This Chapter

- Calculating what is a reasonable amount of leverage
- Controlling leverage when you can't control margins
- Keeping enough breathing room in your trading accounts

In this chapter, we look at one of the aspects of spread betting that people find most attractive – the leverage inherent in the bet itself. We suspect that people feel that if they take on really big positions then they need only a tiny move in their favour to make a decent profit. The opposite is also the case, of course – it takes only a tiny move in the wrong direction to lose money – but it's human nature to gloss over the bad when you want to focus purely on the good.

This dynamic makes for an interesting combination, where traders are excited by the most dangerous aspect of the product that they're dealing with. It means that you must work to control appropriately the amount of leverage that you use to remain in control of your overall trading outcomes.

Leverage Doesn't Have to Mean Massive Positions

Using leverage doesn't always have to mean you take on huge positions with a view to ultra-short-term profits in the market. Traders can employ diversification in order to get more diverse exposure than they might otherwise have been able to. For example, a trader could choose to take the £10,000 he has in his trading account to take on a £30,000 position, or he could build up six

£5,000 positions that he believes are going to trend quite consistently over the next month or so.

Diversification is generally seen as the focus of long-term investors, but only taking exposure to one or two positions may be dangerous because the outcomes you have on a day-to-day basis are very heavily focused on a narrow end of the market. Although you don't want to take on dozens of positions, a decent spread of positions may help to smooth your equity curve. Multiple positions will, of course, mean that you have sufficient money with your spread betting firm to support them.

Just Because You Can Doesn't Mean You Should

Different spread betting providers offer different margin requirements on their bets. Providers that offer the most liquidity generally have the lowest margin requirements, which may be as low as 1 per cent (or even lower in some cases). Based on a margin requirement of 1 per cent you could turn £10,000 into £1 million worth of position if you wanted. If you did, however, a very small move in price would immediately put you in a position where you'd receive a margin call from your broker.

The key is that nothing's stopping you from doing a trade like this, even though the trade makes no sense from a risk-management point of view.

Keep the Leverage Conservative

Even though you won't generally be able to nominate how much margin you pay, you can control the amount of leverage that you employ. For example, if you had £30,000 worth of share-based spread bet exposure and the margin requirement was 5 per cent then you would need to provide £1,500 in margin. If you had £10,000 in your account, you have levered this by three times (3×). If you had fully levered up the position, you could have gone to £200,000 or 20× leverage.

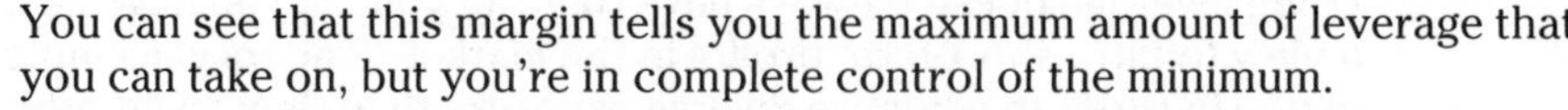

You can see that this margin tells you the maximum amount of leverage that you can take on, but you're in complete control of the minimum.

A 3× leverage is pretty reasonable as a conservative maximum for most people, so try putting a self-imposed cap of a similar amount on your trading.

Different Spread Bets Suit Different Leverage

When you're dealing in share spread bets the spread betting firm places a higher margin on them than it would for a foreign exchange (FX) bet. A big part of the reason for this is because you need more exposure to FX to make US$1 per tick (a tick is just another way of referring to the smallest increment movement of price, often referred to as points in spread betting circles) than you do with share-based bets (where your exposure differs from share to share). In FX, minimum trade sizes tend to be larger because you generally need a high level of leverage to capitalise on changes in the currency markets.

Keep in mind that the amount of margin required gives you an indicator of the risk of gaps in the market. A gap in the share market is common because the market is closed overnight, and prices adjust for news releases that have occurred while the market is closed. In the 24-hour FX markets, gaps are less common and are likely to be of a smaller magnitude.

Bear in mind that not all markets are created equal. A pound a point on shares and FX isn't the same thing, because FX pairs can move quite a lot further in a given session than shares. You may think £5 per point isn't too bad on shares; however, it may prove to be more than you bargained for with FX.

Your exposure to markets also differs due to the way spread bets are priced: even though you may be staking £1 per point on Natural Gas and the UK 100 (FTSE), a 10 per cent move on the latter involves considerably more profit or loss than in Natural Gas. You're betting on how many points that particular market will move before your bet expires – a market at 1.970 and a market at 6700.7 are radically different propositions when spread betting.

Pay attention to how many ticks or points the price moves in a market you intend to trade, because this gives you a good idea of how much leverage you should be using.

Let Your Account Have Plenty of Room to Breathe

The more leverage you use, the less room you have for the market to move against you before you receive a margin call. If you use only conservative leverage, you may go your entire financial spread betting career without ever receiving a margin call, which is something to aspire to because it shows a sensible approach to your leverage management.

If you spend too much time thinking about the profits a high level of leverage can bring, you will ignore the fact that it also reduces the number of times you can be wrong on a trade, as your losses will be bigger too.

Know What You Stand to Lose

Calculating the likely downsides of trading precisely may be difficult, but you can make some good estimations for a day-to-day basis. If you have a decent spread of share bets, you may feel that if a big slide took place in the United States overnight, you could be in for a fall of 5 per cent, which would mean a loss of your entire margin if the share bets require a 5 per cent payment. The difficulty is working out what effect a crash like the stock market crash after September 11 is going to have, and how concerned about it you should be. Clearly, a fall of 20 per cent is going to be very costly to anyone holding long share spread bet exposure, but happily this is a very rare event.

If you're leveraged to only a low level then you can withstand a major fall in the market you are trading. Alternatively, a trader who's very highly leveraged may be totally wiped out. A crash similar to the one after September 11 may be a rare event; however, you only need to be wiped out once.

Simultaneous Long and Short Trades Can Minimise Damage

You may find that carrying long and short exposure in the same market (particularly share bets) reduces your risk at any given point in time. This may mean that in a sharp downturn, losses on the long side are offset (to some extent) by gains on the short side.

Carrying long and short exposure can be very effective in the event of a sudden widely distributed fall in the market. However, a sudden fall in the market won't happen every day, so you need to pick your short positions as carefully as you do your long positions and not just carry short exposure as an attempt at insurance.

A Close Stop Doesn't Make Over-Leveraging All Right

A lot of position-sizing methodologies let you take on a bigger position the closer that your stop loss is to the market. The temptation for traders is to place their stops really close so that they can have a much bigger position for the same apparent amount of risk.

The big downside occurs if a big gap in the market happens, so your stops are gapped over, leaving you with a much bigger risk than you calculated. There isn't a safe way to leverage in an extremely heavy way, so use smaller sizes and focus on the defence of capital.

Even Small Amounts of Leverage Make a Big Difference

If you could make 15 per cent per annum trading shares without leverage (which would be very good) then simply by doubling your exposure to the market using spread bets you're miles ahead of where you'd have been otherwise, with only a small use of leverage. Keep this in mind before you implement a strategy that sees you taking out vast amounts of leverage.

Leverage Your Returns and Your Volatility Too

Returns are increased directly by leverage and so too is volatility. When you look at your expected performance, don't just think about where you would like to be in one year. Instead try to think about what the journey is going to be like.

Making a positive return is one thing, but you must be prepared for dealing with the negative trading sessions and the drawdowns that your trading account faces. The more leverage you apply, the bigger the peaks and troughs, so try to prepare yourself as much as you can. The more you trade, however, the easier the peaks and troughs are to cope with.

Chapter 20

Ten Ways to Plan Your Trades

In This Chapter

- Knowing that planning makes all the difference
- Coping better with changing market conditions
- Improving your skills over time

In this chapter, we look at some of the major advantages that arise from putting extra effort into planning your trading in as much detail as you can. Some eventualities may not be immediately obvious; but it pays to cover as many eventualities as possible in your plan.

You can't predict the outcome when you trade, so you need to build in risk management procedures. Keeping good records helps you to remember the details of trades and fine tune your plan. You can't be right all the time, so devise a strategy that keeps your risk low and minimises damage to your portfolio from losing trades.

Spend Time Building Your Strategy

If you're building a technical analysis strategy then really no substitute exists for looking at lots and lots of charts to determine what works for you. If you're looking at something fundamental you need to master the relevant formulas and analytical methods and/or secure relevant research for your analysis. You can find any number of trading strategies out there to use and a lot of them are very good. The weakness isn't necessarily in the strategy but in the trader using the strategy. You can't shortcut the process of deciding what works for you by opening an account and grabbing another person's strategy.

You can test different strategies for nothing by being diligent with your work with the charts. If charts are your primary means of selecting and managing positions then you need to be sure how the trades you take are likely to behave when you open positions for real.

You need to undertake comprehensive testing to get a good idea of how likely your trades are to be successful, a likely win–loss ratio and reasonable estimates of likely drawdowns that you'll face on your capital. When you get underway you need to give your strategy time to work. Throwing your strategy away if the first two trades don't make money isn't sensible, because you haven't made a proper assessment of the strategy you've employed. So you need to stick with the strategy. As you find problems you can fine-tune them, but don't undertake massive overhauls to your plan on the fly because doing so wastes a lot of the testing that you've done.

Write Down Your Plan

We speculate that for every trader who writes down her plan, ten or more traders don't. Your trading plan doesn't need to be complex at all. In fact, we've heard a very sensible recommendation that your written plan should fit on the back of a coaster.

Your trading plan should specifically deal with your reason for buying and selling and how much you plan to risk on each trade. A plan is only as good as the following two things:

- The plan's profitability
- The trader's ability to follow the plan

Be Explicit in Your Plan

If you're explicit in your planning, you can comfortably respond in a range of market conditions. Of greatest concern is a large and sudden move in the market, when you must be able to respond quickly. Can you hold on or are you going to sell out? Will you be left in a bigger losing position than you originally anticipated? You must be able to answer these questions and respond to all market conditions so you can act quickly in times of uncertainty.

Don't put yourself in the position of knowing that you need to do something but then doing nothing.

Record Your Results

You can refine your planning in even more detail by being diligent with your records of winning and losing trades. Don't try to forget about your losing trades, because they can point you towards problems you're having with your planning. One of the worst things you can do is become frustrated and do the 'trading plan tear down and rebuild' routine.

Unless you've cobbled your plan together, parts of it are sure to be correct. Throwing away your plan is a waste of the effort you put into it. No plan is going to be right straight away, so keep refining.

Psychology forms a huge part of a trader's success or failure. When you modify your plan, be sure that the plan is at fault, not you.

Know Your Stop Loss, So You Know Your Risk

All traders want to think about how profitable a trade may be, but you can't do so at the expense of not properly managing your risk. Before you open any trades you should know exactly where you're going to get out if the trade doesn't go the way that you hoped it would. If you can't say exactly where you're going to get out then you haven't managed your risk. Not managing your risk is one of the worst things you can do, because you're not properly defending your capital.

Planning an exit at a small loss is one thing, but for some people executing the exit can be quite another.

Stop losses should only move in the direction of the trade, not away from it. Moving away from the direction of the trade increases your risk.

Be True to Your Plan

If we ask, 'Is it better to follow your plan and lose money, or ignore your plan and make money?', what is your answer? Answering 'Yes' to the second part of the question is tempting because everyone enjoys a profit; however, this is the wrong answer – but you guessed that already! If you ignore your plan then you may as well not even have one.

One of the hardest times for traders is when they're having a profitable trade and decide that they want to cash it in, even though their plan says to let the trade keep running. They run the risk of leaving a winning trade that could go on to make them even more money. You can convince yourself of anything if you want – all you need to do is recall the adage that 'you can't go broke making a profit' and you're set. Stick with your plan, even when you're tempted not to.

An exception here is not to follow your plan until you have no money left. You may want to put a 'circuit breaker' in your plan where you stop trading and reassess your plan. A good rule is this: when you've lost a certain amount of capital (for example, 15 per cent), you stop trading and work out whether to modify your plan or scrap it and go back to the drawing board.

Test All New Set-Ups

One of the negative impacts on traders is the law of small numbers. People see a small sample size and make an assessment based only on that sample. In trading circles this may mean that you look at a couple of similar set-ups on some charts that look successful and decide that these set-ups are worth trading in the future.

Remember that just because the sample worked once or twice, statistical probability isn't necessarily in your favour. You need to test rigorously every new set-up you consider, otherwise all you're doing is gambling.

Don't Spend All Your Time on Your Entry Plan

One thing that gives people a feel-good experience is opening a trade and having it run quickly in their favour. This is about as close to instant gratification as trading is likely to get. Remember, you only get to keep the profits you've made when you close the trade. Don't just focus on the first part of the trade; focus on the part that dictates how the trade will end. You need to have a very clear plan about the conditions that will trigger an exit from your trade at either a profit or a loss.

Include Targets as Part of Your Plan

Some people are very keen on setting goals for themselves, which is a useful way to improve how you monitor your progress. We recommend setting SMART goals that are Specific, Measurable, Attainable, Realistic and Timely (see Chapter 17 for more on SMART goals). If you can fit your goals into all these categories, you have a good set of targets to work towards. New trading opportunities come along every day, so you don't need to move too far too fast.

Include targets as part of your plan so that you keep modifying your strategy to deliver better results.

Include Market Entry Requirements As Part of Your Plan

Your spread betting provider probably offers thousands of markets for you to trade. Do you want to trade them all? Few people have that much capital to play with and those who do know trading thousands of markets isn't an effective use of their capital.

Your trading plan acts as a market filter so that you focus on looking for a very specific market set-up and ignore anything that's not an opportunity to trade. A detailed trading plan makes sorting market opportunities from market noise easier.

Appendix A

Glossary

2 per cent rule: A risk management technique in which traders vary the size of each new position so that it won't lose more than 2 per cent of their trading capital assuming the ***stop loss order*** they place at the same time they enter a trade is triggered. This technique doesn't guarantee that no loss will be greater than 2 per cent of your trading capital because in some cases ***slippage*** occurs on a stop loss order.

ascending triangle: A chart pattern in which you can draw a horizontal ***trend line*** across peaks of at least two separate trends and you can draw an upward sloping (or ascending) trend line across at least two separate troughs in those trends. The two trend lines thus form the shape of a triangle. A common trading strategy involves entering new positions in the direction of a breakout of the triangle pattern.

average true range (ATR) indicator: A widely used technical analysis tool that's designed to indicate the level of price volatility in a market over a given time. Often a trader uses the ATR to set a trailing ***stop loss order*** after he enters a position.

backtesting: The process of testing the profitability of a trading strategy against Ahistorical price data or charts. Usually, you need at least 30 to 100 past examples before you can regard the test results as statistically significant.

beta: A statistical measure of how volatile an individual security has been compared to the whole market or to an index over a given period. The market's beta is defined as being 1. So a stock with a beta of 0.8 has been 20 per cent less volatile than the market and a stock with a beta of 1.2 has been 20 per cent more volatile.

binary bet: A spread bet based on whether something will happen in the market rather than the change in price. Thus, a typical bet might pay out if an index crossed a specific level before the end of the trading day, or stayed inside a specified trading range. Binary bets also have limited downside – you know how much you will win or lose when you open the bet. Not all brokers offer binary trading.

breakout traders: Traders who use ***breakout trading*** strategies.

breakout trading: Trading strategies based on entering trades after price breaks through a defined ***resistance*** or ***support*** level. A trader enters new ***long*** positions on a break through resistance and new ***short*** positions on a break through support. The strategies are based on the view that after price breaks through support or resistance, a new trend is likely to be established.

cable: common term used to describe the GBP/USD currency pair, ittakes its name from the transatlantic telegraph cable originally used to transmit currency prices between New York and London.

capital: The wealth (whether monetary or in assets) owned by an individual or company.

carry trade: An investment strategy that involves temporarily selling or borrowing an asset with low yields in order to buy a higher yielding asset. The investor is attempting to make a positive return (or 'carry') holding the higher yielding asset compared to the return on holding the lower yielding asset or compared to the cost of borrowing that asset. However, in this type of trade you're exposed to the risk that the market value of the high yielding asset that you now own will fall compared to that of the low yielding asset that you have to repurchase in the future. Traders have made large-scale carry trades in currency markets in recent years – for example, borrowing Japanese yen to invest in Australian debt securities.

charting: A range of techniques that use charts of past prices and other indicators to anticipate future price movements.

close out: Selling a ***long*** position or buying a ***short*** position so that you no longer have any exposure to changes in market price.

commodity: Physical goods that market participants exchanges without any quality differentiation and for which a general market price is established – for example, a pound of copper or a bushel of wheat. This differs to the price of a house, for example, which is likely to be unique and based on individual factors such as location.

commodity spread bets: Spread bets in which the underlying instrument is a *commodity*.

commodity currency: The second currency quoted in a foreign exchange pair. A foreign exchange pair price depicts how many units of the commodity currency you need to buy or sell a single unit of the first currency quoted in the pair. (Confusingly, another common usage of 'commodity currency' exists. In this sense the term refers to the currency of a nation that derives a large amount of its export revenue from ***commodities***. Fluctuations in commodity prices can heavily influence the value of these currencies. The Australian and Canadian dollars and the South African rand are the best known examples.)

compound interest: Where interest is simply reinvested into the underyling capital. The added interest therefore also itself earns interest.

consumer confidence index: An index based on a survey of consumers that asks a number of standard questions, such as whether they expect their financial position to improve or deteriorate over the next year and whether they think now is a good time to purchase major consumer items. Analysts collate the results of the survey into a single index number designed to reflect overall consumer confidence. Consumer confidence indices are widely used to predict future changes in consumer spending.

Consumer Price Index (CPI): A measure of the quarterly changes in the prices of a 'basket' of goods and services commonly purchased by metropolitan wage and salary earners. CPI is the most common method of measuring the rate of price ***inflation***.

contracts for difference (CFDs): An agreement between a buyer and seller that allows them to make a profit or loss due to fluctuations in the price of an underlying instrument such as a share, index, ***commodity*** or ***currency pair.*** If the price of the underlying asset rises between the time an investor opens a CFD and the time it closes, the seller must pay the difference in value to the buyer. If the price falls, the buyer must pay the difference to the seller. CFDs are widely used outside the UK as an alternative to spread bets. They can be traded if you live in the UK, but unlike spread bets, they are subject to UK tax.

core inflation: A measure of ***inflation*** that excludes items that are subject to volatile price movements – for example, vegetable prices, which fluctuate widely based on seasonal conditions.

countertrend trading: The practice of trading in the direction of 'corrections' or 'countertrends'. These are minor trends in the opposite direction to the longer-term trend. They're typically smaller and last a shorter time than minor trends in the same direction as the longer-term trend. Many trading strategies therefore seek to avoid following countertrends because they're often considered poor risk–reward opportunities.

coupon: The periodic interest payments governments make to holders of bonds. Prior to the days of electronic registration, bond owners would tear a coupon off the bond each six months and present it at an agent of the central bank to receive their interest payment.

cross rate: An exchange rate between two currencies other than the US dollar.

crossover method: See ***moving average crossover***.

currency pair: A price quotation of the relative value of one currency in terms of another.

data releases: The release of economic statistics, usually by a government body such as the UK Office for National Statistics. Releases are typically made at regular dates on the basis of a predetermined schedule.

debt to assets ratio: Total liabilities divided by total assets. This ratio shows the proportion of a company's assets that are funded by debt as opposed to equity.

debt to equity ratio: The amount of a company's debt divided by the amount of its shareholders' equity. This is a measure of a company's leverage. A high ratio implies greater risk and may make it difficult for the company to meet interest payments in the event of a downturn in earnings or an increase in interest rates.

delta: The ratio of change in the price of a derivative compared to the change in price of an underlying asset, such as a share. Where a derivative has a delta of 0.5, a £1 change in the share price causes the derivative price to change by £0.50.

demo account: A spread betting account with no money in it, used by traders who want to test trades without risking any capital, or learn how a new spread betting platform works.

deposit requirement: The minimum amount of money a trader needs to hold in his spread betting account to fund his open trades. Some companies will also require a minimum amount is help on deposit before a trader can place any bets at all.

diversification: To vary an investment or a trading portfolio so as to limit exposure to any single instrument. For example, investors may allocate the entire portfolio across a range of different asset classes such as shares, spread bets, property, fixed interest and cash. Within each of these classes, assets may also be varied. For example, an investor may allocate a share portfolio across a range of industry sectors.

earnings per share (EPS): A ratio determined by dividing a company's after-tax profit by the number of ordinary shares it has issued.

economic clock: A diagram in the form of a clock that depicts what is likely to be happening to the prices of various assets (such as shares, property and interest rates) at different stages of the economic cycle as the economy moves between periods of contraction and growth in output.

economic drivers: Changes in the economy that lead to changes in the market price of investments such as shares, commodities or property.

economics: A discipline that studies the production, distribution and consumption of goods and services in human society.

ex-dividend date: The first trading day on which the buyer of a share is no longer entitled to payment of the current dividend.

exiting: See ***close out***.

exposure: Refers to a situation where you have a current or open position. This means you're financially exposed to the consequences of a change in price of the instrument you have open. The larger the size of the position, the greater the exposure to the possibility of financial gain or to the risk of financial loss.

financial ratio: A measure of the relative size of two items in a company's accounts – for example, its debt and equity. Securities analysts and investors use financial ratios to compare different companies, to assess changes in a company over time and to assess companies against a standard benchmark for risk.

fiscal policy: A government's financial policy covering the amount it earns (for example, through taxation), spends, borrows and invests. Fiscal policy impacts on the overall level of economic activity. Where a government runs a deficit (spends more than it earns) it's putting more into the economy than it takes out and so adding to ***Gross Domestic Product***.

fiscal surplus: A surplus of government income over expenditure in a given period. A fiscal surplus has the effect of reducing the overall level of ***Gross Domestic Product*** because the government is taking more out of the economy than it's putting in.

fixed price model: An approach to risk management where a trader calculates the size of every position a trader enters so that if the ***stop loss order*** is triggered the resulting loss will equal the same pound value.

fixed percentage model: A risk management technique such as the ***2 per cent rule*** in which traders vary the size of each new position so that it won't lose more than a fixed percentage of their trading capital if their ***stop loss order*** is triggered.

foreign exchange spread bets: ***Spread bets*** where the underlying instrument is a ***currency pair.***

fundamental analysis: Analysing and valuing financial assets based on factors such as financial statements and earnings forecasts, company strategy and risk assessment, demand and supply forecasts, projections of future economic growth, industry developments and government policy.

Goldilocks economy: An economy that's able to sustain reasonable levels of economic growth without creating too much inflation (that is, it's 'not too hot and not too cold'). In the late 1990s and early 2000s many developed economies had sustained Goldilocks periods where they were able to achieve relatively high growth rates with little inflationary pressure due to the large amounts of excess capacity (that is, unemployed people) created by the severe recession of the late 1980s and early 1990s.

Gross Domestic Product (GDP): The total final value of goods and services produced by a country's economy in a given period of time (usually a year or a quarter).

hedge funds: An investment fund that's open only to high-net-worth or professional investors and has a large minimum investment requirement (for example, $1 million). These requirements mean that the funds are exempt from much of the regulation applying to retail investment funds and they often have very flexible investment mandates allowing them to hold both ***long*** and ***short*** positions, to invest or trade in a wide range of financial assets and to use considerable leverage.

hedged exposure: Where a trader opens a position in one instrument that's opposite to his exposure in another instrument – for example, you may open a ***short*** position in 1,000 BP share spread bets to hedge a ***long*** position of 1,000 BP shares. Any loss of value resulting from a fall in the price of BP shares is then offset or hedged by a profit on the short spread betting position.

highest high value (HHV): The high of any chart candle or bar that's the highest of all the highs in a given period covering multiple candles or bars. For example, each candle in a one-minute chart shows the price high and low in a one-minute period. Over a given 20 periods, the highest high value will be the high of that one-minute candle that's greater than or equal to the other 19 candles.

hyper-inflation: Very high inflation that's out of control. When hyper-inflation is present, the purchasing power of money falls rapidly and large losses result from holding money assets such as cash or debt securities for any length of time.

if done: Conditional spread betting order that only comes into force if another order takes place. It allows the trader to program a level of automation into his trades for the day.

index spread bets: *Spread bets* where the underlying instrument is an index reflecting changes in the value of a group of shares – for example, the largest 200 shares listed on the FTSE.

index fund: A fund that invests in the assets underlying an index (for example, the shares in a share index or the commodities in a commodity index). Each individual investment is weighted so that the performance of the index fund tracks the performance of the index itself. These funds allow an investor to obtain a return equivalent to the overall market and claim to do better in the long term than many managers who seek to beat the market through active asset selection techniques.

index stripping: A trading strategy that involves buying an index spread bet and selling certain ***sector contracts*** or ***share spread bets*** within the index. This is a strategy to use if you believe that an overall index will rise but that certain sectors or stocks within the index will underperform. If you're correct, index stripping will improve the result of a long position in the index.

inflation: An increase in the money value of goods and services over time.

inflation rate: A measure of the extent of ***inflation*** that occurs in a given period – for example, a year or calendar quarter.

initial margin: The amount of cash or other approved collateral a trader is required to have with a spread betting broker in order to open a new position.

interest rate differential: The difference in yield between similar interest-bearing assets or benchmark interest rates in different currencies – for example, the difference between the US Federal Funds rate and the Bank of England's rate.

intra-day trading: Trading where positions are opened and then ***closed out*** within the same trading day.

leverage: The use of debt to partly fund the acquisition of an asset. This has the effect of amplifying profit or loss as a percentage of the trader's equity.

limit-move rules: Rules used by some international futures exchanges that place a limit on the maximum price movement in a market between one day and the next. Where a market is up by more than the limit, no trading will generally occur that day because no traders are prepared to sell under what is regarded as fair value. Typically, no trading occurs until enough daily limits have passed so that trading can occur at the new fair value. The purpose of limits is to create a market breather, avoid panic and allow brokers to call margins in fast-moving markets. However, they can create a new set of problems by preventing people getting out of positions.

limit order: instruction to your spread betting broker to close your trade once a particular price is reached.

liquidity: A gauge of how readily you can make transactions in a market. One of the main measures of liquidity is how long it takes to complete larger transactions.

listed companies: Companies whose shares are available to be traded on regulated exchanges such as the London Stock Exchange (LSE). To be listed companies need to comply with listing rules – for example, reporting standards and minimum size requirements.

longer-term trading: In the context of spread betting longer-term trading refers to strategies where the average duration of open positions would be between a few days and several months.

long trading: Where the initial transaction is to buy and the position makes a profit if price rises but a loss if it falls.

lowest low value (LLV): The low of any chart candle or bar that's the lowest of all the lows in a given period covering multiple candles or bars. For example, each candle in a one-minute chart shows the price high and low in a one-minute period. Over a given 20 periods the lowest low value will be the low of that one-minute candle that's less than or equal to the other 19 candles.

margin: The amount of cash or approved collateral you need to open and then hold a spread bet position or futures contract. You need an ***initial margin*** to open a new position and after that you must meet any losses as they arise in the form of ***variation margin***.

marked-to-market: Revaluing something at market values. In the case of derivatives such as spread bets, the buyer and the seller then make cash payments, representing profits and losses resulting from any changes in value of the underlying instrument.

market capitalisation: The total market value of all shares of a company listed on the stock market, found by multiplying the number of shares on issue by the current market price.

market neutral: A market neutral investment strategy attempts to carry no exposure to changes in the value of the overall market. For example, you may be long in some shares and short in other shares so that theoretically if the whole market goes up or down by 5 per cent you'll have no profit or loss. The strategy is attempting to make money only through the stocks held in long positions doing better than those held in short positions, or vice versa.

medium-term trading: In the context of spread betting this refers to strategies where the trader is prepared to hold positions open for longer than one day but where the average duration of positions would be no more than a few days.

monetary policy: Policies carried out by central banks to set interest rates and control the amount of money in an economy with the aim of keeping inflation and unemployment at acceptable levels.

moving average: A mathematical technique designed to provide an indication of the overall trend in prices by smoothing out short-term fluctuations in price. In a simple moving average, the charting software calculates the average of closing prices over a certain trading period – for example, 20 days or 20 minutes. After trading for a new day or minute finishes, the program drops out the first closing price from the previous average and adds in the closing price for the last day or minute. If the new bit of data is higher than the one dropped out, the average goes up; if it's lower, the average goes down.

moving average crossover: When a shorter-term ***moving average*** crosses through a longer-term one. A cross from above to below indicates a change from uptrend to downtrend. A cross from below to above indicates a change from downtrend to uptrend.

net tangible assets (NTA): Tangible assets are generally a company's physical assets, such as land, buildings and machinery. Intangible assets consist of the value attributed to certain non-physical assets, such as customer goodwill or patents. Net tangible assets refers to the value of all a company's tangible assets less the amount of debt it owes. It gives a view of what may be left over for shareholders if a company is wound up and its assets sold and debt repaid. You exclude intangible assets because they often have no value if the company isn't operating as a viable entity.

noise: Small price moves that turn out to be only minor oscillations and can confuse a trader about the overall price trend.

non-advisory product: A financial product where the provider of the product doesn't provide advice on whether it's a suitable investment for a customer or on whether this is an appropriate time to buy or sell. For example, a spread betting broker may offer the service of a platform you can use to buy or sell spread bets but not provide any advice about whether now is a good time to buy or sell a particular spread bet.

option: A contract which gives the owner the right to buy or sell an underlying asset at a price agreed in advance and at a specific time. It is called an option because the buyer doesn't have to use that right.**order:** An instruction given by a client to buy or sell spread bets. The order stipulates the quantity to be bought or sold and instructions about the price or timing of execution.

oscillating indicators: Mathematical indicators designed to provide insight into whether a market has become overbought or oversold. These are situations where markets are regarded as being more than normally vulnerable to a price reversal because price has moved a relatively long way in a short time or because a trend has been in existence for a long time without correction. The indicators oscillate within a band of values – for example, 0 to 100, or above and below a centre or zero line.

pairs trading: A spread betting transaction in which a trader buys one instrument and simultaneously sells a similar one. For example, you might buy HSBC bank share spread bets and sell Barclays share spread bets. In this example, you're seeking to profit from a change in the price relationship between the two particular banks rather than from an overall movement in bank shares.

paper loss: A loss that has yet to be realised. For example, you have a paper loss where you've bought shares that have since fallen in value but you yet sold the shares. Your statement of assets shows a lower value on paper but this is restored if the shares rise again. The loss isn't realised until you actually sell the shares for less cash than you initially paid.

paper trading: Simulated trading where traders record where they would have bought or sold. This can be a useful way of assessing the likely profitability of a trading strategy before actually committing risk capital to it. You can also use paper trading to practise the mechanics of trading and get a feel for placing orders or what you'd be likely to do after you enter a trade and the price moves.

parabolic stop and reverse (PSAR): A technical indicator designed to show market trends and higher probability points for changes in market momentum. The indicator uses an acceleration factor that often gives it a parabolic shape on a chart. Traders often use it to set ***stop loss orders*** that trail behind a price trend.

pattern recognition: A form of analysis that involves recognising patterns such as ***ascending triangles*** and ***rectangles*** formed by bars or candles on a price chart. Common trading strategies are often based on the assumption that a breakout of these patterns indicates the likely start of a new trend.

pip: The smallest amount by which a foreign exchange quote can vary – for example, .0001 GBP:USD. The name comes from 'price interest point'.

point: The smallest increment a price will move; used as the basis for a spread betting stake. Hence, at £1 per point, you will make / lose a pound for every point the price moves.

portfolio: A collection of investment assets such as shares, spread bets, fixed interest, property and cash.

position sizing: A risk management technique whereby an investor calculates the size of each new trading position so that the maximum likely loss on the trade doesn't exceed a certain amount or a certain percentage of the investor's trading capital. Examples include the ***2 per cent rule*** and the ***fixed dollar model***.

post-market auction: A facility under which traders can submit bids and offers for shares for a limited time after the close of ordinary trading on a stock market. Where the market maker receives bids that are equal to or higher than the lowest offer price, a single weighted average price is established. This becomes the official closing price. The market maker then executes any bids at or above this price and any offers at or below this price at the official closing price.

pre-market auction: A facility similar to the ***post-market auction*** where the market maker(s) establishes an official opening price from bids and offers placed prior to the opening of the stock market.

price–earnings ratio: A ratio calculated by dividing the market price of a share by the company's earnings per share. This is a widely used method of measuring a company's value. It has the advantage of allowing more meaningful comparisons of similar companies or of a single company's valuation over time. For example, knowing that Bank A has a market valuation of 12 times its earnings but investors are only paying 11 times earnings for Bank B makes more sense than comparing the basic share prices of, say, £27.50 with £24.25.

pricing in: A market price (for example, a share price) should, theoretically, reflect the market's assessment of all the known factors that may affect its valuation, including projected future earnings and likely risks. When a factor like a potential law change affecting a company's earnings is 'priced in', it means that an investor considers that the share price already fully reflects the potential change.

pyramiding: This is a staking strategy whereby traders add to the size of their position as price moves in their favour. The strategy aims to increase returns from profitable trades. Traders manage the increased risk by ensuring that any new positions they add are always smaller than the previous one. This means the first position at the base is the largest and the final one added is the smallest – hence the name.

rectangle: A chart formation in which you can draw a horizontal line across two or more trend peaks and across two or more trend troughs.

requote: Spread betting platforms indicate a bid price at which clients can sell and an offer price at which they can buy. A requote occurs when a client tries to buy or sell at the indicated price but the provider doesn't execute the order and instead quotes a new price. The most likely reasons for this are that the client is trying to execute a greater volume of spread bets than is available at the original price or that the underlying market has moved.

resistance: A price level that the market is unable to rise above for some time. When price rises to a resistance level, the weight of selling outweighs the buyers and this pushes down price again. A number of different trend peaks often occur at a resistance level.

scaling in: A staking strategy where traders gradually build a position with several orders at different price levels rather than entering the whole position with a single order.

scaling out: A staking strategy where traders gradually exit a position with different orders at different prices. The most common technique is to have more than one profit objective. You take some profit at the first objective but leave some of the position in place to let the position 'run'. These strategies normally involve moving your ***stop loss order*** to reduce risk as each trade meets each new profit objective.

scanning the market: Searching charts with different instruments to find those where a certain opportunity is close to occurring (for example, a *moving average crossover* involving a 10- and 20-day average). You often do this with technical analysis software, allowing you to efficiently scan large numbers of charts for opportunities.

sector bet: A *spread bet* where the underlying instrument is an index over an industry sector. A sector is made up of listed companies on an exchange that fall within a particular industry, such as healthcare or information technology.

share spread bets: A *spread bet* where the underlying instrument is a share in a company listed on a stock market.

short trading: A form of trading where the initial transaction is to sell. A buy transaction closes the position. The trader profits if price falls and loses if it rises.

slippage: This occurs when the broker can't execute an *order* at the stipulated price. For example, you may have a *stop loss order* to sell *share spread bets* at £1. However, if the market closes one day at £1.02 and opens the next at £0.98 (see *pre-market auction*) then the broker executes the order at £0.98 (or less if insufficient volume exists to execute the order at £0.98). The trader has suffered slippage of 2p or more per spread bet.

softs or soft commodities: Common term used to describe agricultural commodities, in particular coffee, cocoa and sugar.

spot price: The price quoted for immediate settlement (that is, payment for and delivery of an instrument). It's the opposite of a forward price, which is for settlement at some time in the future. Each market has its own convention for what constitutes immediate delivery. On the London Stock Exchange it's T + 3 (three business days after trade day). On foreign exchange markets it's mostly T + 2.

spot rate: An exchange rate for immediate settlement (see *spot price*).

spread bet: A bet on the price move of an underlying security such as a share or a foreign currency pair. Spread betting brokers quote a bid and offer price, or the spread, and investors bet on whether the price of the security will be lower than the bid or higher than the offer. The investor doesn't hold the share but only speculates on the price move of the share.

stop loss order: An order that aims to limit your loss.The trader places a stop sell order at a price below the current market price. It's an instruction to sell at market if price falls to the stipulated price or lower. A trader places a stop buy order above the current price and it's an order to buy at market if price rises to the stipulated price or above. A stop loss order is a stop buy or sell order that the trader places to close an existing position. It prevents (or stops) a loss getting any bigger.

support: A price level that the market is unable to fall below for some time. When price falls to a support level, the weight of buying outweighs the sellers and this pushes up price again. A number of different trend troughs often occur at a support level.

swing techniques: Techniques that aim to position a trader to sell near the end of a price upswing or to buy near the end of a downswing. Swing techniques involve being prepared to hold positions for longer than a single trading day to ensure the swing has time to complete. However, they're based on relatively short-term swings with trades normally lasting a matter of days or weeks, as opposed to ***longer-term trading*** where positions may typically be held for weeks or months.

symmetrical triangle: A chart pattern in which you can draw a downward sloping ***trend line*** across peaks of at least two separate trends and an upward sloping trend line across at least two separate trend troughs. The two trend lines thus form the shape of a symmetrical triangle. A common trading strategy involves entering new positions in the direction of a breakout of the triangle pattern.

technical analysis indicators: Mathematical formulae designed to show whether market prices are trending up or down. ***Moving averages*** are probably the best known example.

terms currency: The first currency quoted in a foreign exchange pair. A foreign exchange pair price depicts how many units of the second currency quoted you need to buy or sell a single unit of the terms currency. See also ***commodity currency***.

tick: The minimum amount by which the price of a particular spread bet can change.

time stop: A strategy to exit a position at the prevailing market price after a certain time has elapsed.

today's money: The value of money today. This may be measured by what it buys – for example, how many pounds it takes to buy a Big Mac today compared to the number required to buy one in the past or the future.

trading plan: A business plan for trading. It may include risk management plans, budgets, operational plans (such as plans for training or backup plans for Internet failures) and specific trading strategies (such as rules for entering and exiting trades).

trading price breakouts: A trading strategy based on buying when price rises above a ***resistance*** level or falls below a ***support*** level.

treasuries: Debt securities issued by a government treasury, such as treasury notes or bonds.

treasury spread bets: ***Spread bets*** where the underlying instruments are ***treasuries***.

trend following indicator: Trend following indicators are designed to provide an insight into whether price is trending up or down. However, because they're based on mathematical calculations they inevitably lag or follow the actual trend.

trend line: Lines used to provide an easy visual appraisal of the direction and momentum of a trend. An uptrend line slopes up and is drawn across at least two or three separate trend troughs. A downtrend line slopes down and is drawn across at least two or three separate trend peaks.

trend trading: Trading strategies designed to profit from trading in the direction of price trends. Traders attempt to recognise the beginning and end of trends as early as possible. The ideal trade involves entering the market near the beginning of a new trend and keeping the position open until as near as possible to the end of the trend.

true range: A calculation of the average or 'true' range within which a market can normally be expected to move during a given period. To calculate the true range take the average of differences between the high, low and previous closing price of each candle or bar in the period.

volatility: A measure of how much the price of an asset moves over a period of time.**variation margin:** Payment of profits or losses resulting from changes in market price of the underlying instrument. These are a requirement of many contracts such as futures and ***spread bets***. Brokers automatically debit or credit variation margin payments to a client's account before closing or formally settling a position.

wiggle room: A small amount of leeway that a trader allows before responding to the breach of a significant price level. For example, when trading range ***breaks out*** some traders may not enter new positions until price has moved a small way beyond ***support*** or ***resistance***. They're looking to reduce the risk of being caught out by a false start.

About the Authors

Vanya Dragomanovich is Commodities Editor at FTSE Global Markets and Commodities and Shares Editor at thearmchairtrader.com. A veteran financial journalist, she spent more than 10 years at Dow Jones Newswires, where she contributed to the Wall Street Journal.

Before immersing herself in financial markets she worked in war zones as part of the United Nations and as a researcher and journalist. She won a DuPont Columbia University Award for Excellence in Broadcast Journalism.

David Land is Chief Market Analyst for stockbroker CMC Markets. David has worked in the financial markets for well over a decade in a wide range of roles. Although his experience is diverse, he has always remained greatly interested in, and focused on, short-term trading methods employed across financial markets.

David started life in the financial markets working for a small Sydney-based stockbroker, before moving on to work for Colonial and the Commonwealth Bank of Australia. These roles led to an investor education role at the Australian Securities Exchange, which really improved his ability to relate to traders and investors from all sorts of backgrounds.

On the work front, these days David divides his time between writing analytical and commentary reports and providing education in trading to clients of CMC Markets. In addition, he lectures for Kaplan Professional and makes regular TV appearances providing market commentary. David holds a Master of Applied Finance from Macquarie Applied Finance Centre. He currently lives in Sydney with his wife and small white dog.

Dedication

From Vanya: This book is dedicated to my husband who is an intellectual daredevil and who taught me everything I know about spread-betting. Here's to you, Zlato!

Authors' Acknowledgments

We would like to thank the Wiley publishing team, in particular Claire Ruston, Erica Peters, Daniel Mersey and Simon Bell.

Publisher's Acknowledgments

Acquisitions Editor: Claire Ruston

Project Editors: Erica Peters and Simon Bell

Development and Copy Editor: Charlie Wilson

Technical Editor: Stuart Fieldhouse

Proofreader: Kerry Laundon

Production Manager: Daniel Mersey

Publisher: Miles Kendall

Senior Project Coordinator: Kristie Rees

Cover Image: © iStockphoto.com/pictafolio

Index

• D •

• E •

• F •

• G •

• H •

• I •

• M •

• N •

• O •

• P •

• S •

• T •

• U •

• V •

• W •

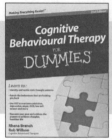

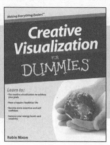

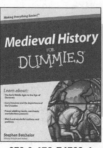